BERGLUND CENTER FOR INTERNET STUDIES

Internet 2.0
After the Bubble Burst
2000-2010

Published by
Berglund Center for Internet Studies
Pacific University
Forest Grove, Oregon

bcis.pacificu.edu

Acknowledgements

Published by Staff of Pacific University Oregon's
Berglund Center for Internet Studies,
Forest Grove, Oregon, USA

Jeffrey G. Barlow, Ph.D., Editor
Theresa Floyd, Managing Editor
Lilly Huynh, Copy and Design Editor
Ben Griffin, Cover Design

Berglund Center for Internet Studies
Pacific University
2043 College Way, Forest Grove, OR 97116
http://bcis.pacific.edu

Library of Congress Control Number: 2011919254

Table of Contents

Forward

The Berglund Center for Internet Studies (BCIS) at Pacific University was created slightly more than ten years ago, just as the global ramifications of the Internet in every sector were becoming impossible to ignore. James and Mary Berglund, both alumni of Pacific University, endowed the center to examine the effects of the Internet on individuals and their communities worldwide. BCIS seeks to study the impact of the Internet on how we work, communicate, teach, and learn.

The funding was to provide startup capital and operating support capital to the Center with the idea that other financial assistance would come from interested parties over time to expand the Center's activities. Director Jeffrey Barlow has been the leader of the Center for many years and also teaches in the Department of History at Pacific University. BCIS is a multifaceted organization within Pacific University and has gained a reputation as a source for solid, understandable information relating to the Internet. BCIS believes that it is important to explore the effects of the Internet on how we, as individuals, communicate and gain knowledge utilizing the Internet.

With that in mind as our starting point, how much has the Internet changed our lives; the way we do business; the way we communicate; how we educate? Change happens on a daily basis and incrementally we incorporate new ways of working into our lives. But, here on the ten-year anniversary of BCIS, it is interesting to note how much has changed since the Internet entered our world. These changes are wide ranging; some small and inconsequential, some toppling governments and influencing elections. Many businesses have disappeared because of the Internet and new ones have been created. Information is readily available from reliable news organizations and others with little more than opinions. A whole new language has been created...Google, blog, tweet, etc., etc...

Forward thinking businesses have had to change their business model to succeed in a fast changing environment. Junk mail has almost disappeared; and in its place are junk emails touting everything from luxury goods, prescriptions and the seamier side of life. It is possible for companies to announce sales instantly…. "free shipping, 15% off, free returns." If you're not on Twitter, it is possible to lose out on a deal. Sign up with Groupon and you'll receive the latest discounts. It is possible to cancel cable television and watch the latest shows on Hulu, not to mention the hours of free entertainment on YouTube. Airline tickets and hotel reservations are now purchased online rather than calling a travel agent. And, really, who uses a phone book or Yellow Pages anymore? Roadmaps….a thing of the past. Receiving and paying bills only takes a few fast clicks to accomplish. Buying a book takes seconds. Meet new friends, Google their names and get their story. Who needs to meet prospective dates the old fashioned way, when E –Harmony, Match.com, or Zoosk will provide you with the mate of your dreams? No need to go out and actually meet your friends, all you need is computer, camera and Facebook.

It seems, though, most of the changes wrought by the Internet all boil down to one essential theme, and that is communicating. We are now able to communicate our ideas in seconds rather than days. Business can advertise a sale in a blink rather than the tedious process of hard copy ads sent through snail mail or magazines. Prices of goods and services change by the second based on the ability to buy or sell. Online auctions have given sellers and buyers the opportunity to communicate quickly and effectively. I can know this instant the prices of a stock rather than waiting for tomorrow's listing in the newspaper. Want to scare yourself to death? You only have to Google your medical symptoms and a dreaded disease pops up. We have the ability to peer into our neighbors' back yards with Google Earth. We can find out what they paid for their house with Zillow.

We can see, hear and read about what is happening anywhere in the world at any given moment. In real time we can Skype across town or around the world. Online newspapers from every reputable news organization are available. It is possible to know the exchange rate for the South African Rand, or any currency, right at this moment. The Internet has given rise to "communities" of folks to discuss, dissect, and research topics. It allows colleagues in faraway locales to communicate with one another, to work from home, and to share ideas. Because of the Internet, we can get a University degree without ever leaving our homes. Students in China can study with students in the U.S. We have become a global world sharing our stories, ideas, and our aspirations. Not so long ago, it took hours for students to research and write a short paper. Students now have access to major libraries and learning institutions around the world.

All of these changes in communicating and doing business are the reasons the Berglund family endowed the Berglund Center for Internet Studies. The goal of the Center is to further the study of the Internet and its applications. To accomplish this, many generations of Pacific University students have been employed, learning office skills, Internet use, program support, and general computer skills. BCIS grants Berglund Research Fellowships to Pacific University faculty members for relevant research assignments. BCIS provides the platform and the know-how for Pacific University to provide distance learning, using the Internet, at venues in the U.S. mainland, Hawaii and China. *Interface on the Internet*, published 10 times per year, explores and supports theoretical and practical discussion of the impact of the Internet on individuals and their communities due to Internet utilization, one of BCIS' core purposes. Lastly, the Center stages a number of Roundtable Discussions each year to showcase current Internet topics by qualified speakers.

Technology will improve and our ability to match the improvements with the way we work will continue to accelerate our ability to communicate, teach and engage in commerce. The Berglund Center for Internet Studies at Pacific University looks forward to the challenges ahead in our fast-paced world. We will continue to study the Internet and study changes we are not even aware of today. We look forward to being a resource for those researching and working in the field as they document all that is possible.

James Berglund,
Julie Berglund Baker, and
Anne Baker

Introduction

This fully peer-reviewed special publication of the Berglund Center for Internet Studies presents essays by some of our regular contributors discussing the last ten years of the Internet, and some of its possible futures. This last decade, 2001 to 2011, corresponds to the period during which the Center first began to study the impact of the Internet. It was merely the fourth decade of the Internet, but the first period during which the Internet became broadly significant.

The first period, from the 1970's through to about 1980, was a geek's paradise—the rest of us are highly indebted to them, but largely unable to understand exactly what it was the techies were really doing. But by 1990 everyone could observe the impact of the Internet, much accelerated, of course, by the events known as the Dot.Com Bubble, usually dated from 1995-2000. It was in the following decade that we began our work at the Berglund Center, hence the title of this work, *After the Bubble Burst, Internet 2.0*.

This work resulted from a query we sent to our regular feature writers. We asked them, "Given that we began publishing just after the Internet Bubble collapsed, what characterized this period of the Internet and what might we expect in its next decade?" Scholars, with some exceptions, do not easily respond to questions about the future, but eight of us chose to answer the question in light of our work in our specific fields.

Librarians have long been the often overlooked heroes of digital information as they, of course, have to make sure that it is not only made available in an efficient manner, but in such a way that it can be accessed for a very long time. Deborah L. Andersen and her husband, David F. Andersen, both of SUNY Albany, put their analysis into the framework established by one of the founders of classification systems in 1876, Samuel Swett Green, in his piece, "Personal relations between librarians and readers." The

Andersen's see the Internet as having made rapid progress in the past decade but also see some important challenges, which they are confident will be met, at least by librarians.

Isaac Gilman and Lynda Irons, Pacific University librarians, also emphasize the progress of the past decade while identifying the essential challenges facing librarians in the next decade as keeping information open and free while training new generations to meet the problems of learning to access it in sophisticated but safe fashions, given the many issues raised by digital data.

Two professors of education, Mike Charles of Pacific University and Steven Rhine of Willamette University, focused upon the impact of the Internet upon education, both in the recent past and in the possible future. Each of them believes that while there are many advantages to the use of the Internet in formal education, it is also serving less useful purposes than might be the case if teachers, administrators, and politicians better understood its possibilities.

David Staley, Director of the Goldberg Center at Ohio State University and both a futurist and an historian, responded by viewing the Internet as an "external symbolic storage system," a result of human choices to make information accessible in a particular manner, both like and unlike earlier systems, ranging from oral exposition through hard-copy texts. He believes that this transition is inevitably a challenging and dramatic one requiring new ways of understanding the Internet and how it is that humanity stores and accesses its collective memory.

I myself wished to understand the impact of the Internet by looking at a literary genre which may seem to have very little to do with it: crime fiction. I survey critically acclaimed works to see how writers of crime fiction have dealt with the reality that the central problem of such fiction has suddenly become not how sleuths gather clues, but how they deal with the enormous expansion in available information presented by the Internet. This

VI

new reality challenges the boundaries of very successful fictional forms to the point where some genres, like classical detective fiction, may prove to be unable to hold their audiences. Other genres, like the thriller, may well benefit enormously from the Internet. The impact of the Internet, then, is to be found everywhere.

Taken together, we all see some major challenges lying ahead if the Internet is to fulfill its promises, but we also believe that both the recent past and earlier human experience working with non-digital information suggests that continued progress will be made, if perhaps it will be substantially less disruptive than the changes of the earlier decade, before the bubble burst.

Jeffrey Barlow
Director, Berglund Center for Internet Studies,
2000-2011

Acknowledgements

This tenth anniversary publication of the Berglund Center is dedicated to two groups; first, to the many authors who have contributed to *Interface* over the decade that we have published. We have been fortunate that so many have contributed selflessly to *Interface*, often on short notice and always with minimal compensation. They have done so because they believed in the importance of the Internet as a communications channel, and have desired to help build *Interface* as a source for analysis, and as a tool for expressing their own voices. We wish that we could thank each and every one of them individually, but this is the best we can do given that hundreds of individuals have contributed. Colleagues, we extend our sincere thanks.

These many voices would have had no outlet, of course, without the services of the second group, the hundreds of Pacific University students who staffed the Berglund Center in its first decade. Associating with them has been the best part of my own work at Pacific University in this period. I hope that in my work as a teacher, my students have learned more from me than I have from them; that is the natural order of things. But insofar as the Berglund Center has been concerned, I have learned far more from the staff than I have taught. Thanks guys, it was always fun, and always educational.

Jeffrey Barlow
Director, Berglund Center for Internet Studies, 2000-2011
Pacific University Oregon
November 2011

Information, Mediation, and Users: A view of the Internet's Evolving Relationship to Information and Library Science

David F. Andersen and Deborah L. Andersen
University of Albany

Beginnings—What Goes Around Comes Around

The challenges facing the field of information and library science today are long standing and persistent. On October 6, 1876, in Philadelphia, Pennsylvania, a group of 90 men and 13 women, including Melvil Dewey (of the classification scheme), Charles Ammi Cutter (of a competing classification scheme), Richard Rogers Bowker (of Books in Print), and Samuel Swett Green, signed a register which made them charter members of what was to become the American Library Association. The goal of this new association was "to enable librarians to do their present work more easily and at less expense."[1] This goal has continued until the present day even as technology changes, information explodes, and users seem to be more and more inclined to use the Internet rather than step into an actual library building.

The question for this article is what difference the Internet has made in information science, and if indeed we are now seeing a stabilizing of information and library science in relation to the Internet.[2] Is the field now at peace with technology and with the

---

[1] See Edward G. Holley. 1976. ALA at 100, in *The ALA Yearbook* (centennial edition). P. Sullivan, Carl H. Milam and the American Library Association, HW Wilson; and Doris Cruger Dale. 1978. ALA and its first 100 years, 1876-1976, in *Milestones to the Present: Papers from Library History Seminar V.* Gaylord Professional Publications.

[2] A shorter article in anticipation of this piece, with the same title, was published in the November 2010 issue of *Interface.* Deborah Lines Andersen. Information, mediation, and users: A view of the Internet's evolving relationship

ways information is stored, organized, and made available for access? Has the field come to some form of mutually agreed upon behaviors with users of information? Samuel Swett Green, the last of those listed above, is notable for having written a seminal piece, in 1876, entitled "Personal relations between librarians and readers."[3] Green's central thesis was that one could not let a reader (the term "patron" was not yet in use, and "reader" was indeed appropriate since individuals did that and only that) into a library on his or her own. Readers needed the guidance of a well-trained, cordial librarian to find what they were looking for. They would be lost at the library catalog (paper cards at the time) and unable to find a print work suitable to their needs.

Green gives many examples of the kind of work a librarian must do in order to help a patron find needed information. In doing so he suggested the title for this essay: "Information, Mediation, and the User." Green's information was in books on the shelves of the library. His mediation was in the form of the well-trained librarian, and his users were "modest men in the humbler walks of life, and well-trained boys and girls," since "scholars and persons of high social position" would not be timid about finding what they need or approaching a librarian for assistance.[4] A central question for this piece is how, if at all, information, mediation, and the user have been changed by the Internet, and if these changes are complete or still evolving.

Public Libraries

Melvil Dewey, another of those present for the ALA's founding in 1876, was primarily concerned about the public library—not private or subscription libraries that were selective about their clientele. The focus for this piece is also the public library more

---

to information and library science. *Interface: The Journal of Education, Community, and Values* 10(9) at http://bcis.pacificu.edu/journal/article.php?id=738 access 11/30/2010.
[3] Samuel Swett Green. 1876. Personal relations between librarians and readers. *American Library Journal* 1 (November): 74-81.
[4] *Ibid.* p. 74.

2

than academic or university settings. Public libraries are at least in part funded by tax dollars and as a result bring with them the challenges of responding to citizens, legislators, public administrators, and various citizen groups that often have the opportunity to advocate for or against the policies of libraries. Drawing on research and experience with public libraries and public library policy in Scotland, Canada, Mexico, Guatemala and the United States, this article explores a variety of ways of dealing with information, mediation, and patrons in a comparative sense, looking at similarities and differences in style to posit potential practices and policies that might be put into effect in the public sphere. Public libraries also cover all ranges of patrons—young and old, educated and becoming educated.[5] Information science is necessarily concerned with all patrons, not just academics in the university library. Information science as opposed to library science also takes into account those individuals who use information but never use the library. In an evolving environment where more and more information is available without recourse to library resources, there are substantial questions about the role and types of information mediation that users will need in the future. What are the mechanisms that might meet those needs?

Libraries Pre Internet

Samuel Green's library of the 1870s had much in common with today's libraries. There were patrons, information, and the librarian to mediate between the two. By way of example throughout this paper, we present a series of vignettes that point to critical themes, both static and evolutionary, about this interface. These vignettes begin with a look at libraries very

---

[5] See for example, Deborah Lines Andersen, 2004. Library as living space: How Glasgow, Scotland defines its public libraries. *JLAMS* (Journal of the Library Administration and Management Section of the New York Library Association), 1(1) at http://www.nyla.org/content/user_10/JLAMS2004-01.pdf accessed 11/30/2010; and Deborah Lines Andersen. 2003. Selling a public good: The case of rechartering public libraries by referendum in New York State." *Public Library Quarterly* 22(4): 5-23.

similar to those that Samuel Green experienced in the 19th century.

Vignette 1—The text-based library of the 20th century

In 1959 a group of volunteers in Upper Saddle River, New Jersey received permission from the town to turn a room in the borough hall into a public library. The local library before the time had been housed in the one-room school house—"two glass door bookcases"—and as a result residents traveled to the neighboring Ramsey and Allendale Public Libraries for their information needs. The new library was to be conveniently located across the street from the new elementary school. A call went out through the volunteer network of mostly elementary school mothers for donations to the collection. The volunteers collected, cataloged and shelved the materials for the public. In 1964 the first salaried librarian was hired by the town.[6]

Vignette 2—The text-based library of the 21st century

In 2009, more than 60 women in La Esperanza, Guatemala City, Guatemala voted to give space to a library which would serve the community as well as the preschool through sixth grade run by their artisan cooperative. There were no public libraries in La Esperanza or in the immediate geographic region surrounding it. The space they assigned was in the same four-story building as the school—a former Internet café and soy yogurt production facility. On the ground floor of the UPAVIM cooperative (Unidas para Virir Mejor) the library was next to both the bread bakery and the homework center run by a set of international volunteers, although there were plans to move it upstairs with a computer and typing center for

---

[6] William M. Yeomans. 1994. *The Lore of Upper Saddle River: From Prehistoric Times to the Present.* Upper Saddle River, NJ: Upper Saddle River Historical Society.

teenagers in the area. Trained by the head of the national Guatemalan library, the UPAVIM librarian was the one with vision who picked out lights, tables, books and more for the library, financed by a major fund drive of a group of former UPAVIM volunteers. Notably, there was a single computer in the library, with its power cord snaking through the door from the homework center next door. The librarian hoped to catalog all the books in the collection on this computer so that her patrons could find information more easily. However, she had no expectations that this catalog would be linked at any time in the future to other catalogs in Guatemala.[7]

These descriptions of libraries from 1876, 1959 and 2009 have much in common although separated by time, and in the case of Guatemala, geography. In all three cases there were individuals who identified information needs of a local population and went about creating a place, the library, where trained individuals (at least two including volunteers) could help to connect citizens to needed information. The two more recent cases look to evolutionary changes in information delivery, although they still have much in common with Green's original vision. First, libraries moved from being the right of the rich to a public good for the many. Education no longer entitled one to the information in the library. Instead, education became one of the critical functions of the library. Second, libraries started using the power of computing to create enhanced access to information sources, first within the walls of the library through simple computerized catalogs. These three stories embody Samuel Swett Green's triple concepts of user, information, and mediation.

---

[7] For information on Unidas para Virir Mejor, its school, tutoring center, crafts and library, see http://upavim.pursuantgroup.net/english/homeeng.htm ; accessed 11/30/2010. This vignette is also based on face-to-face conversations with the UPAVIM librarian in Guatemala in summer 2009.

Green's Users

Public library users exhibit a series of characteristics which define how they use information and need to be helped in the process. Although Green defines men, boys and girls as his patrons, seemingly forgetting that women might also be interested in library materials; his users had a lot in common with those of any time period. First of all, they have always come from a wide range of backgrounds and experiences so that each information need is potentially unique. (This can be contrasted with the academic library in which students have more defined sets of information needs that are dictated often by their coursework.) Second, public libraries today, perhaps more than in Green's time, serve all ages and all information domains. A librarian is just as likely to see a toddler looking at picture books as a teenager doing homework or an adult looking for materials on car repair. All users expect assistance as well as ease of access, but the pre-Internet user did not expect the library to have everything she wanted. In fact, before the Internet and before the system-wide, online public access catalog, the information available to a patron was defined by what the librarian (or volunteer) had brought into the collection. Users defined the library as a place they could go to meet a wide range of their information needs.

Green's Information

Pre-Internet a patron could expect access to the library's information through a card catalog, usually a wooden case filled with small drawers and organized alphabetically by author's last name, book titles, and subjects. Each library maintained its own collection of materials that reflected, to the best of its abilities, the information needs of its particular clientele. Missing from this information mix were computers, online public access catalogs, system-wide union catalogs covering multiple libraries within a geographic area, and "meta-union catalogs" such as WorldCat[8] and

---

[8] WorldCat, at http://www.worldcat.org/ , allows users to locate copies of books geographically by library using searches as simple as typing in zip codes. It describes itself as "The world's largest library catalog"; accessed 11/30/2010.

the Library of Congress[9] covering whole countries and beyond—all systems designed to extend the collection of the library beyond its doors so that patrons could have access to materials wherever the materials and the patrons resided. The pre-Internet library collected physical objects such as books, magazines and newspapers, and maintained clipping files on materials that librarians thought would be pertinent to patrons.

Green's Mediation

Key to Green's view of libraries was the role of the professional librarian as the mediator, connecting users to information. Pre-Internet one might expect that a librarian knew the collections of other libraries in the area, and would not hesitate to call other libraries in order to find materials for patrons. This form of mediation meant that the librarian had to have acquired a wealth of information for dealing with patron requests on site. It would not be unusual for the librarian to annotate the library's card catalog to provide important notes about additional materials. (One of the laments of librarians when the New York State Library (Albany, NY) went from a card catalog to an online access system in 1978 was that all those years of annotations were lost.)

The pre-Internet library as defined in many ways by Samuel Green was (and still is in the library at UPAVIM) thus an information island with tenuous connections to other resources in the community, the state, the country, or the world. Individuals' best access to information required that they walk through the library's doors. Librarians provided mediation in order to connect users to the information that they needed, within the walls of the library.

---

[9] See the extensive Library of Congress website at http://www.loc.gov/index.html , accessed 11/30/2010. "The Library of Congress is the largest library in the world, with nearly 145 million items on approximately 745 miles of bookshelves. The collections include more than 33 million books and other print materials, 3 million recordings, 12.5 million photographs, 5.3 million maps, 6 million pieces of sheet music and 63 million manuscripts," and collects materials "in some 470 languages."

Post-Internet Users, Information Delivery, and Mediation

Getting people to walk through the doors of the public library has become more and more of a challenge for librarians in the Internet age. As individuals use their computers from home, order inexpensive books through Amazon, or find materials on the World Wide Web, librarians are faced with fewer patrons on site, even if they are using the library's resources through its website. How can a librarian be a helpful mediator if individuals are not available face-to-face for assistance? The two vignettes that follow highlight strategies that libraries put in place in order to evolve in the time of the Internet and thus get individuals to show up at the library's doors.

Vignette 3—Library as social space in Internet time

The 33 libraries of Glasgow, Scotland are a well-run organization that provides sources, services, and mediation to the nearly three quarter million individuals who live there. In order to get individuals into the library, library administrators have focused on user preferences and how to attract individuals. In particular, Glasgow has concentrated on attracting children, young adults, international populations, and those who are interested in cultural and athletic facilities that are housed in the same building as their libraries. Unlike many libraries in the United States, food and beverages are allowed and sold, newspapers are thrown out at the end of each day, and furniture tends to be sofas, upholstered chairs, and coffee tables. The feeling is of a living room rather than a research center. Individuals stop in after work to read a newspaper in their native tongue, attend a class on personal computing, or view the latest art exhibition. The 33 libraries are placed throughout the city so that citizens may easily walk to their local libraries. Glasgow maintains its branch libraries as places to visit, while maintaining the central Mitchell Library as a research center for the entire city.[10]

Vignette 4—Library strategy in Internet time
Montréal, Canada is a city that works in two languages. There are public schools for French- as well as English-speaking students although the population also contains individuals who speak Spanish, Greek, and Chinese, among other languages. Public libraries in Montréal are numerous (over 40 in all), cater to different populations in their catchment areas, and must respond to government regulations about language policy. Not only are there issues of language choice for collection development in each library, but staffing, signage, webpage design and programming all must take language into account in this multilingual environment. In 2005 the Biblioteque Nationale was constructed as a flagship repository for French language and culture in the national province of Quebec, creating a magnet for francophone users in all media from print to digital. Libraries in Montréal are being designed to attract and support the francophone population of the city, relying heavily upon computers in each library and Internet resources to support their collections.[11]

The vignettes above highlight some strategies to get patrons to come into the library and use its resources. In particular, they highlight the growing trend toward multilingual collections in public libraries. If the Internet were not evolving as it is, providing more and more resources to individuals outside the library, perhaps these strategies to attract patrons would be enough. Situating the public swimming pool and public library in the same building, or offering assistance to new immigrants, surely cause

---

[10] See Deborah Lines Andersen. 2004. *Op. cit.*
[11] Marc V. Levine. 1990. *The Reconquest of Montreal: Language Policy and Social Change in a Bilingual City*. Philadelphia: Temple University.

individuals to walk through the door. But, as discussed below, the arrival of the Internet has driven change in many ways—for the information user, information, and the bounds of mediation in this environment.

Characteristics of the New User

Samuel Green would not recognize the library of today, and would undoubtedly be mystified by users who find information in a wide variety of venues that have little to do with the physical library. Robert Marshall, a fictitious character, is one such Internet example.

> ### Vignette 5—A user post Internet time
> Robert Marshall is an 11th grade student with an immediate information problem. He was assigned a term paper in social studies weeks ago but has let the paper go in a rush of other activities both educational and social. The paper is due tomorrow and will constitute a major portion of his grade for the quarter. Robert went to the high school library with his class but he needs additional references and a lot of text to reach the ten-page minimum requirement. Rather than going to the public library tonight Robert turns on his Internet-connected computer at home and calls up Google. He plans to find full-text articles on his topic, collect as much text as he can find that seems to work together, quote some materials directly, per his assignment, and use other material more or less as is. He rationalizes that since it is on the World Wide Web information really does not belong to anyone in particular and he can freely repurpose what he finds to fit his own information needs.

Robert Marshall presents a particularly challenging case for any information professional who is interested in helping a user to navigate today's information sphere. A central tenant of information and library science service is to know the user. The purpose of acquiring, organizing, and making information accessible is for the user. However, understanding that user, and that user's behaviors and needs is a complex task since all users are not the same and all require specialized attention. In library science we speak of the "reference interview" in which we ascertain the specific information needs of specific individuals.[12] All of this ascertaining, knowing, and interviewing is theoretically independent of the media through which a user will receive information, although more and more we must also consider mode of access and delivery as well as the informational content itself. Robert Marshall is problematic because he has chosen not to use the library as a place or as an information venue (through its website). Librarians understand that there are users who never come through the physical doors of the library, but if the user also avoids the virtual door—the website—there is no opportunity for librarians to provide any sort of helpful mediation.

In fact, online media are changing information consumers in a variety of ways that are challenging as well as disturbing to information professionals. Robert Marshall's vignette points directly to the concept of intellectual property and the linked concept of plagiarism. Although individuals from a very early age tend to understand the idea of owning a toy, a book, a car or a house, the concept of owning an idea is less distinct. Ideas can be multiply distributed. Many individuals can possess the same piece of information without having any single piece diminished in the process—decidedly different than sharing ownership of a house or a piece of land. Grandma's recipe for rhubarb pie is information

---

[12] See, for example, Patricia Dewdney and Gillian Mitchell. 1996. Oranges and peaches: Understanding communication accidents in the reference interview. *RQ* 34(4): 520-535; James Rettig. 2003. Technology, cluelessness, anthropology, and the memex: The future of academic reference service. *Reference Services Review* 31(1): 17- 21; David Tyckoson. 2003. On the desirableness of personal relations between librarians and readers: The past and future of reference services. *Reference Services Review* 31(1): 12-16; and Jack O'Gorman & Barry Trott. 2009. What will become of reference in academic and public libraries? *Journal of Library Administration* 49(4): 327-339.

which could potentially be broadcast on the Internet for all to read and use. After it has been published online, who now "owns" the recipe? Could anyone take it and create a book, for profit, that includes it in its pages? Here is where the next generation of information consumers arises, or, as the New York Times headline named them—"Generation Plagiarism."[13] If one of the functions of a public librarian is to help users understand the difference between citation and plagiarism, how will this mediation take place if the user and the information professional never have the opportunity to interact?

It would appear that the next generation of information consumers' definition of intellectual property is far less clear than that of past generations. One college student in the "Generation Plagiarism" comments section stated that, "In the digital age, plagiarism isn't and shouldn't be as big of a deal as it used to be when people used books for research." He or she did not elaborate on why this might be the case but other students have. An earlier piece in the New York Times[14] quoted students, saying that pages without author information and, in particular, articles in Wikipedia did not need to be cited because they were unsigned and collectively written, therefore "common knowledge." The article's author went on to state that "concepts of intellectual property, copyright and originality are under assault in the unbridled exchange of online information." This "evolving view of authorship" was supported even further in Germany when a 17 year old author created an award-nominated novel that turned out

---

[13] This is a social media site that allows individuals over the age of 13 to comment on questions presented by the moderator. The focus of this session was "tell us what you think about plagiarism." Montgomery, Carrie. Are you part of "Generation Plagiarism?" *New York Times*, August 3, 2010.
http://*learning*.blogs.nytimes.com/2010/08/03/are-you-part-of-generation-plagiarism/ ; accessed 11/30/2010.
[14] Gabriel Trip. 2010. Plagiarism lines blur for students in digital age. *New York Times*, August 2: A1.
http://www.nytimes.com/2010/08/02/education/02cheat.html ; accessed 11/30/2010.

to be a collection of materials taken (plagiarized?) from other sources. The article noted that her work was:

> Representative of a different generation, one that freely mixes and matches from the whirring flood of information across new and old media, to create something new. "There's no such thing as originality anyway, just authenticity," said Ms. [Helene] Hegemann in a statement released by her publisher after the scandal broke.[15]

Is this the new user of information, who will grow up, become an adult, and supplant those of us who presently recoil at the idea of plagiarism in any form? What has happened to the ideas of information property and information authorship? Of creation of new ideas that will in turn need to be organized and made accessible to others? How worried should information professionals get, and what kind of actions might they take now to evolve gracefully in this world that has been decidedly changed by the Internet?

A user of today who is 20 years old or less has never known a time without the Internet. She is comfortable with a variety of media. She is also probably the owner of a cell phone, can instant message, and knows how to search the Internet for information. More and more applications are becoming available for this user, for free and for a fee. These include star charts, geographic information systems, dictionaries, games, and books. This user posts on Facebook and spends a large amount of time being electronically connected.[16] The probability is very high that she

---

[15] Nicholas Kulish. 2010. Author, 17, says it's "mixing" not plagiarism. *New York Times* February 12, A4.
http://www.nytimes.com/2010/02/12/world/europe/12germany.html ; accessed 11/30/2010.
[16] See Amanda Lenhart, Kristen Purcell, Aaron Smith & Kathryn Zickuhr, Pew Internet & American Life Project. 2010. Social media & mobile Internet use among teens and young adults. *Pew Research Center Publications*, November 28 at http://pewresearch.org/pubs/1484/social-media-mobile-internet-use-

believes that all needed information is on the Internet. Frightening for educators and librarians alike is this user's complete trust in the veracity of information on the Internet.[17] Perhaps more frightening is her belief that she is really good at searching and really does not need any help at all. Like Robert Marshall, she does not come into the library as place, wanting instead the ease of getting information quickly on the Internet. In fact, she will sacrifice depth of information for enough information to get by.[18] If information professionals were only dealing with technology-savvy 20 year olds, the path would be fairly straightforward. We would teach our new information professionals and equip our libraries to target this group. Instead, and rather obviously, we have individuals of all ages visiting the library (or not) and wanting to make use of an enormous variety of resources, sources, and services available there (or somewhere on the Internet where there is little hope that they will be guided by information professionals). We are also experiencing a surge of globalization in which our information users are literate, but not necessarily most fluent in English.

Characteristics of Information

Expansion of information has indeed gone so far beyond the library's shelves that there are vast stores of information that might be accessed through the library's computers but that could

---

teens-millennials-fewer-blog for statistics on age and use of social media and computers; accessed 11/30/2010.

[17] William Dutton & Adrian Shepherd. 2006. Trust in the Internet as an experience technology. *Information, Communication & Society* 9(4): 433-451.

[18] See James A. Buczinski. 2005. Satisficing digital library users. *Internet Reference Services Quarterly* 10(9): 99-102; Yazdan Mansourian & Nigel Ford, 2007. Search persistence and failure on the web: A "bounded rationality" and "satisficing" analysis. *Journal of Documentation* 63(5): 680-701; and Claire Warwick, Jon Rimmer, Ann Blandford, Jeremy Gow & George Buchanan. 2009. Cognitive economy and satisficing in information seeking: A longitudinal study of undergraduate information behavior. *Journal of the American Society for Information Science & Technology* 60(12): 2402-2415 for studies of individuals "satisficing"—making due with less than complete information.

just as easily be found without once using the library. Not all, but an overwhelming amount of information is free for the finding, if one knows where to look. There is an abundance of policy questions for libraries about what kinds of resources patrons need, about redundancy of information in print and electronic forms, and about patron education as a balance to online information that is abundant but dubiously accurate. Inevitably the question of resources comes to play in this debate. Where should libraries direct funds in order to provide the best services to the greatest numbers of individuals? How much of budgets should be spent on education rather than resources, and how can libraries provide education (thus mediation) to individuals who do not use their services?

While Robert Marshall from the previous vignette may seem a bit like a rogue information user, his mother Ellen certainly is not. In the following vignette, Ellen Marshall, Robert's mother, is seeking to use information as a tool to become a more value-driven, environmentally and socially-aware consumer. The next two vignettes are purposely set outside the public library, illustrating a critical point about information use today, and the potential for public libraries to tap into social computing as a means of connecting to patrons.

Vignette 6A—Buying coffee today
Ellen Marshall has always considered herself to be a careful shopper. Living with her husband and three children on a limited budget, it has been a struggle to make ends meet while at the same time making purchases that reflected her personal commitments to social justice and environmental sustainability. She pays more attention to the unit pricing label than to the price itself, but has difficulty finding trustworthy non-price information that she cares about. She does not have time to search the Internet for information on each product, and she does not know which information to trust. Today Ellen is shopping for coffee. She returns automatically to the fair trade and organic shelf in

15

her local supermarket because over time she has discovered that this is the place where her price- and value-conscious shopping seems to take her. She relies on the store manager to offer the products that she hopes are consistent with her values. She also knows that the manager, however well meaning, selects and places products to serve the interests of the supermarket, but it is the best she can do.

Ellen, like her son Robert, probably feels no need to go into a public library for any additional help mediating her information environment as she seeks to create a more value-based coffee purchase (although, perhaps she might go to her public library to learn more about what the labels "USDA organic" or "fair trade" actually mean). Nonetheless, Ellen must navigate her way through and around an information environment that is much more complex than that facing Samuel Green in 1876. Green's marketplace was much more face-to-face, where most of the products that he purchased were grown or produced by farmers and manufacturers who sold these goods directly to the consumer, or where the supply chain was short enough that the producer was directly known to the retailer.

Today, Ellen's grocery store is part of a market operating under conditions of asymmetric information, where some players (the sellers) have better information than others (the buyers) about product quality. Although in most markets it is possible to find "good" and "bad" products, both kinds of products may be sold at the same price because consumers have difficulties telling the difference between them. Pricing mechanisms in an information asymmetrical market offer an incentive to sellers to offer low quality products, driving out the high quality products, which cannot survive in the market because producers cannot afford to produce them.[19] Ellen is a consumer who cares about

---

[19] See G. A. Akerlof. 1970. The market for "lemons": Quality uncertainty and the market mechanism. *The Quarterly Journal of Economics* 84(3): 488-500; K.

environmental impacts, fair wages, and social justice but often lacks the information that would allow her to base purchases on her values because these are unobservable product attributes. Ellen can observe the taste and color of the coffee, but she has no way to observe or confirm anything about where and how the coffee was grown. As a consumer, Ellen seeks trusted information (presently provided in the form of product labels such as "fair trade," "organically grown," or "shade grown" coffee).[20] In present markets, unobservable attributes mean that Ellen makes her coffee purchase based on judgments with missing cues, creating biased judgments.

The information environment present in Ellen's coffee purchase contains a vast amount of potential information (most of which is hidden from Ellen as a consumer). There is more information than any individual can handle, so part of the challenge for Ellen is to obtain what information is pertinent (information professionals refer to this as the precision dimension of an information search—obtaining relevant information) without obtaining everything (the recall dimension of a search—she does not want so much information that she is overwhelmed and has to weed out a lot of irrelevant or repetitive materials). In addition, all of this product information is distributed across a large variety of sources and is neither cataloged nor available in any one place. Much of the information that could help Ellen to make values-based purchases

---

Giannakas. 2002. Information asymmetries and consumption decisions in organic food product markets. *Canadian Journal of Agricultural Economics* 50: 35-50; and M. S. Sriram 2005. Information asymmetry and trust: A framework for studying microfinance in India. *The Journal for Decision Makers* 30(4):77-85 for information on information asymmetries and trust in the marketplace.

[20] See A. Abdul-Rahman & S. Hailes. 2000. Supporting trust in virtual communities. In *Proceedings of the 33rd Hawaii International Conference on System Sciences*. Maui, HW, USA; S. Ba & P. Pavlou. 2002. Evidence of the effect of trust building technology in electronic markets: Price premiums and buyer behavior. *MIS Quarterly* 26(3): 243-268; J. Golbeck. 2005. *Computing and Applying Trust in Web-Based Social Networks*. Ph.D. Dissertation, University of Maryland, College Park for examples of research that deal with trust in the online marketplace.

is proprietary information that the public would like to have but that private sector organizations do not make publicly available (e.g., the addictive nature of cigarettes).

Furthermore, the complexity of the information environment that Ellen faces as a consumer (of coffee and almost any other product in her retail world) is matched everywhere else in Ellen's life. As a client of medical, financial, or other professional services, Ellen daily makes choices that can take into account only a small portion of the information that could potentially inform her choices. As a citizen, Ellen's taxes support a wide range of governmental products and services that presumably have been provided to meet citizen needs and respond to the preferences of citizens such as Ellen. Ellen today lacks the information mediation tools necessary to sort through all the information potentially available to support values-based decision making. Like her son Robert, Ellen must rely on what she knows, ignorant of information that is hidden from her view, purchasing and deciding as best she can while swimming in a sea of unknowable information.

Although the previous paragraphs relate specifically to consumer information, it is important to note that information seekers, in general, whether in libraries, or supermarkets, or online, find themselves facing information gaps as well as information overload. Mediation, as discussed below, opens up the possibility of guiding users to find the information that they need, when they need it, in a form that is appropriate to their requirements. The Internet has created a wealth of possible information sources. In the process it has made it possible to circumvent the very institution that Samuel Green discussed as the primary information mediator for the public.

Characteristics of Mediation
Both Ellen and Robert need help mediating their modern, immensely more complicated information environments. Today's mediation could be in the form of the friendly librarian, but librarians today continue to lament how few people come into the

library and how those who do often want to use just the computer terminals. Reference questions for onsite users have devolved for many to issues of computer settings and broken printers. Off-site use of libraries has its own set of choices in terms of telephone, instant messaging, 24/7 reference, websites, wireless, wikis, and blogging, to name just a few. Social media hold out a promise of bringing individuals into the library, virtually if not in person, but librarians are faced with choices about what services to provide for which users—especially potential users who might be lured into the library with the right choices.

An important policy and program question for libraries will be how to use the power of new technologies, including social computing, to create value for all their stakeholder groups. Information mediation is no longer limited to the purview of public libraries. A look at how Ellen might purchase her coffee in the near future tells us why.

Vignette 6B—Buying coffee in the not-very-distant future

Ellen was the first in her network of friends to adopt the I-Choose application to load on her hand-held shop-mate device as soon as it became available. She appreciated its ability to scan the UPC sticker on many products that she was considering, getting more information about those products, particularly about how they were produced and by whom. She especially appreciated that I-Choose allowed her to create her own value profile. Product ratings that she got from her I-Choose reflected her personal values, creating a price-value rating that she could tailor to meet both her budget and her personal values. Originally, the I-Choose rating just augmented unit pricing with value pricing. Today she was surprised that her I-Choose scan revealed a new product on the shelf that made an even better price and value fit for her. This particular package of coffee had received a 9.5 out of 10 rating by the Green Dot sustainability index. She probed the I-Choose profile on this

19

product. By drilling down with several clicks on her shop-mate device, she found that this product, in addition to being distributed by Star Cents, a coffee distribution firm that was excellent at holding down shipping and distribution costs, was also shade grown at the Velasquez Coffee Cooperative in Mexico, with a much higher environmental sustainability index at the point of production. Two more clicks confirmed to Ellen that the Velasquez Cooperative had been certified by the United Fair Trade Association (UFTA), and was well rated by the Consumer Values Institute, an online social network of consumers who share Ellen's values. Ellen especially trusted ratings from the Consumer Values Institute because she herself was quite active as one of its peer raters. She knew that Consumer Value Institute ratings reflected the tastes, values, and opinions of experts and consumers whom she could trust. Ellen picked up this new brand and dropped into her cart to give it a try.[21]

In our future vignette a number of technical and policy developments have added complexity to the retail market, but have also provided additional information mediation for Ellen. This mediation gives her information that she can trust. For example, the Green Dot product rating was made available to Ellen on her hand-held device via an app that could scan a UPC barcode. Systems such as this already exist, allowing for online price comparisons within a defined geographic area, searching for product toxins, or even looking for specific types of allergens (such as peanut allergies) within prepared foods that can be identified via a UPC. The NuVal nutritional index, for example, can be accessed via UPC bar codes even if the index rating is not printed on the product package.[22] Or, for consumers who are disposed to

---

[21] The reader should note that both of the Ellen vignettes are the product of several National Science Foundation projects and proposals that were originally written by the authors and their research colleagues in 2009 and 2010.
[22] See information on NuVal at NuVal LLC, www.nuval.com/ ; accessed 11/30/2010.

surf the web, unique product identifiers created by producers and associated retail outlets can allow consumers to examine information such as the bill of lading for the Darjeeling tea that they just bought.[23]

In addition, existing product rating systems move beyond merely providing labels on the packaging. Fortunately for Ellen, coffee has a relatively large amount of non-price information that can be routinely attached to product packaging via trusted product labels, and a trend to provide more of this type of information is emerging. The hypothetical "Green Dot Product Rating" cited in the vignette is an example of a growing number of product rating schemes that can be attached directly to product labeling or made available via a UPC code on the Internet. For example, the Walmart corporation has committed to placing a "sustainability" index on all the products that it sells in the near future,[24] while the NuVal nutritional rating system for packaged foodstuffs provides a single index between 1 and 100 to summarize the nutritional value per calorie of foods sold in packages that can be identified by a UPC code. As product ratings such as these proliferate, consumers such as Ellen will have access to detailed, high-level information that can help them to make more informed purchases in more efficient markets with fewer information asymmetries and fewer unobservable costs to consumers (such as the destruction of rain forests or the impoverishment of farm laborers through long hours and low wages).

Some aspects of this vignette move beyond technologies that currently exist. For example, new research on interoperable data architectures will enable widespread information sharing among

---

[23] See information about Darjeeling tea at https://www.bostonteacampaign.com/en-us/3_14/trace-your-tea.html ; accessed 11/30/2010.
[24] See information about Walmart's rating system: Walmart announces sustainable product index. 7/16/2009. Walmart Corporation Press Release. http://walmartstores.com/pressroom/news/9277.aspx ; accessed 11/30/2010.

communities of stakeholders in new information-rich markets.[25] In Ellen's future search for the right coffee, the creation and common adoption of an over-arching information architecture made it easy for the Green Dot product rating to be augmented by information provided by the Star Cents coffee distributors as well as information from the Velasquez Coffee Cooperative. But product specificity is a critical limitation of the current emergent class of product rating applications being brought to markets. Widespread replication of these prototypes will require stakeholders (producers, supply chain managers, consumer advocates, and product certifiers such as the USDA's certification of "organic" products) to adopt standards and practices for creating such an information architecture.[26]

New technologies, still on the drawing boards today, will further help to mediate between Ellen and the complexities of retail information environments. In the vignette, the final technical innovation that will enable the I-Choose system is the creation of trusted product ratings by the Consumer Values Institute. In this possible future, the Consumer Values Institute is a social computing platform that supports consumer activists in rating a wide range of products and services along dimensions that cannot otherwise be directly observed in the marketplace. There is still a need for a set of design principles that can be used by the managers and designers of such systems. Indeed, these new technologies hold the promise of creating value for libraries, public and private, which must deliver trusted information,

---

[25] See the U.S. National Science Foundation's INTEROP program: *I-Choose: Building Information Sharing Networks to Support Consumer Choice*, which was submitted by the authors' research group and funded in October 2010 by NSF.
[26] N. Hu, P. A. Pavlou & J. Zhang. 2006. Can online reviews reveal a product's true quality? Empirical findings and analytical modeling of online word-of-mouth communication. *Proceedings of the 7th ACM Conference on Electronic Commerce*, Ann Arbor, Michigan, USA, pp. 324-330; G. Jahn, M. Schramm & A. Spiller. 2005. The reliability of certification: Quality labels as a consumer policy tool. *Journal of Consumer Policy* 28: 53-73; and S. M. Mudambi & D. Schuff. 2010. What makes a helpful online review? A study of customer reviews on Amazon.com. *MIS Quarterly* 34: 185-200.

gleaned from an ever-widening reservoir of information sources, in such a way that it is truly useful to its intended recipients. Technologies that were developed for an initial purpose (e.g. the research function of the Internet, or the military purposes of RFID) tend to migrate toward more common, public purposes. As an important outgrowth of the Internet, social computing appears to be a technology ready for a variety of applications in the library setting.

Current Challenges to Information Mediation for Public Purposes

Samuel Green suggested nearly a century and a half ago that libraries needed to perform the function of providing professional and trusted mediation between users and information sources. Now more than ever before this kind of trusted mediation is needed. In an era of information asymmetry in retail markets, the marketing departments of major corporations prey on Ellen Marshall's laudable desire to make value-based purchases by "green-washing" the images of their products, projecting prominently on their packaging a view of "green" and "sustainable" product attributes while the reality of what is inside the packages may be quite different. There is an enormous ground swell toward all individuals including private corporations being potential creators of the information that Ellen needs to rely on to make her value-based decisions and choices. While a large amount of information might be available through public sources such as public libraries, increasingly much information is potentially located in grey areas that are not easily accessible. One example is of cloud computing in which individuals are unaware of the actual sources of their data, which sit "in the cloud" of the Internet without clear indicators of their geographic location. Used through a single port of entry, cloud computing has the advantage of collecting vast amounts of information,[27] but it has the potential

---

[27] The Wikipedia article on "cloud computing" provides a very strong bibliography of materials on this topic at http://en.wikipedia.org/wiki/Cloud_computing ; accessed 11/30/2010.

to obscure factors, such as creator or owner of information, that individuals want in order to create trust. Although increasingly large amounts of standards-based information such as library databases are updated on a regular basis, the open web is not peer-reviewed in the same way, increasingly leading to issues of what information to trust. Still, while sources such as Wikipedia give basic information, contributors are no longer peer-reviewed experts—and hence the accuracy and potential bias of information become important factors.[28]

Furthermore, unlike print, information on the Internet can change in content and/or location without notice. Web pages appear, disappear, and are updated. There has been some movement toward fixing information in time, archiving pages before they change yet again. The Internet Archive Wayback Machine, for example, seeks to archive pages before their content changes.[29] PURLs and DOIs are designed to provide permanent addresses for materials that migrate from one site to another.[30]

What is needed today and in the future has much in common with what Green envisioned—a public place where information is open to all and trusted mediation is provided as a public good. The notion of "public" is critical to this discussion. Information provided with public purposes in mind is essentially different from information provided through private markets—information

---

[28] Various articles have documents as well as commented upon bad information on Wikipedia sites. For example, see Brock Read. 2006. Can Wikipedia ever make the grade? *Chronicle of Higher Education; Information Technology Section* October 27 at http://innovations.oise.utoronto.ca/~jhewitt/ctl1602/papers/Read%202006.pdf ; accessed 11/30/2010 ; or Besiki Stvilia, Michael B. Twidale, Linda C. Smith & Les Gasser. 2008. Information quality work organization in Wikipedia. *Journal of the American Society for Information Science and Technology* 59(6): 983–1001, DOI: 10.1002/asi.20813.

[29] The Internet Archive. Wayback Machine. http://www.archive.org/web/web.php ; accessed 11/13/2010.

[30] Carol Anne Germain. 2000. URLs: Uniform resource locators or unreliable resource locators. *College & Research Libraries* 61(4): 359-365.

not necessarily designed to serve public purposes. The public libraries envisioned by the founders of the American Library Association created public goods—not selling a product but providing information mediated to professional standards.

In their many roles as consumers, clients, and citizens, Ellen and Robert need access to information from the point of view of trusted full information—information in service of the public good. By making mediation a public good, Green envisioned an institution—the public library—that could harness the full power of information mediated in service of the public. But who should pay for these mediation services? Funding public goods has always been a persistent problem in public policy. An obvious solution was to seek direct support from tax dollars for public libraries to create the 19th century equivalent of the information commons, mediating and serving as an agent for all individuals. Indeed, Andrew Carnegie devoted his personal vast fortune to promoting this view of open and trusted information mediation provided through publicly-funded libraries.[31]

But as Vignette 6B makes clear, open access to trusted mediation of information in the 21st century is a challenge that will require more resources than are likely to be provided via public library budgets in the future. Hence, our last question, "Whither Public Libraries in the Post-Internet Era of the 21st Century?"

Whither Public Libraries in the Post-Internet Era of the 21st Century?

Working within the resource constraints and institutional boundaries imposed on them, public libraries have been responding rapidly to shifts in their users as well as the information environments to which their users respond. As discussed below, these responses are many and diverse. In some

---

[31] Andrew Carnegie Corporation of New York. Our Founder, at http://carnegie.org/about-us/foundation-history/about-andrew-carnegie/ ; accessed 11/30/2010.

cases libraries have yet to capture the full power of new technologies and resources. The list that follows explores both present-day applications and those that might find their place in the libraries of the future.

Public Libraries Responding to the Challenges of the Internet
There is little doubt that technology and user preferences will require that libraries quickly evolve or be ignored in the face of new ways of seeking and using information. As children of the information age become adults, and as individuals such as Robert Marshall become the primary potential users of public libraries, their needs and behaviors must become the focus of public library programming and policy.

Indeed, across the history of library development the major question has always been one of service delivery choices. Samuel Green believed that readers needed guidance from a well-trained librarian in a library where they were looking for printed works suitable to their needs. His collection development policies (a formal term librarians use to discuss how they will employ the resources—time, talents, and funds—that they have at their disposal) centered on this mission. The volunteers in Upper Saddle River, New Jersey and La Esperanza, Guatemala City realized that there was an information gap. Citizens were lacking critical services that would change the way they accesses information sources and that gap could be filled by a physical public library.

Two critical shifts occurred in public library development policy with the advent of the Internet. First, information was now available in a multiplicity of forms. Collection development decisions had to take into account whether the library should buy and own a print volume, or pay for access to a source that was available on the Internet. Every time a new website surfaces, an old one changes, or a private sector firm creates an information source (e.g., Kindle, the Nook, or iPad), collection development professionals need to make service decisions about that new venue of information delivery. Second, since materials were

26

available on the Internet it was possible to make these sources available to patrons off site, from computers in their homes, offices or coffee shops. These service decisions had profound effects on library traffic. As seen with the Robert Marshall vignette above, libraries have opportunities to deliver critical services without ever having a patron come through their doors.[32]

On occasion, in order to expose potential patrons to a wealth of library services, librarians will create programs that require that individuals come to the library. Guilderland Public Library (Guilderland, New York), instituted a gaming night for teens that attracted teens as well as college students to socialize within the walls of the library. They created a large graphic novel collection for this same age group. Looking at a different segment of the population they created a homeschooling library that has become a resource for homeschooling parents throughout the area.[33] Albany Public Library (Albany, New York) hosted a library school intern at one of its branches. Two factors came into play to create a new library program for teens. The first was that the intern happened to be a very good, locally prominent skateboarder. The second was that there were teens outside the library every

---

[32] It is important to note that this discussion ignores those individuals who come to the library for socialization, story hours, and other programs. Other individuals just want to browse the stacks, wanting physical volumes to read at home or on the bus, and having no desire or perhaps technical skills or inclination to download books from the library's website. It also ignores the fact that not all individuals have computers and not all materials are available online despite such phenomena as Google Books and Project Guttenberg. Citizens can create their own collections of materials through purchase of books, actual volumes or downloaded versions, but then they make a choice to pay for this information when it could be available free at a library. Potential users of libraries vary greatly. Some will always want to come into the physical library. Some may never come through its doors.

[33] See Laura Shin. 2008. A home away from home: Libraries and homeschoolers. *School Library Journal*, August 1; at http://www.schoollibraryjournal.com/article/CA6582320.html; accessed 2/9/2011; and the Guilderland Public Library website which maintains an evolving list of games and programs for teens including graphic novels and gaming nights at http://www.guilpl.org/index.php ; accessed 2/9/2011.

27

afternoon using sidewalks and library plaza for skateboard practice. Capitalizing on an obvious pairing, the intern created a skateboarding program for these teens, drawing them into the library to watch and discuss video about skateboarding and at the same time exposing them to other library services on site. Several of them signed up for library cards and came to use the library's resources and computers even when there was no skateboarding session.[34]

Libraries have explored various information venues as technology changed post Internet. Blogs and Twitter are the most recent forays into social computing, stepping beyond the face-to-face, telephone, email, and instant messaging reference interviews that still exist but have been enhanced by technology services. Libraries rarely give up services (the paper card catalog is an example of actually throwing out an old system), instead adding services to those that already exist. The challenge is to keep up with technology change and remain relevant in this shifting environment. If 2010 articles in both Wired and Public Libraries are correct and individuals are moving toward apps on their handheld devices, how will libraries respond and use these new technologies to help citizens find the information they need?[35]

---

[34] Michael Janairo. 2007. Albany Public Library librarian wins national excellence award. *Times Union*, August 8; and Albany Public Library. 2007. Albany Public Library wins national excellence award from the Young Adult Services Association of the American Library Association, July 18; at http://www.albanypubliclibrary.org/news/?p=83; accessed 2/9/2011
[35] Chris Anderson & Michael Wolff. 2010. The web is dead. Long live the Internet. *Wired* (August 17, 2010). http://www.wired.com/magazine/2010/08/ff_webrip/ ; accessed 11/30/2010; and Joseph Janes. 2010. As the web fades away (Users are gravitating toward special-purpose utensils like apps, gadgets, and widgets). *American Libraries* 41(10): 35.

Embedding Information Mediation in the Structure of the Information Environment

In the end, public libraries with their existing resource and institutional constraints will not be able to fully meet all of the information mediation needs of their 21st century users with just the traditional professional librarian-as-information-mediator model. The full needs of modern consumers, clients, and citizens for mediation of trusted information cannot be met entirely within the confines of existing public libraries.

While the goal of providing open and trusted mediation is the same (the same function), new tools and approaches beyond hiring expensive professional librarians will be part of the library's future. Hints can already be seen of the outlines of this new future in the form of existing technologies currently under development such as .standards-based inter-operability between communities of users, the emerging power of the open source movement, and the emergence of social computing systems to help structure vast amounts of information.

Standards-based Inter-operability between Communities of Users

Communities of users who need to do business with each other on a day-to-day basis need to create and maintain ways to reliably exchange information between members of their communities. Information needs to be transparent and trusted to be useful within these communities. For example, medical professionals who contribute information to a digital medical record need to be able to know when, how, and by whom previous entries on the record were made. They need to be able to trust the professional competence of those adding to the medical record in the past. Because the medical community needs such trusted information about its patients to do its work, professional norms must emerge that will generate the needed information systems. Users such as Ellen and Robert will benefit from the efforts of the professional medical community to mediate standards and norms for digital medical records.

Similarly, managers of commercial supply chains need access to reliable, transparent, and traceable information interchange standards in order to do their jobs efficiently. Part of these supply chain systems gets down to the details of tracking particular cartons of product identified by an RFID chip from point of manufacture to the final retail site. When this type of fully traceable and auditable information finally makes it to the information package that Ellen and other consumer advocates have to examine in order to make value-based purchases, consumer activists will have greater trust in the information because of the industry-enforced standards (sometimes backed by government-sanctioned standards such as the current USDA organic information standard) behind such information sources.

Financial information, especially inter-institutional exchanges starting with simple credit card transactions, and leading up to and including complex capital financing transactions, need to be characterized by a high degree of trust, transparency, and clarity about who is making the transaction, when, and how. All such transactions need to be able to meet the requirements of a formal financial audit, guaranteeing to all members of the community that the information associated with a given financial transaction can be trusted. Here, mediation is being performed by the financial community itself as it produces the information.

When communities of professionals get serious about setting information standards to mediate inter-operable information exchanges in their day-to-day work, ordinary consumers/clients/citizens gain access to trusted and open information that is being continually "mediated" by the standards and norms of professional practice. Surely, the advent of such community-based standards will also shape and inform how librarians do their business within the context of public libraries as a formal institution, changing the information sources available to patrons, as well as the methods of accessing these records through online tools. The librarian's skill set will need to change to accommodate such new information venues.

The Open Source Information Movement

Software systems such as Linux, Firefox, and Open Office are examples of the products of open source collaboration that create innovative software products. One key to creating such open source software is a legal framework that opens information to a community of users while not allowing that same information to be taken into the private intellectual property domain of future system developers to fuel personal gain. But "open source" is much more than a legal framework to foster some types of software development—it is a broader philosophy and set of practices for organizing information on the Internet. It relies on the power of shared contribution to create and transfer new ideas versus a quid pro quo view of information transactions. Enlightened self-interest with one eye on the public good promotes the information needs of the many, while seeking to preserve rights of information creators. This open source philosophy is moving beyond software development into the arena of scholarly publication, threatening to overturn the financial structure of the academic publishing industry as we know it. The Google Books project, while running amok in issues of copyright and orphaned works, is a prime example of the types of policy and management issues that surely will characterize a future of a more open-source view of mediating the information environment.

The mindset and working philosophy of Green's public librarians will be sorely needed as our society seeks to steer itself toward a fully open source view of the knowledge base held and needing to be shared by humanity as a whole. Indeed, the current move to create a National Digital Library (NDL)[36] can be seen as perhaps the ultimate expression of the potential for the open source movement to provide trusted and open mediation to immense information resources for the consumer/client/citizen/user of the

---

[36] Robert Darnton. 2010. Can we create a national digital library? *New York Review of Books* 57 (16; October 28): 4; and Steven Bell. 2010. Fit libraries are future-proof. *American Libraries* 41(10): 37-39.

21st century. The very definition of "library" will necessarily change to deal with global, multilingual, digital, multimedia information and the tools needed to access such a vast collection. The Internet creates the potential for a library without walls, encompassing all available information. It remains to be seen how libraries will meet the challenges of information overload in such an environment.

Social Computing Systems Provide Trusted Mediation of Information Sources

Vignette 6B, Buying coffee in the not-very-distant future, clearly suggests how the trusted mediation of open information will be supported by the emergence of advanced social computing systems. The Consumer Values Institute system that Ellen consulted was the result of a carefully created social computing system designed to elicit, merge, and present the organized opinions of consumer advocates about the coffee that Ellen was seeking to purchase.

Already millions of users voluntarily contribute their time and resources to create shared communities of trusted information. As with Facebook, trust begins with and is tightly embedded within a network of known personal relationships.[37] But other social computing systems such as Wikipedia mediate shared information (while aspiring to create trusted information) in a more anonymous environment. Product and producer rating systems such as those in Amazon[38] and E-Bay[39] rely on fully anonymous

---

[37] C. Dellarocas. 2003. The digitalization of word-of-mouth: Promise and challenges of online reputation mechanisms. *Management Science*. 49(10): 1407–1424; M. Parameswaran. 2007. Social computing: An overview. *Communications of the Association for Information Systems* 19: 762-789. http://crec.mccombs.utexas.edu/attachments/105_Social_Computing_An_Over view.pdf ; accessed 11/30/2010; and R. Sinha & K. Swearingen. 2001. Comparing recommendations made by online systems and friends, in *Proceedings of the DELOS-NSF Workshop on Personalization and Recommender Systems in Digital Libraries*, Dublin, Ireland.

[38] Marjorie Kehe. 2009. Furor over Amazon ranking system. *The Christian Science Monitor*. April 13.

social computing systems to provide evaluations that customers and consumers can rely on.

Surely problems exist with existing social computing systems. They are subject to non-representative bias and they can drift into directions indicated by early users, exhibiting a kind of macro-path dependence where the final ratings depend too heavily on who comments first and with the most force. But these are problems that over time will be solved as social computing systems increasingly mature to mediate between the modern consumer/client/citizen/user and the immense information bases that they rely upon on a daily basis.

An Ending—What Goes Around Comes Around
In 1876, Samuel Green laid out a tidy vision depicting the future of public libraries. He envisioned a publicly funded institution that provided trusted mediation of information contained primarily in books held within the library for the edification of literate users from specific walks of life. This vision has proven remarkably durable as modern libraries continue to evolve and respond to changes in both their user base and the amazing shifts in the nature of information brought about by the Internet. Libraries continue to respond, grow and adapt. However, in the end they will soon be partnering with system developers and information scientists as trusted mediation comes to play an increasingly important role in all aspects of modern consumers', clients', and citizens' information lives. Recent innovations coupled with inventions yet to be imagined will continue to transform information mediation well into the 21st century and beyond. Vignette 7 presents one possible future.

---

http://www.csmonitor.com/Books/chapter-and-verse/2009/0413/furor-over-amazon-ranking-system ; accessed 11/30/2010.
[39] Jack Schofield. 2008. Sellers negative on EBay feedback change. *The Guardian.* February 21. http://www.guardian.co.uk/technology/2008/feb/21/ebay.consumeraffairs ; accessed 11/30/2010.

Vignette 7—A scenario for the information workplace of the future

Robert Marshall is now in college and working on a research paper for his political science class. Sitting in his dorm room he opens up his writing tablet and plugs in his cell phone. He has already outlined his paper, knows the arguments he wants to pursue and wants to look for references that will support his point of view. Using his cell phone as an information conduit to the library, he knows there are at least five apps that will be important tonight. First, there is a virtual librarian on duty 24/7 who will help him if he cannot find materials. He trusts this app's reliability and has rated it highly when asked to evaluate its merits. He knows that he and other students have also made online suggestions about improving its functionality. Next, there are a number of databases that he will access in the area of political science, all with full text available. He does not know or care who manages these databases or where the server resides. With the advent of standards for open source information, the library app simply gives him access. He knows that his topic has been discussed in detail in France so he might find himself using the library's translation program. The citation app will help him to create references to the materials he has used. As a final precaution, when his paper is done he will call up an app that will check his entire paper for materials that might be considered plagiarized so that he can go back and add appropriate citations. He has come a long way since high school and is grateful that his freshman year coursework included a full tour of library apps and their usefulness in the research process.

Information and library science might indeed be moving toward a time "after Internet time" in order to evolve and remain viable in providing and mediating information. At present, in 2010, information and library science would appear to be both moving in this direction and still responding to the forces of a rapidly changing Internet. As usual, it is not that public libraries will totally shift to a new medium, totally dropping old formats and technologies, but rather that they will continue to add to their collection of viable tools be that card catalogs, online public access catalogs, web pages, blogs, wikis, apps, or technologies that are still only on the drawing boards or in the minds of information engineers.

Endnotes

*The work presented in this paper was supported in part by the U.S. National Science Foundation INTEROP Program Grant #0955935, Consejo Nacional de Ciencia y Tecnología de México, and the Fulbright Carlos Rico Scholars Program (supported by COMEXUS in Mexico and the Canadian Fulbright Commission).

The Impact of the Internet on Crime Fiction

Jeffrey G. Barlow
Director of Berglund Center for Internet Studies
Pacific University

Abstract

This paper draws on reader-response theory and anthropological discussions of performance theory to analyze the impact of the Internet upon crime fiction and associated sub-genres, detective fiction (both "soft-boiled" and "hard-boiled"), police stories, and the thriller. Because of its nature, crime fiction has always reflected changes in the societies in which it is written and read, including the impact of wars and of rapid changes in technology.

This being the case, it is not surprising that the Internet is indeed having an impact upon these genres, particularly, among the most popular and tightly defined of them, detective fiction. Other genres, especially the thriller, have benefited from the impact of the Internet. Authors are responding to the Internet in a number of different ways, some of these resistant, others adaptive. Some authors, in attempting to respond to changes in audience behavior related to the development of the Internet, are transgressing the traditional boundaries of the genres.

In effect, earlier notions of ritual performance encapsulated in the interaction between author and audience in mystery fiction, and particularly in its most popular form, detective fiction, are yielding to new concepts of performer and audience. There are trends suggesting that the genre may well be enriched by the impact of the Internet as authors employ the Internet in creative ways to expand the form. But there are other indications that the genre may be forced to evolve beyond recognition in order to maintain an audience.

Keywords: Detective Novel; mystery fiction; internet mystery fiction

Introduction

This paper analyzes the impact of the Internet upon a popular literary genre, crime fiction. We argue here that crime fiction inevitably reflects social changes in the society in which it is written and read, and that the Internet is having a profound impact upon it. This impact, however, is mediated by the genre itself, so that some sub-genres (defined below), such as the detective story, are much more impacted than others, such as the thriller.

While this thesis may seem straightforward, it is a complex task to try to analyze the impact of the Internet upon even a narrow literary genre such as the crime story with its sub-genres of detective story, police story, and thriller. In our analysis we are relying upon two linked methodological approaches. One, a variation on reader-response criticism, comes from literary theory. The other is rooted in ritual performance viewed from an anthropological perspective. Each of these embraces, we believe, a common notion of performer and audience united in a highly structured activity, which can be viewed as ritual performance, whether written or physically performed.

Because it is the most tightly constructed of the crime genres, we concentrate primarily upon the detective story. This genre offers us a very large sample of works written over more than one hundred and fifty years by many creative minds. Glenn Most and William Stowe (1983) argue in the introduction to *The Poetics of Murder* that there are three major explanations for the popularity of the detective novel.

First is its narrativity; the detective story is almost pure narrative concentrating upon weaving elaborate plots within which the reader can play. The second reason for its success is its utility in sociological analysis; as a form of popular entertainment, detective stories tell us much about popular tastes and concerns. A third school believes that the power of the genre lies in its psychoanalytic appeal. Freud loved the genre and, Most and Stowe believe, modeled his own exploratory practices upon those of the detective (Most & Stowe, 1983).

George N. Dove, while benefiting greatly from the work of Most and Stowe, goes in a rather different direction. He focuses upon the differences between the detective genre and its parent genre, the mystery story. Relying upon reader-response criticism, he believes that the detective story is "essentially play transformed into art..." (Dove, 1997, p.1). It is this factor which places the reader/audience into a participatory stature. The author and the reader are engaged in the same game and each must respect the rules.

This notion of play leads us to the twin motifs "Performance and Participation" of the occasion for which this piece is written, the 12.0 conference of the Association of Internet Researchers (http://ir12.aoir.org/). One of the critical aspects of "performative behavior," according to the anthropologist William O. Beeman, is precisely this link between performer and audience. Performance, according to Beeman, is "socially co-created." (Performance theory). Victor Turner, perhaps the single most influential scholar in the study of the intersection between ritual and theater, further expands upon the notion of ritual as social drama. For Turner, all social dramas proceed through stages much as Dove argues, does the detective story: "breach, crises, redress, and either reintegration or recognition of schism." (Turner, 1982, p. 68; Turner, 1990).

The detective story can, we agree with Dove, usefully be analyzed as ritual and as social drama. It is our social dramas that are being narrativized, but we look, with the detective, for the culprit and for appropriate forms of reintegration. Sometimes we fail to find them and must live with the painful recognition of schism.

Definitions of the literary genres with which we propose to work while necessary, can be only partially successful. A genre usually evolves from an earlier one, and then may give birth to yet another. All variations may survive and bear various traces of their linked descent. Here we deal with three such overlapping types of crime fiction: detective stories, police stories and thrillers. All the works, whether shorter stories or books, which we will examine in any detail, fall into one of these categories; some into two; we attempt to define the three sufficiently tightly below so that no given work belong to all three.

Crime fiction evolved from an earlier broader genre, mystery fiction. If we define mysteries as fiction works which center around an unknown, then we can identify mysteries well before we encounter crime stories. Dame P. D. James, herself a very distinguished author of detective novels, argues that Jane Austen (1775 –1817), Charlotte Bronte (1816 -1855), and Anthony Trollope (1815 –1882) can all be thought of as mystery writers, though clearly in a very restricted sense, and crimes sometimes do feature in their plots (James, 2009, Loc. 57-69).

The boundary between mystery and crime stories becomes obvious with the development of the detective story. The essential element lacking in the mystery genre (Herbert, 1999)[1] before the detective novel could emerge was an actual detective. This character type was provided by an American writer, Edgar Allen Poe. In our definition, then, the boundaries of the "classical" detective genre begin with Edgar Allen Poe (1809-1849) and end following the British fiction of the "Golden Age"—sometimes

---

[1] We do not attempt to define the mystery genre in detail here. Many have argued that the genre grows out of European gothic tales. See "Gothic Novel" in Herbert, (ed.) *The Oxford Companion*…See also Alewyn, 74-5.

referred to as "soft-boiled" novels—in the period between the First and Second World Wars (James, 2009, Loc. 311-323). By that time, the essential form of the detective novel was set. We get variations with regard to content, for example, the "hard-boiled" sub-genre, but the form itself remains fixed for reasons explained below.

The detective story is usually said to begin with Poe (Alewyn, 1983, pg. 74; Dove, 1997; Herbert, 1999, pg. 141)[2] because he introduces in the *locus classicus* of the detective story, *The Murder in the Rue Morgue*, two elements essential to the classical model. The first of these is a detective who works in a logical fashion. The detective is Chevalier C. Auguste Dupin, who works largely with his wits. This type of detective, like Dupin, may not ever actually visit crime scenes, but relies upon published accounts or the labors of others.[3]

The second critical element in the detective story also introduced by Poe is a reader who is in possession of at least as much information as is the detective. Poe, then, first gives us the critical elements of a detective performance, actor and audience united by a common base of knowledge. We might define Bronte, Austen, and Trollope as mystery writers, but just as they lack a detective, they likewise fail to systematically offer knowledge or clues, including false ones, to their readers.

---

[2] Dove reiterates throughout *The Reader and the Detective Story* the primacy of Poe, writing "…in a sense, every detective story is a retelling of Poe's "The Murders in the rue Morgue." P. 9. Alewyn, however, argues that the German Romantic writer E.T.A. Hoffman (fl. 1819) is the earlier originator of the genre. Alewyn, p. 74; See also Herbert. *Oxford Companion*, p. 141.

[3] The contemporary equivalent of Dupin is Jeffrey Deaver's *Lincoln Rhyme series*. Deaver has taken this type of physically passive detective to its apogee, and unfortunately, well beyond. This novel, as well as all others mentioned here, was reviewed by me in *Interface*, the e-journal of the Berglund Center for Internet Studies at Pacific University. See the reviews in alphabetical order by book title in References II, below.

Short stories such as Poe's featuring detectives were quickly augmented by novels. The first detective novel is usually said to be Wilkie Collins' *The Moonstone*, published in 1868 (Anderson, 2007, Loc. 273-275). The success of the genre is clearly related to the development of industrial society and hence to the ebbing of Romanticism and the beginnings of the Modern. Whether we are discussing the earlier mystery store or the classical detective story or novel, each is greatly affected by the larger society around them.

It is clear, for example, that cataclysmic wars affect both writers and audiences, and following wars, genres frequently evolve from earlier types. Science and technology are also important influences. This is, after all, our thesis: that the dominant technology of our era, the Internet, has impacted these fiction genres in a definitive manner.

Insofar as the larger society of the Victorian era of the early mystery stories was concerned, it is evident that the leisure time which had earlier made Romanticism possible both created a larger market for fiction and made the profession of writing more accessible. The emerging technologies of the Modern age increased both the audience and the possible length of fiction. Cheaper printing methods reduced costs; public transportation such as rapidly expanding railroads both moved printed products and produced captive audiences, who could in turn pick up novels at W.H. Smith bookstores and stalls strategically located at railway stations. Longer materials such as the detective novel were desirable to both the author and the reader. The author desired a larger stage for his or her detectives; more realistic characters sketched at length, more complex crimes, and more convoluted searches for solutions. The reader wanted to pass increasingly longer lengths of leisure time in pleasurable reading.

The master of this transition is Charles Dickens in his command of both the social context of industrial England and his understanding of such relatively new media as serialized newspaper pieces. The Dickensian scholar Joel J. Brattin believes that Dickens was the first to plan his work for both serialization and for later publication as a whole (*Dickens and serial publication*). Others, like Trollope, wrote the whole work, and then broke it up for serialization. Wilkie Collins was among Dickens' friends; some have argued that Dickens encouraged him to write (Anderson, 2007, Loc. 273-275; James, 2009, Loc. 165-173).

Following the development of the detective story, its leading artificer, Sir Arthur Conan Doyle (1859-1930), produced its greatest detective, or at least its most popular one, Sherlock Holmes. Holmes first took the stage in *A Study in Scarlet* in 1887. Holmes soon became the quintessential detective, despite the fact, some have argued, that Doyle played fast and loose with his audience, resorting to plot devices that violated many of the rules which would later define the detective story (Anderson, 2007, Loc. 290-294).

Part of the appeal of Doyle at the time was his use of the advanced science of the era as E.J. Wagner, herself a serious student of forensics, has shown. Doyle, a physician by training and practice, had a keen interest in the forensic sciences of the times. Holmes often uses scientific information which was not widely known at the time but largely the province of specialists. In some cases, Holmes speculates about future developments which, in fact, came to pass, such as tests which could accurately identify bloodstains long after they had dried, impossible at the time of writing (Wagner, 2007). Holmes also made a full use of new developments in communications, deriving critical information from cables and telegrams, and employing the fastest transportation possible to outwit his villains. Had the Internet been available, certainly both Doyle and Holmes would have employed it.

Poe gave the detective his or her first tool: logic. Doyle gave them a critical second tool: science. The astonishing modernity of the

Holmes stories is, of course, lost to us today. But science and logic remain the twin foundations of the genre to the present.

Doyle was also very familiar with the crimes and criminal trials of the period and often borrowed freely from details of actual crimes to shape his plots. Plot elements which may now seem to us to be outlandish or contrived often had a basis in events with which the readers of the time were familiar (Wagner, 2007, Loc. 1812). Doyle was also the first author to discover a mass audience for detective stories, and the viability of a series featuring the same characters (Anderson, 2007, Loc. 372-379).

Poe is clearly a transitional figure between the Romantic and the Modern. His poetry is often gothic in the extreme; some have taken his killer ape in the *Murder in the Rue Morgue* as representative of the out-of-control nature abhorred by Romantics (Lehman, cited in Anderson, 2007, Loc. 266-270). Doyle, while he had his Romantic moments, might be said to be almost the apotheosis of the Modern.

By 1928, the detective story had become such a well-defined type that the American author, Willard Huntington Wright (1888 - 1939), writing the Philo Vance series as S.S. Van Dine, was able to state twenty "rules" for the genre (Van Dine, "Twenty rules). Perhaps because of his status as an important English theologian, Ronald Knox, also a prolific author of detective novels, produced another version, the Decalogue or "Ten Commandments of Writing Detective Novels," a year later in 1929 (Harrington & Knox, 1929).[4]

---

[4] These were published in Knox' introduction to *The Best English Detective Stories of 1928*, ed. Horace Liveright 1929. They were among the club rules of a group organized by English writers of detective novels, which included as founding members: G.K. Chesterton, Agatha Christie, A.A. Milne, and Associate Members Helen Simpson, and Hugh Walpole. The rules were known as "The 10 Commandments for Detective Novelists." These were:

1. The criminal must be someone mentioned in the early part of the story, but must not be anyone whose thoughts the reader has been allowed to follow.

In the period between the World Wars, often referred to as "The Golden Age of detective fiction," these rules were usually followed, and no wonder, since many noted authors had a hand in producing them. Stripped of their humorous sallies, these might be boiled down, following the points where Van Dine and Knox largely agree, to be, in the words of Van Dine (1928) (http://ronaldknoxsociety.com/detective.html):

- The reader must have equal opportunity with the detective for solving the mystery. All clues must be plainly stated and described.
- No willful tricks or deceptions may be placed on the reader other than those played legitimately by the criminal on the detective himself.
- The detective himself, or one of the official investigators, should never turn out to be the culprit.
- The culprit must be determined by logical deductions — not by accident or coincidence or unmotivated confession.

---

2. All supernatural or preternatural agencies are ruled out as a matter of course.
3. Not more than one secret room or passage is allowable.
4. No hitherto undiscovered poisons may be used, nor any appliance which will need a long scientific explanation at the end.
5. No Chinaman must figure in the story.
6. No accident must ever help the detective, nor must he ever have an unaccountable intuition which proves to be right.
7. The detective must not himself commit the crime.
8. The detective must not light on any clues which are not instantly produced for the inspection of the reader.
9. The stupid friend of the detective, the Watson, must not conceal any thoughts which pass through his mind; his intelligence must be slightly, but very slightly, below that of the average reader.
10. Twin brothers, and doubles generally, must not appear unless we have been duly prepared for them.

- The detective novel must have a detective in it; and a detective is not a detective unless he detects. His function is to gather clues that will eventually lead to the person who did the dirty work in the first chapter...
- There simply must be a corpse in a detective novel and the deader the corpse the better. No lesser crime than murder will suffice.
- The problem of the crime must be solved by strictly naturalistic means. Such methods for learning the truth as slate-writing, Ouija-boards, mind-reading, spiritualistic séances, crystal-gazing, and the like, are taboo.
- The culprit must turn out to be a person who has played a more or less prominent part in the story — that is, a person with whom the reader is familiar and in whom he takes an interest.
- There must be but one culprit, no matter how many murders are committed. The culprit may, of course, have a minor helper or co-plotter; but the entire onus must rest on one pair of shoulders.
- Secret societies, camorras, mafias, et al., have no place in a detective story. A fascinating and truly beautiful murder is irremediably spoiled by any such wholesale culpability.
- The method of murder, and the means of detecting it, must be rational and scientific.
- The truth of the problem must at all times be apparent — provided the reader is shrewd enough to see it.
- A professional criminal must never be shouldered with the guilt of a crime in a detective story. Crimes by housebreakers and bandits are the province of the police departments — not of authors and brilliant amateur detectives. A really fascinating crime is one committed by a pillar of a church, or a spinster noted for her charities.

This list clearly defines a very specific genre. The emphasis is on enabling an active audience—the reader must be given adequate information, and the killer and his or her methods must fall within well-defined boundaries. Given adherence to these rules, then the game is, indeed, afoot.

Below we will describe the detective novel as a sort of text-based "game" of a special sort. But because of its strict rules, it is simultaneously a ritual performance in an anthropological sense which depends on audience familiarity with the ritual structure for its success. It is this relationship between author and audience that distinguishes the detective story from mere narrative; the author narrates a story, of course. But the audience must work hard at assembling the story from the fragments provided. Authors have violated these rules well before they were written, and would frequently do so after, but they provide a basis upon which to separate the detective genre from the mystery story, and from the later police story or thriller as well (James, Loc. 81-110).

The body of work that most directly adheres to the strictly defined rules is the British dominated literature of the inter-war period, the so-called "Golden Age." Four women, the *Queens of Crime*, Agatha Christie (1820-1976), Dorothy L. Sayers (1893 –1957), Ngaio Marsh (1895–1982) and Margery Allingham (1904 –1966) dominated the field (Herbert, 1999, p. 436, 423).[5] Their works, particularly those of Christie, are often set in carefully isolated sites such as villages, manors, or even on islands where victims, suspects and the detective, amateur or professional, must work in a very circumscribed society. Such techniques easily lent themselves to tightly constructed stories which closely followed the rules outlined above.

---

[5] http://en.wikipedia.org/wiki/Detective_fiction#Golden_Age_detective_novels
Although this is a Wikipedia article and hence anonymous, and in this particular case, although generously sourced, it also depends on a relatively narrow bibliography. However, those sources are excellent ones, and the article itself has very broad coverage and many branches to other useful Wikipedia locations on related subjects.

In this period, while the form remained fixed, the content was free to evolve considerably. The detective type changed from the somewhat cold and forbidding Holmes—the very essence of scientific objectivity—to Christie's very human, frequently comical Hercule Poirot. We also get variations upon the formal detective figure, the "Surrogate Detective," and the "Spinster Sleuth," perhaps the best known of which is Christie's Miss Marple, although there are dozen of this latter type, if not hundreds (Herbert, 1999, p. 436, 423). These developments open up the genre and give it new life. But despite these changes the highly ratiocinative detective of the earlier type continued to find a ready audience, as do the Spinster Sleuths, some of whom flourish today. This evolution of the detective story raises some important questions: Why did leading authors in this genre almost uniquely codify its rules? And why have these rules been so successful that they continue to define the genre today? We believe, with many others, that the unique feature of this genre is a virtual contract between author and audience (Dove, 1997, ch.1; Heissenbuettle, 1983, p. 79-93; Stowe, 1983, p. 373-374). The essence of the genre is a highly stylized search for information, most usually for "whodunit," though the missing information may also include the "why" and more often the "how" of the crime, almost inevitably a murder.

This contract, the unique feature of the detective novel, is an agreement on the part of the author to not break the "rules" in major and egregious ways. To George N. Dove, following Hans-Georg Gademer, the detective novel can be analyzed as "play" of a particular sort. It is a game, in the sense of a pastime with rules and boundaries, which can only be played if those rules are followed (Dove, 1997, pp. 14-17). No rules; no game; no play. For this reason, the detective story is uniquely composed of both its structure and its conventions.

The audience for the detective story is usually assumed by the author to be an experienced one; most readers have read many such stories and are, as a result of their experience, intuitively familiar with the rules, although they may not be able to state them in any didactic sense. The readers' goal in this game is a hermeneutic one, that is, to construct a whole, an understanding of the crime, from its parts—the clues offered in the story as it develops.

The satisfaction is a special one, of course, when the reader achieves a *verstehen*[6] in advance of the detective. This however, is not ultimately necessary to the enjoyment of the genre. Simply realizing at the end, that in fact, there was a whole, and that the author has hidden or partially hidden it from the audience, is akin to the admiration we achieve from watching any star performer. It is, however, even more intense because we, as audience, have participated in a very active sense, quite unlike that of reading in other genres.

The fact that the detecting game has been played by thousands of authors and audiences in the millions for nearly two centuries has many additional consequences. Out of repeated performances by virtuoso artists and their highly experienced audiences, extended frameworks of implicit understandings have grown up. There are a number of expectations layered on top of the rules themselves. We regret that we cannot go into all of these in detail, but to mention only a few:

- The most likely suspect is probably innocent.
- Anything mentioned however lightly in the story is probably a clue and should move the story forward.
- Detectives never get to take vacations unmarred by murder; if they go to a play or an opera, it probably will not be concluded satisfactorily for all performers or audience members.

---

[6] I use this term in a Dilthean sense; an understanding reached by an active participation in the process of knowing, by recursive movement between the part and the whole, or between the particular and the general.

- An unidentified body will probably be misidentified at least once.
- Missing people are probably either dead or guilty.
- If somebody contacts the detective with an intention to pass on information but defers doing so, they are probably as good as dead. (This is referred to as the "death warrant.")

Despite these conventions each performance, however stylized, is unique. The game is played not only in the conventions, but also between them, in the "probabilities" listed above. These are "blanks," and have a heuristic purpose; they are intended to provoke the reader to fill them in for him or herself, thus driving the internal analysis forward (Dove, 1997, p. 42).

Even the structure of the performance has become as stylized as a kabuki play. Dove identifies seven stages in the development of a mystery which are almost invariably followed:

1. The statement of the problem. (Somebody has been murdered. But how? Why? And importantly, by whom?)
2. The first solution: Often the arrest of the innocent, or at least the suspicion of such a character.
3. The complication. Often that character is murdered!
4. The period of gloom. We may never know! The detective drinks, or if he is Nero Wolfe, goes back to his orchids.
5. The dawning light. New clues. The Watson rouses the Holmes from his apathy.
6. The solution. The key clue is found.
7. The explanation: often a soliloquy in which the detective explains all (Dove, 1997, p. 8). Poirot first misleads, then pounces!

Over the extended performance of the detective story, we have come to accept the structure as part of the rules. This gives the audience additional imperatives. We are not satisfied with anything less than a solution. In the earlier periods of the detective story, down to the period after World War I, audiences expected that the ritual would result in reintegration: All Will End Well; The criminal would be found out and appropriately punished. Hence, readers were able to tolerate the human depravity and copious amounts of blood and gore laid before them. They were engaged, but also comfortably aware of participating in a highly stylized ritual performance.

This leads us to an important exception to fixed "rules." We think that this very historicity of the detective story has introduced a certain amount of flexibility to the rules. Because we have read so many examples, each of which has its own set of "blanks," we do not insist on a slavish following of the rules. Any story can deviate from them at points, providing that these do not break the contract between author and audience. The writer must "play fair." But there are points beyond which we will not go. Anderson puts this very well in acknowledging some of the difficulties of the plots of Raymond Chandler, often lauded as the best of the 20th century writers in the hard-boiled sub-genre:

> At some point the reader has a right to say, "What the hell is going on here?" A lot depends on the context. We tolerate Chandler's plots for the sake of his characters and his prose. My problem with *The Chill* starts with the fact that it is extremely hard to follow, and when you do decipher it you have to accept that the same woman would kill three people over a twenty-year period (Anderson, 2007, Loc. 1104-1109).

As the detective story evolved changes in the rules were legitimated, almost required, by social change. The Golden Age of the British detective stories had among other conventions, the expectation that the crimes would occasion a minimum of bloodshed and suffering, and that the results would ultimately be comforting ones.

But some social events, such as wars, rapid changes in media and technology, even in transportation, inevitably impact both writers and audiences for mystery fiction. This reaction can go in two possible directions, however. Some writers and audiences of detective fiction clearly become prepared for greater extremes of violence and bloodshed. Others reacted by attempting to reaffirm the status quo ante. These correspond, of course, to Turner's notion of rituals ending in either reintegration (the status quo ante) or schism—a new stage in the society and in the genre as well.

The British readers and writers of the late 19th century participated in or were influenced by successive colonial wars. They were no less marked by war than later veterans—whether combatants or civilians—of the later "Great" wars would be. We can see the effects of the British colonial wars all through the literature of the earlier era. Doyle wrote several works justifying the very controversial Boer War. Colonial wars or their effects are mentioned repeatedly in his works. It is clear from the beginning, for example, that one of Dr. Watson's defining characteristics is his recently completed service in Afghanistan. It is the first thing that Holmes tells Watson about himself: "You have been in Afghanistan I perceive (Wagner, 2007, Loc. 90)." This is the Afghanistan of which Rudyard Kipling, at almost the same time, wrote:

> When you're wounded and left on Afghanistan's plains,
> And the women come out to cut up what remains,
> Jest roll to your rifle and blow out your brains
> An' go to your Gawd like a soldier.[7]

The many African adventure novels of the very popular and influential H. Rider Haggard (1856 – 1925) were drenched in blood (usually that of people of color), but the violence was mostly

---

[7] See complete poem at: http://wonderingminstrels.blogspot.com/2003/01/young-british-soldier-rudyard-kipling.html

of a tasteful and Romantic sort.[8] Haggard, Kipling, and Doyle all knew each other and often appeared in the same serial publications; for example, *The Strand Magazine* published each of them between January and June 1892.[9]

But then Romanticism died an unnatural death in the industrialized slaughter of the trenches of World War I. Kipling pulled strings to get Jack, his barely 18-year old son into the British Expeditionary Force. Jack died in his first battle, at Loos in 1915, along with 75,000 other men in less than two weeks (Kipling, 1915). Doyle wrote of a visit to the Front:

> [a] shattered man, drenched crimson from head to foot, with two great eyes looking upward through a mask of blood . . . might well haunt one in one's dreams (Doyle, 1920, p. 312).

The Romantic enthusiasm for war flagged significantly after World War I, but the level of violence remains reflected in some later

---

[8] See a graphic from one of Haggard's illustrated works at:
http://www.google.com/imgres?imgurl=http://upload.wikimedia.org/wikipedia/com
mons/d/d1/Thure_de_Thulstrup_-_H._Rider_Haggard_-_Maiwa%27s_Revenge_-
_Fire,_you_scoundrels.jpg&imgrefurl=http://en.wikipedia.org/wiki/File:Thure_de_T
hulstrup_-_H._Rider_Haggard_-_Maiwa%27s_Revenge_-
_Fire,_you_scoundrels.jpg&usg=__pSJZnUYVrcUK6GjRm8O2bcIZjTA=&h=5140
&w=7388&sz=14530&hl=en&start=0&sig2=lGv7Nps--
FWXeexhJnjqcQ&zoom=1&tbnid=vpmw3viAA8D0BM:&tbnh=141&tbnw=182&ei
=3VTxTc7FDYf4sAP529mpDg&prev=/search%3Fq%3DH%2BRider%2BHaggard
%2Bgraphic%26um%3D1%26hl%3Den%26safe%3Doff%26client%3Dfirefox-
a%26sa%3DN%26rls%3Dorg.mozilla:en-
US:official%26biw%3D1035%26bih%3D630%26tbm%3Disch&um=1&itbs=1&iact
=hc&vpx=354&vpy=92&dur=13573&hovh=187&hovw=269&tx=162&ty=115&pa
ge=1&ndsp=17&ved=1t:429,r:2,s:0&biw=1035&bih=630 Accessed June 9, 2011

[9] See the volume for sale at: http://www.mynotera.com/1892-THE-STRAND-
MAGAZINE-Bound-Volume-ARTHUR-CONAN-DOYLES-ADVENTURES-OF-
SHERLOCK-HOLMES-Rudyard-Kipling-Alexandre-Dumas-H-Rider-Haggard-F-C-
Burnand-May-Queens-and-much-more,name,149491,auction_id,auction_details
Accessed June 9, 2011

fiction. The problem of the post-war veteran was quick to enter plot lines. Margery Allingham, for example, one of the Four Queens of golden age British detective stories, married a World War I vet and subsequently dealt with related social issues in several of her stories (Anonymous, The unpleasantness).

Other authors, and their grateful audiences, however, retreated behind the comfortable bulwarks of the classical form and returned to reintegrative ritual. This seems to be especially true for most of the female writers of the Golden Age. Agatha Christie, for example, was no less touched by the war than was Allingham; her first husband flew in France in the Royal Flying Corps. But Christie seems deliberately intent on constructing a generously warm and humane atmosphere—despite occasional outbreaks of poisoning and other complicated forms of murder--so as to restore normality (Anderson, 2007, Loc. 409-415). These differences may well reflect gender differences in male and female experiences of war in Anglo-American cultures.

The Golden Age was quickly overtaken by World War II, but the detective genre novels of the era continue to be emulated today, and have spun off another definable sub-genre, the modern "Cozy," intended for largely female audiences, in which all forms of unpleasantness, including murder, are deliberately soft-pedaled (Cozy, 2011).

As global wars accumulated, however, very important elements of the earlier pre-war frame for detective stories would be changed. As in the earlier period when the detective story evolved, there are also simultaneous changes in media. The war time rationing of paper and the great demand for reading material on the part of millions of men in English-speaking armies who became well accustomed to hurrying up and waiting had created a vast new market for the paperback novel or "pocket book."[10] This process again amounted to a sort of increased democratization of literacy, just as had the newspaper serializations and the dime novels of the late Victorian era.

Sub-genre: The American Detective Story

The earlier forms discussed above usually had one element in common: a detective who ratiocinates his or her way to solutions. But now the more physical and often markedly less thoughtful American "hard-boiled" detective was introduced. Authors and audiences continued to want to focus upon the pure sleuth (Most & Stowe, 1983, p. 80), but the classical boundaries of the genre were greatly enlarged.

Dashiell Hammett and Raymond Chandler are almost unanimously given the credit, if not for introducing the hard-boiled detective, for showing how much could be done with stories with central figures such as Sam Spade and Philip Marlowe (Anderson, 2007, Loc. 703-709). Hammett himself had been a Pinkerton detective, and Sam Spade's cynicism and suspicion of authority and power found an immediate response with American audiences first, then with the world. Anderson argues that Spade replaces the cowboy as the iconic American hero, but he might well have argued that in fact, Spade was the cowboy (Anderson, 2007, Loc. 511-514). But it was Chandler who fully anchored the now venerable genre into the fabric of American life, notably in Southern California (Most & Stowe, 1983, p. 123; James, 2009, Loc. 703-709).

The hard-boiled detectives were often professional "private eyes" who worked for a salary. While this achieved a greater realism, it also necessitated alterations in earlier conventions. Private eyes do not investigate murder. However, murder by then had been defined as the significant event of almost all detective novels. We

---

[10] There were more than 123 million military editions of paperbacks in circulation by the end of the war. See Books in Wartime, 1941-1947, at:
http://www.yankreenactment.nl/pagina16.html

therefore get a convention or a "blank" wherein the detectives are hired to investigate a minor crime, but murder quickly intrudes.

Maureen Reddy demonstrates in her definitive work *Sisters in Crime* that the hard-boiled detectives had something else in common: a negative view of women, amounting perhaps to pathology in Chandler's case. Their villains are frequently stereotyped *femme fatales*, and there is a clearly demonstrable fear of unbridled female sexuality among the boys. This motif continues among many of their successors, particularly Mickey Spillane's ultra-violent Mike Hammer (Reddy, 1988, p. 97).

The hard-boiled detectives often also had in common contacts in the criminal world, and a willingness to dive into it in search of the killer. This effectively opened up new sources of information and the plot as well. In the hard-boiled type there are few isolated villages or locked rooms, but rather mean streets which might well lead the detective, and the reader, anywhere.

Even the point of view of the detective story often changes from a largely detached one in which a "Watson" or another sidekick relates the story, or it is told in an authorial third person voice. Now the voice is often the detective's, giving us much more insight into that troubled individual's opinions and psychoses. This permits a much wider panorama in which the audience learns about many other factors—such as food, drink, and fashion tastes. These humanize the detective but do not necessarily forward the plot.

The creation of the hard-boiled detectives is the most significant change in the detective novel after Poe, Dupin, and Doyle's Holmes. They permit authors a more introspective, critical, and even angry look at the injustices of American society than had usually been the case for the more formal British detectives. The type was so successful that their ranks would swell to include drunks, bullies and near—some might say actual—psychopaths. In this period, then, there were remarkable changes in the content of the detective story, perhaps driven by the continuing violence of large-scale global wars supported by changes in media.

The above are but a few of the significant changes in this genre. Even these changes are nonetheless minor ones when viewed against the extreme conservatism of the form. The quest is still for information and the basic rules of the detective novel continue to be important. The audience still must have access to information or discover it along with the detectives, and complex tricks or illusions are still cheating.

An important variant form, now a well-established sub-genre, was the "police novel." This also flourished in the United States, although there are many British and continental forerunners. In these, it is often said, procedure replaces insight. Policemen think, of course, but it is usually the relentless grinding of routine that solves crimes. This form is now much more frequently encountered in film and TV than the classical type, but because it is a significant variation on the detective novel, we discuss it here only for what it tells us about the latter.

This genre is not defined by plot, the very essence of the detective story, nor even by procedure, though they are often referred to as "procedurals," but by character. The cops, just as the private eyes, are individuals and their individuality often drives the plot (Panek, 2003, p. 1-2). The development of this genre shows both the importance of the critical elements of the rules of the detective story, and the impact of social change upon the larger mystery genre.

The police novel violates critical aspects of the earlier rules. Although character development is critical, it is not the character of a lone wolf like the detective. The police represent society and work very much in a social organization. Panek develops a number of characteristics of police novels, drawn from a broad survey of the field. These functions must loosely adhere to the earlier rules, but are less admonitory than descriptive. The police novel is about "The Job." Police work is just that, work. It has its own jargon, much of which has seeped via film and TV into colloquial English, and its own family rules cannot be violated except at great hazard from other police. The job is to a high degree a hereditary occupation. It has its own mode of learning, "on the job"; its particular pains—paperwork, politicians, and civilians; its own dangers—drinking, divorce, and violent death (Panek, 2003, p. 37).

The fact that the police novel took so very long to flourish tells us much about the detective. There were police forces in the 19th century and policemen walk on and off stage in most of the classics, but they are usually comic relief or reminders of the degradation of crime. They are often described by their physicality—strong, brutish, large, and often, stupid. They were also notoriously corrupt, particularly in the United States.

Dupin and Holmes work with some enlightened police who become unofficial sidekicks, though rarely the Watson. Police allies are sometimes necessary to the soft-boiled surrogate detectives of the Golden Age, but are often the actual enemy of the hard-boiled private eyes.

All of these qualities are not only a reflection of nineteenth century and early twentieth century social realities, but also relate to the compact between writer and author in the detective story. The audience wants to encounter a like mind at work, usually an admirable mind embodied in a character of equivalent or higher social status to his or her own. The peasant wit is a recognizable American and British type, but we do not encounter them as detectives until perhaps Columbo in the late 20th century. Policemen simply will not do.

The compact in its purest form also requires as protagonist a single mind with which the audience can interact. If we get a buzzing hive of characters, as in Ed McBain's ensemble in the 87th precinct stories, we get easily confused, and so does the plot, amidst the welter of love affairs, anxieties about promotion, and random crime (Anderson, 2007, Loc. 951-1020; Panek, 2003, pg. 55-62).

Because audiences are attached to the detective type, there has been a tendency for police novels to move closer to the detective story, perhaps in an attempt by writers and publishers to pick up both markets. This is sometimes done by making the policeman a lone wolf, much like a hard-boiled detective. Michael Connelly's Hieronymous (Harry) Bosch, for example, although nominally a cop, is such a rogue that he is often either detached to work on cold cases alone, or is temporarily—but regularly—in such disgrace that he is free to work as an individual. This gives him a sense of freedom, like both the detective and the private eye, to follow not the orders of superiors, but his own values. The same conditions occur on the other side of the water too, where Ian Rankin's Tartan Noir cop, Inspector Rebus, freely interprets the limits of police work.[11] The redoubtable Tana French's Irish cops, Frank Mackey and Cassie Maddox, work out of a Dublin station but are usually found well off the reservation (French, 2008, 2010). Lee Child's surrogate detective, the wandering Jack Reacher, was a military cop and Child's plots often require flashbacks into the back-story, and Reacher occasionally relies upon his old army contacts to solve current crimes.[12] Like Bosch and Rebus, Reacher was a loose cannon as a cop and frequently disciplined for it. Even Ed McBain, arguably with Joseph Wambaugh, the top practitioner of the cop novel, once killed off Steve Carella, his central protagonist in the 87th Precinct novels, only to have to resurrect him later, due to audience response (Dove, 1997, pp. 97, 105).

With the police novel we reach the latest development in the detective story. The former is a genre in its own right and has its own sub-genre of cop detectives which closely follows the usual

---

[11] See Rankin's website at: http://www.ianrankin.net/

[12] See Child's (and Reacher's) website at: http://www.leechild.com/

rules of the latter genre. With the present, we also, of course, enter finally into the Internet era, and the rapid development of yet another genre, the thriller.

Enter a New Technology: the Internet

The Internet is clearly a major development in human culture. It would be difficult to minimize its impact. Here we propose to first trace the development of the Internet while observing some broad impacts on crime fiction. Then we will turn to specific examples of the ways in which it has affected the genre.

We can see the antecedents of the Internet from the 1970's through to about 1980. These beginnings were a geek's paradise—the rest of us are highly indebted, but largely unable to understand exactly what it was the techies were really doing. The next stage of the Internet, we believe, is the decade from 1980-1990. At that time the technology behind the Internet was of primary interest to those trying to develop systems to interconnect isolated computers and systems. This process had actually begun several decades earlier, but the protocols necessary for true networking were not standardized until 1982. But by 1980 the visionaries among us had already begun to apply the Internet to their work.

By 1990, everyone (except those who would not see) could observe the impact of the Internet all around us. This awareness was much accelerated, of course, by the events known as the Dot.Com Bubble, usually dated from 1995-2000. In that third stage the Internet became widely used; in 1992 the millionth host was added to it. Only then did the Internet become truly influential and begin to have a significant cultural impact.

Writers quickly began to weave the Internet into their stories. This was inevitable because professional writers early took to computers. Every writer of a certain age can remember the time when they put aside their beloved typewriters (and their less beloved carbon paper and white-out) and took, however warily, to a computer. Once comfortable with a computer, the next step was computer-mediated communication; E-mail, gophers, list-serves, bulletin boards, then the World Wide Web followed quickly. It was impossible not to begin to consider what could be done with computers and the Internet in plots as well as in methods of production. Because networked communications systems had long been a staple of science fiction, it is difficult to say which author was the first to actually bring the Internet into his or her work. Vernor Vinge, a computer scientist, wrote a Sci-fi piece "True Names," a 30,000-word novella, which envisioned a networked world (Hafner, 2001). William Gibson is usually given credit for first using the term cyberspace, in 1982.[13] In 1993 Neil Stephenson's Snow Crash deals prominently with networked computers, but it is set in the 21st century, so it is again, Sci-Fi.

One suggestive indication of the penetration of the Internet is the early work of Dan Brown. He published *Digital Fortress* in 1998. *Digital Fortress* was clearly aimed, however clumsily, at the emerging market for books dealing with this weird new thing, the Internet. One of the back-cover blurbs refers to it as a "realistic technothriller" and another promises that it will "rivet cyber-minded readers." The book itself is confusing and muddled, and in fact has little to do with the Internet. It did not do well. It was, however, probably about the best that could be done in 1998, given limited public awareness and understanding of the Internet.

But in 2004, *Digital Fortress* was buoyed by Brown's success with *The Da Vinci Code* (then in first place in hardback bestsellers on *The New York Times* bestseller list) and with his paperbacks *Angels & Demons* and *Deception Point*, in first and second place respectively. When it was reprinted and four-walled *Digital Fortress* rose to 8th place.

---

[13] See http://www.etymonline.com/index.php?search=cyberspace

Development of the Thriller

The thriller, sometimes related to the mystery, and occasionally to the detective story, was emerging at the same time as was the Internet. By 2006, thriller writers had their own professional organization, International Thriller Writers, Inc. In 2006 the organization collectively published *Thriller*, edited by James Patterson, a book of short stories intended to represent both the organization and the genre.

James Patterson is perhaps the ultimate thriller factory—he is the author of one out of 17 hardback books sold in the U.S. Patterson first lauds the "openness to expansion" of the thriller, then states:

> ...what gives the variety of thrillers a common ground is the intensity of emotions they create, particularly those of apprehension and exhilaration, of excitement and breathlessness, all designed to generate that all-important thrill. By definition if a thriller does not generate that thrill, it's not doing its job.

Even granted that Patterson is not especially noted for the precision of his prose, this definition is nonetheless puzzling. It moves the definition of a genre from its subject—the works themselves—to the audience. This makes for an impossibly subjective definition, though it certainly gives us a feeling for the effects which Patterson feels critical to the thriller.

A more useful definition comes from Patrick Anderson, no fan of Patterson—he refers to him as "...the absolute pits, the lowest common denominator of cynical, scuzzy, assembly-line writing (Anderson, 2007, Loc. 4237-4239)." Anderson became the reviewer on the "thriller beat" for *The Washington Post Book World* beginning about 2002. He became the definitive source on thrillers when he received an Edgar award for the Best Critical/Biographical work of 2008 for *The Triumph of the Thriller:*

How Cops, Crooks and Cannibals Captured Popular Fiction. He defines the thriller as:

> Just what is a thriller? How is it different from a mystery or a crime novel? The terminology is far from precise, but let me suggest a few guidelines. Agatha Christie and her imitators wrote mysteries that stressed intellectual solutions to crimes... In this country, around 1930, Dashiell Hammett invented the American crime novel, also known as the detective or private-eye novel, and Raymond Chandler built on Hammett's work. Their hard-boiled tradition prevailed for several decades, but by the 1970s the crime novel began to mutate into something that was bigger, darker, more imaginative, and more violent: the modern thriller (Anderson, 2007, Loc. 70-88).

Although this definition is infinitely more useful than Patterson's, it is still evident that the thriller is a somewhat elusive genre. Anderson is clearly discussing the most recent evolution of the thriller and puts it as occurring after 1970, and later defines the "tipping point," when thrillers began to dominate best-seller lists, as occurring in 1981 (Anderson, 2007, Loc. 1169-1177).

Andersen may well be right about the modern thriller, but like all genres we have discussed here, it evolved over a much longer period. John Reilly and Clive Bloom state that "thriller" refers to "stories of heroic adventure set in criminal situations (Bloom & Reilly, 1970, pg. 460)." This generous definition could at times include detective novels, but is sufficiently broad to include a much wider range of works.

We will define "thrillers" for our purposes, as works usually involving crimes, but which do not have a detective or surrogate detective as the protagonist and are heavy on characterization as opposed to plot, which is often loose and freewheeling. Most importantly, thrillers emphatically do not share the crucial compact between author and writer wherein there are structured rules of play. The most critical distinction is that the reader need not have all the information which the protagonist has.

Thrillers often focus not on detective or on victim, but upon the criminal, who is often a collective of shadowy figures—terrorists, neo-Nazis, or communists—or, increasingly, a psychotic figure whose motives are inhuman, thus rendering the crime unsuitable for a classic detective story which presumes a rational motive. A sub-genre, the "action thriller," is even farther distanced from the detective story. The action thriller's characters are expressed almost solely in action, the central character is often impossibly heroic, and "the possible replaces the probable (Bloom & Reilly, 1999, p. 461)." Other definable sub-genres include the psychological thriller, the spy thriller, and the serial killer thriller (Cobley, 2000, pp. 460-461).

Thrillers violate so many of the classical rules of detective fiction that there is often no relationship between the two at all. Anderson believes that just as World War II prepared both writers and audiences for the hard-boiled detective, so did the Kennedy Assassination, the Vietnam War, and we would ourselves add, the events of 9/11, prepare us for the thriller (Anderson, 2007, Loc. 1171-1173). Reilly and Bloom argue that the thriller provides a sort of "magical and (or) fantasy resolutions" to our inchoate fears of such threats as anarchy, the Cold War, arms smugglers, and insurrections (p. 461). Again, we see Turner's discussion of ritual performance as evocative here; the thriller can confirm the status quo and reintegrate it, or it can remind us that there has been an irreparable schism in our order.

We are not sure that Anderson is correct that the thriller is increasingly the dominant form of the mystery genre. Below is a chart from a Google Ngram (an application for measuring the occurrence of search terms in the huge database of works scanned by Google world-wide).[14]

Ngram Graph 1

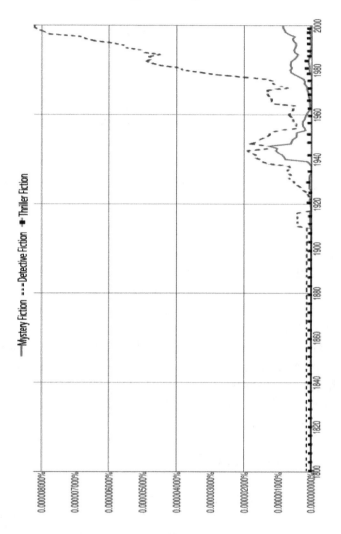

---

[14] See "Google's Ngram Viewer" at:
http://ngrams.googlelabs.com/ngrams/graph?content=mystery+fiction%2C+detective+fiction%2C+thriller+fiction&year_start=1800&year_end=2000&corpus=0&smoothing=3

The search terms we used were the cap-sensitive ones, "Detective Fiction," Mystery Fiction," and "Thriller Fiction." The occurrence of these terms in the corpus is very low as shown by the vertical axis. Because these terms are subject to so many interpretations, too much should not be made of this graphic.

Because the statistics for the term "Thriller Fiction" were extremely low relative to the other two categories, the green/thriller line appears flat. Here is an Ngram chart dealing only with "Thriller Fiction" (Be careful in comparing the charts— the line for Thriller Fiction is with squares in Graph 1, but a solid line in Graph 2 and the scale is very different). Graph 2 does indeed show a bump in the use of the term "Thriller Fiction" at 1980+, just as Anderson states, but one quickly followed by considerable gyrations.

Ngram Graph 2

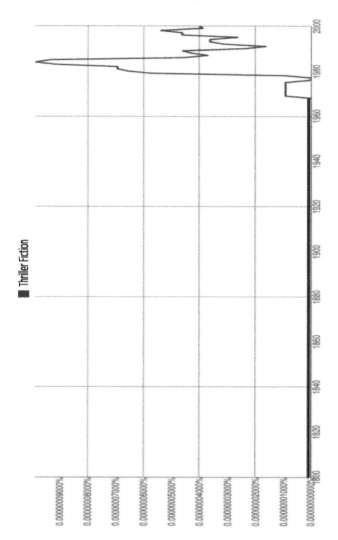

However, the combined Graph 1 very clearly shows that the "Detective Fiction" genre is mentioned much more frequently than is thriller or even mystery fiction in the Ngram database of works in this same period. This may indicate that, just as some authors and audiences took refuge following World War I in the reintegrative detective story, perhaps they are also doing so following the horrific events listed above, after the supposed tipping point.

What we perhaps can conclude from looking at both the development of the Internet and the rise of the thriller is that changes are occurring in audience tastes, and there is possibly a symbiotic relationship between the two. The detective story, however, is, if anything increasingly popular.

The Internet and the Thriller

The thrillers mentioned above, as well as many others we have read and reviewed, indicate that the advent of the Internet has done much for the genre. We cannot, of course, attribute direct causation but we believe that the growth of the Internet may well have stimulated the growth of the thriller. We say this for a number of reasons. First, the Internet has created a new arch-criminal type, the hacker.

At first computer or Internet-based thrillers were necessarily the provinces of those who had some background in technology and knew what they were doing. One such series, beginning in 1989, was the Kidd series which ran from 1989 to 2003 (Sandford). The writing was supple, the characters very interesting. The protagonists, Kidd, a male hacker and LuEllen, a female burglar, largely functioned as surrogate detectives. Though the series was clearly a thriller, there were many similarities to the hard-boiled school of detective novels. The author was John Camp, a Pulitzer-prize winning journalist, writing as John Sandford, and an early enthusiast of computers and computing.

Camp/Sandford is most noted for his later "Prey" series, featuring Lucas Davenport, a Minneapolis police detective. In the Kidd series, computers are central to both crimes and solutions. The first book in the series introduced such "cutting-edged technology" (Sandford's words, http://www.johnsandford.org/kidd01c.html) as:

His (Kidd's, the protagonist—a hacker) main computer is
an Amiga 2000. Even with the best accelerator card you
could get, its top speed was 30MHz. That is 1/100 the
speed of typical desktop computers today, and the chip is
much less advanced anyway.

Kidd uses modems for everything, usually at 1200 baud.
The Internet didn't exist back then. Or at least, for the
public it didn't exist beyond special (usually university-
based) connections to ARPAnet.

Nobody uses encryption. With the exception of academics
specifically studying it and certain governmental agencies,
encryption effectively didn't exist.

Over the years during which the four books were published they
showed a complex story arc which made them almost one work.
The use of computing grew ever more sophisticated. But by the
fourth book, even an enthusiast begins to feel that perhaps the
long explanations of technology necessary for a naïve audience are
taking some of the thrills out of the work. We return to this
problem below.

Sandford's Kidd, while a criminal, had a much more refined day
job as a consultant, and later, as a successful painter. He was too
much the "White Hat" to be a true villain. But the real world was
beginning to produce increasing numbers of these. By 1996, when
Kevin Mitnick, the first infamous hacker, was finally indicted for
illegal entry into corporate computers, he had been active for a
number of years. (Recall that the millionth host computer had not
been added to the Internet until 1992). In 1990 there were only 42
references to "computer hacker" in *The New York Times*, many of
which referred to the same several stories and often to phone
hacking rather than computer hacking.[15] In 1995 there were only

---

[15] See:
http://query.nytimes.com/search/query?frow=0&n=10&srcht=a&query=computer+h

62 such references, most of which were to Mitnick himself.[16] One of the first highly publicized virus incidents was the Melissa Virus, which affected 1.2 million computers, in March of 1999 (http://www.lycos.com/info/computer-hacking--cases.html).

Mitnick published his memoirs, first in 2002, then an additional work in 2005 (Mitnick & Simon, 2002, 2005). Almost simultaneously with Mitnick's 2002 book, Ejovi Nuwere and David Chanoff (2002) published *Hacker Cracker*, a much richer work than either of Mitnick's. From this point forward the notion of the hacker was firmly embedded in the minds of reading audiences, and easily researchable by thriller writers. As of 2005, computer hacking was still not in truth a major threat in the real world, but the perception of hacker criminality was widely known and increasingly feared.

The criminal hacker easily blended into other types of criminals and soon we have rapists and serial murderers stalking their prey on-line. M.J. Rose, a contributor to the 2006 short story collection *Thriller*, was herself a very knowledgeable computer user who had developed her career by clever uses of digital marketing techniques. Her 2006 work *The Venus Fix* featured a killer who accessed video cams to stalk young women (Rose, 2006). Of the 29 stories compiled in *Thriller* in 2006, six mentioned computers, but only two the Internet.

In 2008, two major writers, Michael Connelly and Jeffrey Deaver, each featured killers who, having mastered accessing the "hidden Internet, " lined up their victims through very sophisticated data mining, while simultaneously pinning the crimes on others, also with the use of computers (Deaver, 2009; Connelly, 2009).

---

acker&srchst=nyt&submit.x=30&submit.y=8&hdlquery=&bylquery=&daterange=period&mon1=01&day1=01&year1=1990&mon2=12&day2=31&year2=1990

The use of the computer and the Internet for evil goes on and on, of course. Andrew Vachss in a series of novels beginning in 1985 introduced a seriously twisted criminal, Burke, who later in the series focuses on child abusers who use computers for pedophilic crimes (Vachss, 2007). Child abuse was to become a frequent plot element in works dealing with the Internet. In between these examples, there were hundreds of other works of greater or lesser quality. By 2006, the computer-enabled criminal had become a staple in the thriller market.

As well as introducing a new type of criminal and opening out the possibilities for criminal activities, the Internet and "white hat" hackers also frequently assist the hero. This rapidly changed many of the conventions of the pre-Internet mystery story. Let us use an example from Michael and Daniel Palmer's (2006) thriller short story, "Disfigured." The son of the protagonist, Maura, has been kidnapped and is being held in order to force her husband, a noted plastic surgeon, to disfigure a patient who is scheduled for an operation. Maura is a rather typical thriller hero/heroine. Everyman, who has to draw on her native skills to survive an unexpected threat, usually of staggering proportions. "She was an egghead—a usually gentle scholar, not a woman of action. Now she would have to change, and change in a hurry (Loc. 2147-2149)." Fortunately, Maura is the sort of egghead who teaches Computer Science, at Cal Tech no less, and naturally has talented hackers among her students.

A common convention of the mystery or detective novel as well as the thriller is the shadowy automobile which begins to tail the protagonist. This is often the clue that opens up the solution, enabling the protagonist to identify the criminal or criminals. In pre-Internet plots, identifying the car was often a task assigned to a Watson or a friendly cop with access to a DMV database—the very sort of tiresome detail that would only bog down a thriller. Maura simply picks up her cell phone and calls "Hack" Burgess—her student, who "...put the 'eek!' in "geek." She soon has not only abundant information on the patient whose fate is tied to that of her son, but the identity of the owner of the automobile which has begun to menace her—it is the husband of the patient! Eureka!

There are many other advantages of the Internet for the thriller writer. The hacker who threatens the national interest—or even the entire world—by intruding into a computer quickly became a common type. For example, in 2003, R.J. Pineiro published *Cyber Terror*. This work deals with "an enemy determined to unleash a wave of destruction on America" by hacking major utilities and other vulnerable computer-operated control systems.

Information concealed in a computer also became an element of many thriller plots. "Man Catch," (2006), a story from *Thriller* by Christopher Rice, deals with a woman's use of her boyfriend's computer. Her search for "Mapquest" is auto-completed by the computer to send her to "Mancatch." This is a homosexual hook-up site of, what is to her, a shockingly overt low-rent sort. The plot depends upon her finding out how that information got into his computer, and into her life.

Despite the many advantages of the computer and the Internet to the thriller, they also have serious limitations as plot devices. Computers and the Internet quickly segment the audience, the opposite of what a thriller author wishes to accomplish. Digital technology opens up plots and speeds up the action, but to be persuasive it requires so much explanation that the plot easily loses all but the most technologically savvy members of the audience. But, lacking such explanation, less sophisticated audience segments cannot understand what is transpiring. And even the techies are going to be upset when the technology inevitably comes to seem dated to them.

In discussing the Kidd series in an interview (Sandford, The Fool's Run synopsis) Camp/Sandford raises a serious problem in writing realistically about computer-related crime. By the time a novel can go through writing, editing, publication in hard back, and finally reach a mass-market paper-back edition, the technology will be so dated that the work will then seem unrealistic. Possibly for this reason, Sandford abandoned the Kidd series and now works largely in the hugely successful Prey series.

The problem of dated technology can be overcome by extrapolating somewhat from current technology. But this solution runs the risk of moving too far into science fiction or fantasy. The works which feature J.D. Robb's female cop, Eve Dallas, a bodice-ripper/sci-fi thriller heroine who works for a sort of elite digital crimes bureau in the 2060 New York police department, are of this sort. Robb has an enormous audience and writes well in a number of genres. Her work *Fantasy in Death* is very well done. Robb makes many real-world references to current technology before slipping smoothly into describing future developments. Still, despite the latter, the work somehow seems realistic.[17]

This device can easily veer toward the ridiculous, however, as in Daniel Suarez' 2009 work *The Daemon*. Here, what starts out as a fairly rational explanation of artificial intelligence turns into a slam-bang thriller with autonomously driven killer vehicles making an absolute mess of both the plot and miles of highways. The work is noteworthy, however, because Suarez has excellent credentials as a systems developer, and the technology is carefully introduced in measured doses to the point where many readers would be quite content. A wide range of technological mavens, including Stuart Brand, Billy Brand (The former Director of Cybersecurity and Communications Policy for the White House), and Robin Cook reviewed it positively, all affirming it as presenting a possible future, given the direction of current technology.

But there remain numerous risks for a thriller writer who goes too deeply into technology, unless it is the sort of technology that very

---

[17] See the review by 'Toon reviewer IProfess at:
http://bcis.pacificu.edu/journal/article.php?id=752#1

rapidly goes bang! or boom! and the author is actively seeking the young or nostalgic aging white male demographic. But they are probably all reading a Tom Clancy novel, in any event.

The Internet has had a very positive impact on the thriller. It has provided classes of new villains, many of them the shadowy super-criminal type the genre prefers. These are now armed with digital tools of which we can believe just about anything—the word "hacker" has acquired new resonance. Heroes and their sidekicks too have taken on new dimensions. The thriller was able to accommodate these changes because of the fluidity of its structure. The detective story, however, is inherently burdened with much tighter boundaries, indeed, is defined by those boundaries and by the pact that the audience and the detective must proceed together in understanding the crimes at the heart of the genre.

The Detective Novel and the Internet

The Internet presents particular advantages and disadvantages to the detective genre. Some of these are similar to those impacting the thriller, but because the detective story has a much tighter structure, it has greater difficulty in adapting to the impact of the Internet. This is particularly true of the essence of the detective story as we have defined it—the contract between author and reader.

We discuss the advantages first. One of these is that the Internet opens up new types for the Watson. In both the high-tech content thrillers and detective stories, the Watson is often a low-tech personality who can ask the questions necessary to let the high-tech protagonist explain to the reader the nature of the technology. One of the old rules for the Watson was that they be a person slightly less intelligent than the reader, letting the reader feel superior while still getting necessary insights.[18] An example

---

[18] This is the 9th of Knox' Decalogue: "The stupid friend of the detective, the Watson, must not conceal any thoughts which pass through his mind; his intelligence

of this type is Camp/Sandford's LuEllen in the Kidd series. Although Sandford writes thrillers, he hews fairly closely to the model of the classical detective story and tries to play fair with his audience, and LuEllen is very much a Watson, though she also has attributes of the type Anderson labels "The More Dangerous Sidekick" (Anderson, 2007, Loc. 3091-3094).

Thrillers also, however, often have a pressing need for a new type of Watson, the hacker, who can carry much of the burden of dealing with the technology so that the hero can be physical and appropriately thrilling. But the hacker-Watson cannot be too successful or he or she can easily overshadow the hero. This is the case for the troubled Lisbeth Salander in Stieg Larsson's "Millennium series," who becomes progressively more central to the series until the original protagonist becomes largely her foil. Salander is perhaps the new arch-type of the geek Watson, a much more active and sometime threatening figure than the classic type (Larsson, 2010; Stevens, 2011).

One method of subordinating the hacker-Watson is to present him or her as a socially or economically disadvantaged hacker, often a person of color or of a markedly lower class who becomes the Internet specialist in the partnership. Lawrence Block's Matthew Scudder, a former alcoholic hard-boiled Private Eye, has his TJ, a black Times Square hustler (Block, 2000). TJ becomes ever more important in the series which grew to eight books into 2011, enabling the defiantly retro Scudder to keep up with the impact of the Internet.

Camp/Sandford's protagonist Kidd, himself a formidable hacker, nonetheless depends very heavily upon Bobby, a hacker who is both crippled and black. Bobby was once a phone phreak, and as the Internet developed he became the master of massive and carefully protected governmental and corporate databases, the

must be slightly, but very slightly, below that of the average reader."
(http://www.mysterylist.com/declog.html)

"Dark Internet" where only the most skilled can maneuver. Bobby does not make a physical appearance until the last book in the series, when Sandford opens the plot with his murder, as effective a declaration that the series is over as killing off Kidd or LuEllen, and emotionally a lot easier for the fans to swallow.

Maintaining the boundaries of the detective story, scrupulously following the rules, has always had its own complexities, but the Internet presents entirely new sets of challenges. A number of these occur over the issue increasingly not of how the detective "knows" but why he or she does not know. There is simply so much information on the Internet that the reader sometimes grows impatient with the detective who insists on plodding along, neglecting resources of which the audience is aware.
In surveying winners and nominees for Edgar awards we have begun to see a number of related ways of circumscribing the Internet within plot-appropriate boundaries. And however important the Internet may be in terms of its impact upon human society in general, it is important to remember that the publishing industry is market driven and that driving force is the need to sell books. So while the Internet may be important to those of us trying to understand it, to the detective author it is nothing more than a tool for advancing plot and a decidedly double-edged one as well.

Writers need not deal with the Internet at all, of course. Many authors have, for a variety of reasons, simply set their work in a time or place where the Internet is irrelevant. One who has been highly successful is Sue Grafton author of the Kinsey Millhone series. Grafton is quite conscious of the issue of technology and how it might affect plotting. In an interview in 1999, Grafton was asked (http://www.suegrafton.com/interview99.htm):

> Q. You admit that your books take place in a time warp—currently Kinsey is living in 1986, where she's been for the last few books. With ten letters of the alphabet to go, do you think you'll bring her into the present? If so, how will

you...and Kinsey...deal with the explosion of technological developments in her field in the past ten years?

Grafton answers: I'm still debating the issue of whether to jump Kinsey Millhone from 1986 into the present. For the moment, I prefer not to do so. When I started writing these books, I was interested in continuing the tradition of the hard-boiled private investigator. My heroes are still Raymond Chandler, James M. Cain, and Ross Macdonald. The stories they tell have nothing to do with technology and everything to do with human nature. Obviously, the modern day private detective and law enforcement experts have at their disposal a vast array of equipment and scientific techniques to aid in their pursuit of the criminal element, but I'd be willing to bet that much of the crime-solving process still comes down to skill, intuition, and experience.

Grafton may well be right, but if Kinsey ever comes into the present—and in the six books in the series published after that discussed above, she has not done do—she will find that many things have changed, and that plots set in the present simply must deal with the Internet in a convincing fashion, or come up with reasonable explanations for why they do not do so.

Contemporary settings, however, are important to audiences and to publishers. History is no longer even taught in many middle school systems and while there are plenty of successful works in the intersection between history and the detective story, the imperative is always to seek out the mass audience and new readers. Grafton's Kinsey is written in such a way that she appeals to both feminists and to fans of the hard-boiled school, precisely because while she appeals to feminists, she does so with a minimum of ideology. Grafton then, while doubtless she appreciates new readers, can draw on a well-established audience for each new work, and Millhone can live forever in 1986, if Grafton wishes.

Other authors, however, are less well-established. Some of these choose to place their stories in the present and simply ignore the Internet when it is not convenient. Sometimes they explain the lacuna, other times they just plow forward. One of these was David Cristofono's work, *The Girl She Used to Be*, nominated for an Edgar in 2010. This is a very interesting work with an almost unique MacGuffin,[19] a young woman who enters the Witness Protection Program because she saw the murder of her parents. But when she becomes bored, as she repeatedly does, she pretends that she has been discovered and takes on another identity at federal expense. She is extremely lonely because she fears to make friends lest her true identity be uncovered. She is burdened with both loneliness, and as she enters maturity, with her virginity. She is a very sophisticated user of the Internet when she needs to be, but makes no use at all of social media and hence only increases her isolation. This latter failure is completely inconsonant with everything else we know about her, and ultimately rings false. We enjoyed the book, but we think the evasion of the full impact of the Internet contrived and somewhat clumsy.

If the author does admit the Internet fully into the plot structure, it immediately raises difficult issues; an important element of detective stories has often been the delay following the murder and unsuccessful initial attempts to solve it. This stage of the structure amounts to almost a caesura in the plotting, a long delay until something new happens. Dove feels that this interim— termed by him the "period of gloom," is a key part of the usual structure of the detective story (Dove, 1997, pg. 78). In Turner's

---

[19] A MacGuffin is defined as "a plot element that catches the viewers' attention or drives the plot of a work of fiction" (http://en.wikipedia.org/wiki/MacGuffin) I find this Wikipedia site sufficiently authoritative to use here, although it deals largely with films, because of its thorough analysis of plot elements in a great number of films, and a bibliography which is adequate.

analysis of ritual, this is the period of crises, before redress can be achieved.

This period is a very valuable one, a "blank" when both detective and audience can mull over the many possibilities open to them, and a period when the author can more fully develop character and culture. It is often in these periods when the detective is fully humanized, when we learn about their back-story of lost loves, critical friendships, and even their tastes in fashion. This period usually is terminated when new clues critical to the solution to the crime are discovered. In this era, it is inevitable that the Internet frequently will be the source of these new clues.

The timing of these new Internet-born clues is critical. If they arrive too early we truncate the period of gloom and fail to develop suspense and possibly characterizations as well. Too late, and the audience grows impatient and begins to wonder, "What is the deal with the Internet, anyway?" We find several examples among recent Edgar winners which reveal common strategies for maintaining the caesura and prolonging the necessary period of gloom/crises while still eventually solving the crime via the Internet. One of these we typify as the God from the Machine strategy.

In C.J. Box' work *Blue Heaven*, the 2009 Edgar Award Winner for Best Novel, the surrogate detective, rancher Jesse Rawlins, is dependent for much of his information upon Villatoro, a friendly Los Angeles retired cop who comes to Wyoming in pursuit of a group of rogue cops who had robbed a race track years earlier. Villatoro has a loosely described Watson, a minor character who runs some simple computer searches which effectively uncover the evildoers. But to prolong the period of gloom/crises and postpone the conclusion, she cannot get in touch with Villatoro because he keeps missing her critical calls. In addition, in much of the area there is no cell or Internet service, so Villatoro cannot warn Jesse, even after he gets in touch with the Watson.

In this fashion, the utility of the Internet is effectively suspended, and then suddenly enabled just in time to solve the crime. But any good reader of detective stories interrogating the plot is perhaps already asking Anderson's fatal question: "What the hell is going on here?" (Anderson, 2007, Loc. 1104-1109).

Another example of the suspended use of the Internet comes from John Hart's *The Last Child*, the Edgar winner for best novel for 2010. This is a novel with a broodingly Faulknerian air about it which garnered much critical praise. It is set in a timeless southern locale. All we really know about the time frame through much of the book is that it is somewhat after the Vietnam War. The Internet and cell phones are kept well out of the Mise-en-scène, but because of the strong sense of place and implied time, we do not miss them.

The detective is a surrogate, a child hunting for his missing sister. The police have law-enforcement computer networks and there are any number of worried adults missing friends and children. The chief evildoer finally is caught because of his collection of Internet child pornography. But a simple Internet search of missing children in the region would certainly have set off a major search, and much useful ratiocination, much earlier. The transition in apparent time, from the timeless brooding south to the near present is shockingly abrupt. The work is well written and certainly deserves its Edgar award, but for one detail: the suspended use of the Internet.

Another novel which successfully sets an atmosphere which permits the author to ignore the Internet until after the period of gloom is Tom Franklin's *Crooked Letter, Crooked Letter* (2010), a 2011 Edgar nominee for Best Novel. It begins in 1979, when the crimes are committed. The time frame then jumps to an unspecified present when email is common and so is the Internet. The surrogate detective, a lower-level local lawman, gets caught up once more in the old case when other girls disappear. Because the setting is isolated and backward, we do not really think much about the Internet, nor about serial killer databases, or any other attribute of digital technology. Once again the isolation of rural communities which are the scene of racially motivated violence allows an author to finesse issues of Internet use by playing upon our stereotypes of rural areas. This is, of course, ultimately illogical because the Internet is now ubiquitous, particularly in law enforcement agencies, no matter how isolated or Faulknerian the locale.

Another work which plays upon our stereotypes of local culture is Timothy Hallinan's *The Queen of Patpong*, a 2011 Edgar nominee set in Thailand. Here the Internet is available, but not so available as to simplify the plot before the author can build suspense. The means of doing this is to have waiting in the off-stage area an American intelligence agent who reluctantly periodically feeds critical information to the protagonist—a surrogate detective— from databases to which only he has access.

The identity of the criminal, a serial killer of Thai prostitutes, probably could have been resolved much earlier with a Google search. The emotionally satisfactory conclusion in which the killer is undone could have been much more easily accomplished with the Thai equivalent of twitter than was the case. Nonetheless, this is another excellent work. And we buy into the plot because, knowing little of the local culture, we have to trust the author's presentation of the Internet and digital communication in general.

Box, Hart, Franklin and Hallinan have, we believe, resorted to a very old theatrical device, the *Deus ex Machina* or "God from the Machine" sometimes used by Greek playwrights and as often roundly condemned by Greek critics. We agree with Aristotle that this device is ultimately a dramatic cheat, and breaks the compact with the audience in that it introduces elements at the last moment for which the audience has not been prepared. We expect, given the problems presented by the Internet, to see much more of it, Aristotle notwithstanding.

As is clear here, we regard this device as unacceptably clumsy. It can be obscured by deft evocations of local culture which suggest a pre-Internet setting, but the point at which we suddenly realize that we are in the present is unacceptably abrupt to us. It may be that the conventions of the timeless South, frontier West, or mysterious East are such that the convention can continue to be followed, but we think younger audiences in particular will soon grow tired of it.

Fortunately there are also other, more acceptable, ways for the author to maneuver his or her detective around the obstacles presented by the Internet. One of these is the split time frame: the plot is divided into pre- and post-internet stages. The crime is set in the pre-Internet era. We have as long as the author may take to prolong the period of gloom, then the problem can be solved with or without the Internet depending on how the plot was developed. The longer the Internet is suspended however, the more awkward its absence becomes.

Tana French's wonderful *Faithful Place*, a candidate for the Edgar Award for Best Novel of 2011, illustrates a new problem impacting the detective novel: time and the Internet march on, and the Internet 2.0 and social media develop relentlessly. *Faithful Place* has a critically split time frame. The plot opens in 1985, when Rose, the love of Dublin police detective Frank Mackey's youth, disappears on the evening the two were to run away to London. When Rose does not show for their rendezvous, Frank believes that she did not truly love him as he had loved her, and she simply left without him.

Twenty-two years later, in 2007, Rose's body is found in the basement of the deserted tenement where they were to meet before running away. With the discovery of the body, we are fully in the age of the Internet. Even Mackey's nine-year old daughter Holly is an avid computer user who IM's with other children, and Mackey has access to all the digital panoply of police tools.

The book, like, in my humble opinion, all of French's, is wonderful. The sense of place, as in all excellent detective stories, is very strong (Geherin, 2008). Dublin, dark and brooding, seems almost an accessory to the crime with its medieval strictures. But, all that said, now we come to the Internet. We have no problem dealing with the lack of the Internet at the time of the original crime. The early setting then gives us time for the many consequences of the crime to echo down the decades. Nor would the crime have been solved more easily with the Internet; the murder is proven to have grown out of purely local history and relationships. As in the Golden Age novels, criminals, victims, and detective all knew each other. But the problem presented by the Internet also lies in the intervening 22 years. MacKay sincerely believed over this entire period that Rose was alive; so sincerely that his love for her interferes with his later marriage and subsequent relationships. He prowls police databases periodically looking for some evidence of either her death or her life.

It requires a considerable suspension of disbelief, however, to accept that for 22 years Rose had escaped being somehow referenced on the Internet. This is particularly true because her very purpose in running away was to make a career in the counter-cultural music world in London. She has no *Facebook,* no Flickr site, no sound files on ITunes, no video clips of her bands on *YouTube.* The only possible explanation for her complete disappearance simply has to be that she is dead.

Once that realization occurred, a search of the area where she had last planned to be would have turned up her body quite easily. But then there would have been no story line. The lengthy development of the work depends in large part upon the caesura, which is very effectively related in flashback as the crime is solved in the present.

Another recent work, Steve Hamilton's *The Lock Artist* (2010), which won the Edgar Award for Best Novel for 2011, also employs a split-time frame. As in French's work, the crime, insofar as there is one, occurs in the pre-Internet era. Then the protagonist is arrested for burglary and behind bars as the Internet comes upon the scene. By the time he is released and plot issues resolved, it has become irrelevant.

All of these works depend for their suspension of the Internet as a factor in the solution. In the works of Box, Hart, Hallinan, and Franklin, its impact is postponed until the electronic god descends. In those by Cristofono, French and Hamilton, it is simply but somewhat illogically ignored. The partial success of these strategies depends, paradoxically, on a very strong sense of place. Box' *Blue Heaven* constructs a Western environment so marked by horses and ranches, even by a cowboy detective, that we do not even think about the Internet unless we are a jaded scholar trying to assess its impact. John Hart's *The Last Child* and Tom Franklin's *Crooked Letter, Crooked Letter* presents a timeless south of gravel roads and long-concealed racial tensions. Again, we feel in such a familiar and so gothic an environment that we happily suspend disbelief until the authors finally trot out the Internet to solve the crime. In French's work, the poverty of the Dublin neighborhood and the generational conflicts of its denizens work much like Hart's and Franklin's south. But we, at least, feel somewhat manipulated—not the way a detective story of classic quality should end.

In addition to the problem of timing, the Internet presents other issues for the author striving to perform within the classical bounds of the detective story. One of these is the critical sense of place (Geherin, 2008). Although a strong sense of place can finesse our concerns about an appropriate use of the Internet, the Internet raises some particular issues with regard to locale, however convenient and traditional a strong sense of place may be.

One of the key rules of the genre has always been that crimes and their solutions be rational; if it is not, the contract is broken. But rationality depends very much on a strong regard for physical laws and scientific explanations for events, a la Sherlock Holmes and thousands of later sleuths. Western science demands proximate causes. If a book falls off my desk, the cause must be local—some measurable physical force acted upon it; an object at rest tends to stay at rest. We cannot say, as might a Chinese Daoist thinker, that it had a "tendency to fall."

If a murder occurs, the causes must lie in local issues, proximate to both the killer and the victim. The more removed the causes, the less opportunity a sleuth or detective has to understand the crime, and hence the more difficulty the reader has. There are good reasons that detective stories and police procedurals are usually placed in local environs, but thrillers on the other hand, like the Bond or Bourne series, feature exotic locales and quick switches in setting; it is a large part of their appeal.

But to center the plot upon the Internet is in effect to put it nowhere. No matter how often the author pictures for us a killer crouching over his or her computer, the contract is strained if not broken from the outset. This is equally true if the detective spends a great deal of time working with computers. For example, Jeffrey Deaver's paraplegic sleuth *Lincoln Rhyme* was, in my opinion, initially both very interesting and entertaining. But despite Deaver's remarkable efforts, the series—nine books from 1999 to 2010—became increasingly static. Deaver cleverly blends the roles of the Sherlock—Rhyme, and the Watson—Amelia Sachs, Rhyme's very vital and physical lover, a police detective who does everything a heroine should do. But the increasingly laboratory based nature of the series, best exemplified in *The Broken Window* (Deaver, 2009), ultimately begins to seem decentered.

The Broken Window has all the problems of the high-tech thriller: technology which overwhelms the reader; a break in the compact as the killer very much becomes the center of the action rather than the detective, so that the audience ultimately is left to wonder only how the creep will eventually be caught; a series of increasingly high-pitched life-threatening crises—Oh no! Is

Amelia going to die?—And the problem of a complete decentralization of place. Early in the series, New York, both historic and contemporary, was, like French's Dublin, effectively a character. Now we see mostly Rhyme's high-tech apartment and the Internet, including pages and pages of the results of database-driven surveillance records which certainly thrill us by bringing our inchoate fears of identity theft, digital crime, and murder by a stranger to the foreground, but at the last is unsatisfying.

While the problems discussed immediately above raise many issues for authors working in the detective genre, they are by no means insuperable. When they are overcome, the audience is able to enjoy a writer who is dealing with complex challenges in very satisfying ways.

Effective Uses of the Internet

Several recent detective novels have made an excellent use of the Internet while adhering to the rules of the genre. One such was Harlan Coben's *Caught*, a 2011 nominee for the Edgar award for Best Novel. The protagonist, "Wendy," is a TV journalist (the journalist surrogate detective is a very common type in the genre) who has exposed "Dan" on the air for stalking a teen-ager on the Internet. However, her exposure of Dan leads to his murder by a vengeful relative of a missing girl.

Coben presents the Internet in a very realistic fashion. It becomes a major factor in both the crimes and in their solutions. Wendy is a facile and experienced Internet researcher. She moves from simple uses of the Internet to accessing large databases and then on to Facebook, which turns out to be a critical source of evidence. For an audience with some experience with similar social sites, her path seems both logical and self-affirming—this is the way we would do it, too.

Caught was successful throughout in incorporating new media, the Internet, pop culture (particularly music), a poor economy, dying newspapers, and all the tropes of our present digital world.

Wendy seems an appropriate hero for the present who employs the tools of her profession in solving crime, much as Sherlock Holmes employed his own scientific knowledge.

Another 2011 Edgar nominee, Laura Lippman's *I'd Know You Anywhere* also shows an effective use of the Internet. The protagonist, Eliza Benedict, had been kidnapped and held for six weeks in 1985 by a serial killer, Walter Bowman, and was the only surviving victim of his spree. Now, in the present, he contacts her from death row. This might have been another opportunity for employing a split time frame evasion, but Lippman rather incorporates the Internet in clarifying both the pre-Internet past and the present.

Eliza has little or no memory of the earlier trauma and must uncover the past to understand the present. The author uses Internet searches by the protagonist to unfold the back-story, a storytelling technique we have not seen before—a modernized version of the familiar protagonist-or-Watson-goes-to-the-library. By searching her maiden name, Eliza turns up the past details of her life, and the reader is quickly brought up to speed on her earlier very complex relationship with the spree killer, Bowen. This is a very clever Internet-enabled device which facilitates a plot that can take radical twists and turns without the reader at any point calling foul. We learn what the Internet knows, but do not know what Eliza herself no longer does.

Eliza is no über-geek such as Stieg Larsson's Lisbeth Salander, but merely a competent computer user with whom the reader can easily identify. Her use of the Internet is consistently dogged but never spectacular. The author is also very conscious of differing stages of the Internet and repeatedly plays successfully upon changes between them. For example, in the pre-Internet era following her kidnapping, a not very talented writer had written a true-crime exposé in which he had speculated that she had been not a victim but the female member of a spree-killing team, perhaps even the initiator of the crime for which Bowen was convicted. Eliza once had hoped that her story would die down and she could live a normal life. Her husband tells her, however:

> But his book is out there. Nothing really disappears anymore. Once, that kind of true-crime crap would be gone forever, gathering dust in a handful of secondhand bookstores, pulped by the publishers. Now, with online bookstores and eBay and POD technology, it's a computer click away for anyone who remembers your original name. For all you know, he's uploaded it to Kindle, sells it for ninety-nine cents a pop (Lippman, 2010, Loc. 501-504).

The Internet, in Lippman's work, is very much a part of the environment. When we might turn to it, so does the protagonist. But neither the central mystery nor its unraveling depends in any critical way on the Internet. We are not left with any questions as to why the protagonist had missed easily retrievable information, nor are we overwhelmed with technology. It is a very nice updating of the classic detective story, and once again the compact between author and reader is left intact.

Our survey of mystery stories, including the general mystery, the detective, the police story, and the thriller sub-genres, leads us to believe that there are essentially three ways to deal with the Internet, in descending order of desirability given the nature of the genres. The first is simply to inappropriately ignore it. This leads the reader to question the authenticity of the work, and is not a good long-term strategy for an author who wishes to capture a digitally sophisticated market as well as other groups. It is a particularly chancy strategy for the detective story, with its engaged audience attempting to follow the rules and quick to call foul at the violation of the contract if the Internet is either neglected or inappropriately trotted out at the last minute.

The second is to attempt creatively to negate its impact. We have seen several ways of doing this among the works we have analyzed here. The first is to somehow delay the employment of the Internet as a device until it is fully useful. Some authors have used the *Deus ex Machina* approach with mixed success in otherwise excellent books. Others have employed a split-time frame, putting important parts of the action in the pre-internet era, and then moving forward to a time when the issue is irrelevant.

The third approach, and obviously the one anyone seriously interested in the Internet or in writing a plot appropriately embedded in contemporary culture would employ, is to work the Internet into the plot where useful without being overwhelmed by the technology, which, like ignoring it inappropriately, could cost the author audience, or at least readers for his or her next book.

Conclusion

What we are now experiencing, and what Internet researchers study, is the impact of a broad new stage upon which to perform, a digital one embracing the World Wide Web and all its emerging socio-economic practices. Rituals are almost by definition in Turner's sense, comforting and hopefully, stabilizing. Even If they prove rather to be schismatic, that also reintroduces stability, although perhaps in two newly constituted social organisms. In an important sense the Internet recapitulates earlier forms of ritual which were truly performative in that the community were either players in the ritual or it was their reception of the ritual which sacralized it. Such rituals are truly commanding. They are effectively multimedia, addressing audience concerns directly through music, dance, and theater.

But the mystery genres, particularly the detective story, even the thriller, are truly but shadows by comparison to the Internet, inherently restricted in cast, impact, and potential audience. Few can write them, and not that many—perhaps decreasingly many—can comfortably read them at the highest level. But we can all, for better or worse, text, Tweet or browse, even post our digitized performance clips for a global audience.

But what happens when a comfortable ritual is threatened by a new form of ritual so discontinuous that it opens up huge schisms between age groups and genders, destroys long-established media, threatens established hierarchy and simultaneously empowers both the oppressed and the oppressor? We cannot of course, begin to answer these questions merely by examining the impact of the Internet upon one small genre of literature. But no matter how opaque the clues, there are nonetheless some tendencies that must be regarded as threatening to the old textual rituals, and particularly to the detective story.

Literature is always necessarily in search of an audience, particularly in a highly commoditized environment such as our own. Increasingly, authors must choose between fidelity to the form—to the rules of the game—and the need to find an audience. We have seen a variety of ways in which authors have reacted to the impact of the Internet, from simply ignoring it, to restricting its impact, to working it smoothly into the plot. Clearly each of these has its limitations. The first make a work seem almost archaic, particularly if that work is set in the pre-Internet era, a time as far away to the modern reader as was the First World War to the Second World War, or either to the Vietnam generation. The second approach, what we have called the God from the Machine and the split-context, renders a work contrived. The third is difficult to accomplish, though immensely satisfying when done well.

There is, however, a fourth choice, suggested by the thriller: for authors to accommodate to the sensitivities of the post-Internet audience. We have seen several such attempts in our reading for this piece. In our search to understand the impact of the Internet upon mystery fiction we focused primarily upon seasoned writers. The Edgar Awards, however, have a number of categories, including Best First Book. In 2011 a nominee in the category was David Gordon's *The Serialist: A Novel* (Gordon, 2010). Gordon says of himself (http://www.amazon.com/David-Gordon/e/B002EJ3UO8):

> David Gordon was born in Queens and lives in New York City, with stops in New Jersey, London, and Los Angeles along the way. He attended Sarah Lawrence College, holds an MA in English and Comparative Literature and an MFA in Fiction Writing, both from Columbia University, and has worked in film, fashion, publishing and pornography.

The book, like Gordon's thumbnail bio above, suggests a romp through popular culture, and attempts to establish a distance from traditional models, either of authors, or of plots. The protagonist is a writer attempting to survive despite the adverse impact of the Internet on publishing. Here is a bit of the flavor of the character and of the author's style:

> Still I'm a professional, of sorts, and since this is a Mystery/Suspense (shelve accordingly), I want to open in the classic style, with a hook, a real grabber that holds the reader hostage and won't let go, that will keep your sweaty little fingers feverishly turning the pages all night long. Something like this: It all began the morning when, dressed like my dead mother and accompanied by my fifteen-year-old schoolgirl business partner, I opened the letter from death row and discovered that a serial killer was my biggest fan (Loc. 49-54).

In *The Serialist*, the Internet serves as a symbol of the whirl increasingly overtaking our culture. It has destroyed the small serial magazines that were the protagonist's primary market and reduced him to ghosting term papers for wealthy prep school students. But the Internet is not otherwise particularly important. This may be said to be a very realistic use of the Internet—as we all know, sometimes it is useful, other times not.

We are less interested in Gordon's use of the Internet than we are in the authorial posture which he adopts. It is, we think, much closer to a post-Internet sensibility than to the classical model. Gordon's plot is not so much driven by a search to discover information as by events. The plot, such as it is, is pushed forward when things happen to the protagonist, who is, by nature, out of control.

Another work, this by a highly published writer, shows us, we think, the same sort of authorial stance. Charlie Huston's, *The Mystic Arts of Erasing All Signs of Death*, was nominated for an Edgar Award for Best Work in 2010. The protagonist, Webster Fillmore Goodhue, belongs to the "clueless sleuth" category, a hapless soul—described by the author as "a slacker"—who blunders into a crime requiring that he solve it to survive.[20]

The impact of this work lies in large part in the unique employment of the protagonist. After failing at everything he has tried, Goodhue winds up cleaning trauma sites, such as suicide locales, and the residences of recluses discovered weeks, if not months, after their death. While this might initially seem an unpromising, if not totally off-putting premise, the author has previously demonstrated his mastery of contemporary popular culture. He has several fiction series going, including super heroes, a vampire detective, and comic books, as well as, based on *The Mystic Arts of Erasing All Signs of Death*, what once seemed likely to be an HBO series (http://www.pulpnoir.com/).

The work is post-modernist and contemporary (Huston refers to his style as pulp.) in that it has an ironic undercurrent in which the author continually signals his distance from not only the protagonist, but also from the audience. The gruesomely

---

[20] See a Wikipedia page for Huston at: http://en.wikipedia.org/wiki/Charlie_Huston I have no judgment on the veracity of the material covered there and suggest that the avid fan crosscheck it on other sites. A good place to begin doing so would be at: http://www.pulpnoir.com/, where Huston maintains a blog.

described trauma sites are nothing if not sensationalized, as though to draw attention from an otherwise rather thin plot.

Huston has suggested that his style has in part been driven, as were earlier pulp authors, by the need to write very quickly to survive as a writer. The quality he seeks is described as "velocity." Huston's style is distinctive, relying heavily upon dashes in lieu of quotation marks to develop velocity, and indicating changes in voice by identifying the speaker's actions rather than using the "he said..." of conventional fiction. These devices result in passages such as these:

> I walked to the section of bookcases that was in line with the open bathroom door.
> —He had some nice books.
> She watched me.
> —Yeah, he loved his books...
> She dropped her voice an octave.
> —Too much to do sweetheart, why bother reading about some made-up life when you can live it yourself?
> She brushed dark curly hair from her forehead, and bit her lip.
> —Is that bad, that it makes a kind of sense to me?... [21]

These devices make the dialogue a series of statements interrupted by physical action used to identify the speaker, as in the above series, where the female speaker is watching, dropping, biting, and brushing, while quoting her dead father as well, all within three statements. The author certainly achieves velocity, but perhaps at the expense of clarity.

This is not a style which can sustain complex plot development or intricate dialogue. It is intended to leap off the page and be

---

[21] The elisions signaled by "..." are my own in order to shorten the passages in which they appear.

apprehended more emotionally than intellectually. It seems to me that the author desires to break with conventional fiction, both speeding up narrative through a variety of devices such as those discussed above, and by embedding the story in a horrific context of mindless violence, both the commission and the messy aftermath of which is described in detail.

Among the icons of pop-culture frequently dissed in this work are both computers and videogames. Computers are portrayed as ultimately a shallow entertainment, comparable to television, merely a way of filling time. The poor quality of the Internet and of its audience is suggested by a humorous passage in which one of the more witless characters (among many such) details plans to make his fortune by investing in the careers of two video artists who attracted a large audience on YouTube by showing video clips of animals eating their own feces (Huston, 2005, p. 215).

One charge often leveled at the Internet is the entire category of offenses which we might call "dumbing down." These attacks have it that the Internet has attenuated our attention spans, reduced our tolerance for complex and extended treatments, whether these are news analysis or fictional narratives. These range from the scholarly and thoughtful to sensationalist diatribes.[22]

Lest this analysis be taken as a simple longing on my part for the back-in-the-day Miss Marple-style of crime fiction—which I personally find laboriously slow—I think that, in fact, Gordon and Huston are addressing a real problem. Fewer and fewer young people read mystery fiction; its audience is aging dramatically. The goal now for an author, like Huston, is to find new audiences by breaking into television, film, and adult comics, thus becoming a one-person media conglomerate. These all require an increasingly violent pace and necessarily must be deeply imbedded in pop culture, because the desired mass audience is an

---

[22] See Barlow, J. The Madness of Crowds: Recent Criticisms of Web 2.0
http://bcis.pacificu.edu/journal/article.php?id=7

impatient one that increasingly shares no other cultural reference points.

All of these characteristics can be attributed in part to the Internet. The audience for fiction is increasingly less educated; the pace is necessarily fast so as to suit a web-speed attention span, the level of information conveyed and depth of plot necessarily ever more shallow. In this, as in the eras when the detective story and later the Golden Age developed, and when the hard-boiled school and later the thriller emerged, technology has influenced genre. Writing has often adapted itself to changes in the wider culture, and cultural authorities, usually self-appointed ones, have often attacked these whether for the assault upon the classical canon or for contributing to the decline of the West.

Huston's career shows that his velocitized approach, whatever else may be said of it, works. He has a large audience in a variety of genres. However, the author, at bottom, in this work at least, seems almost contemptuous of his characters and his audience, and would like, I think, to be accepted as a WRITER. The fact that the work was nominated for an Edgar suggests that other writers feel these same contradictory pressures.

The mystery story and its modern sub-genres offers us, we think, something very like a tightly controlled social experiment, a very difficult thing to achieve in the real world—if we change this one rule, by introducing the Internet, what consequences do we see? And obviously, we see many. The Internet has contributed, we believe, along with many other obvious social changes, particularly a series of wars, to the development of the thriller. At its best the thriller offers some of the same challenges as does the detective story, but it also can so demolish the rules of the older genre that it becomes a pastiche in search of ever larger mass audiences. Many thriller authors—and probably most of their agents and publishers—no longer aspire to be or to represent Conan Doyle or Agatha Christie, but rather Tom Clancy or James Patterson. It is hard to believe that the culture is markedly enriched by these latter models, as it surely was by the former two.

Of the impacts we have discussed above, we believe that several are positive in that they can modernize a venerable genre and push it forward. The Watson of recent writers is much more interesting and socially varied than those of Holmes or Poirot, as he or she is increasingly required to be intelligent and "wired." Plots can be opened up considerably, pushing out the sometimes confining walls of classical models. Using the Internet can also embed a story much more in contemporary culture as in the examples from Coben and Lippman discussed above. This will be, we believe, very important if the genre is to continue to find an audience.

But we need to be reminded continually that mystery stories, even finely crafted detective stories, are ultimately a commercial endeavor. Without profits for a chain of people, there are no works. As much as we admire the British detective stories of the Golden Age, we suspect that nothing like them could develop under present social conditions. What we observe in the impact of the Internet upon mystery fiction is two rituals in collision, as the pre-Internet age and its characteristic ritual performances meet those of the Internet age. We cannot now know if this collision will be reintegrative or schismatic.

Acknowledgements
I am very grateful to the Berglund Center for Internet Studies for kindly supporting this work, and to its wonderful staff, particularly ace Copy Editor Lilly Huynh. I am very grateful to Dr. Cheleen Mahar, my colleague at Pacific University, an anthropologist of note and a fan of both the Golden Age detective literature and of the modern "Cozy," for leading me through the labyrinth of Performance Studies. I am also grateful to my colleague in History, Dr. Lisa Zefel, who has read through "O" in Grafton's Kinsey Millhone series, and was a great help in understanding feminist perspectives on the genre. And as always, I am thankful for the support of my kindest if most serious editor, and sometime co-author, my wife Christine Richardson.

References

Alewyn, R., Most, G.W., Stowe, W.W. (1983). The Origin of the Detective Novel. In Most G.W and Stowe, W. W (Eds.), *The Poetics of Murder: Detective Fiction and Literary Theory* (pp. 62-79). Ann Arbor, MI: Harcourt Brace Jovanovich.

Anderson, P. (2007). *The Triumph of The Thriller: How Crops, Crooks, and Cannibals Captured Popular Fiction*. New York, NY: Random House (Kindle Edition).

Anonymous, http://en.wikipedia.org/wiki/Detective_fiction#Golden_Age_detective_novels Accessed July 9, 2011.

Anonymous, http://en.wikipedia.org/wiki/The_Unpleasantness_at_the_Bellona_Club.

Anonymous, MacGuffin. Wikipedia Retrieved from http://en.wikipedia.org/wiki/MacGuffin. Accessed July 9, 2011.

Barlow, J. (2011, June 16). [Edgar Award Nominees, 2011, and the Impact of the Internet]. Interface. Retrieved from http://bcis.pacificu.edu/journal/article.php?id=779.

Barlow, J. (2011, July). The Madness of Crowds: Recent Criticisms of Web 2.0 http://bcis.pacificu.edu/journal/article.php?id=7.

Barlow, J. (n.d.). Google's Ngram Viewer. Retrieved from http://bcis.pacificu.edu/journal/article.php?id=778.

Barlow, J. (n.d.). Reviews of 5 Edgar Nominated for Best Mystery Novels for 2010. Retrieved from http://bcis.pacificu.edu/journal/article.php?id=793.

Beeman, W. O. "Performance Theory in an Anthropology Program" at http://www.brown.edu/Departments/Anthropology/publications/PerformanceTheory.htm accessed June 30, 2011.

Block, L. (2000). A Dance at the Slaughterhouse. Waterville, ME:

Thorndike Press.

Bloom, C., & Reilly, J.M. (1970). "Thriller: Introduction". Herbert, R. (ed.). The Oxford Companion, 460-461.

Brattin, J. (2011, May 19). Dickens and Serial Publication: Retrieved from http://www.pbs.org/wnet/dickens/life_publication.html.

Brown, D. (n.d.). Dan Brown. Retrieved from http://www.danbrown.com/#/home.

Burroughs, E. R. (n.d.). The Efficiency Expert. *All-Story Weekly Magazine*. N.p. Kindle edition.

Caillois, R. Most, G.W., & Stowe, W.W. (1983). "The Detective Novel as Game." In Most G.W and Stowe, W. W (Eds.), *The Poetics of Murder: Detective Fiction and Literary Theory* (pp.1-13).

Coben, H. Caught. (2010) Penguin Group USA – Dutton.

Cobly, P. (2000). "Thriller: Psychological Thriller". Herbert, R. (ed.). *The Oxford Companion*, 460-461.

Cozy Mystery (2011). Cozy Mystery List: A Guide to Cozy Mystery (and Other Favorite) Books and DVDs. Retrieved from http://www.cozy-mystery.com/Definition-of-a-Cozy-Mystery.html.

Cristofano, D. (2010). The Girls She Used to Be. New York, NY: Grand Central Publishing.

Dan Brown. (2011, May 28). Retrieved from the Dan Brown Wiki: http://en.wikipedia.org/wiki/Dan_Brown.

David, C., & Nuwer, E. (2002). *Hacker Cracker*. New York, NY: Harper Collins Publishing.

Deaver, Jeffery (2009). *The Broken Window: A Lincoln Rhyme Novel*. New York, NY: Pocket Star Books.

DeSilva, B. (2011). *Rogue Island*. New York, NY: Forge Books.

Doiron, P. (2011). *The Poacher's Son*. New York, NY: Minotaur Books.

Dove, G.N. (1982). *The Police Procedural*. Bowling Green, OH: Bowling Green State University Popular Press.

Dove, G. N. (1997). *The Reader and the Detective Story*. Madison, WI: University of Wisconsin, Popular Press.

Doyle, A. (2011, June 9). *The British Campaign in France and*

Flanders, 1920, p. 312. See
http://elizabethfoxwell.blogspot.com/2011/05/conan-doyle-and-war.html.

Franklin, T. (2011). *Crooked Letter, Crooked Letter*. New York, NY: Harper Perennial.

French, T. (2008). *The Likeness*. New York, NY: Penguin Books.

French, T. (2010). *Faithful Place*. New York, NY: Viking Press.

Geherin, D. (2008). *Scene of the Crime: The Importance of Place in Crime and Mystery Fiction*. Jefferson, NC: McFarland.

George, D. (1982). *The Police Procedural*. Bowling Green, OH: Bowling Green State University Popular Press.

George, D. (1997). *The Reader and the Detective Story*. Bowling Green, OH: Bowling Green State University Popular Press.

Grafton, S. (2011). Sue Grafton: Author of the Kinsey Millhouse Mysteries. Retrieved from http://www.suegrafton.com/interview99.htm.

Gregoriou, C. (2007). *Deviance in Contemporary Crime Fiction*. New York, NY: Palgrave McMillan.

Gordon, D. (2010). *The Serialist*. New York, NY: Simon & Schuster.

Hafner, K. (2001, April 2). *A Scientist's Art: Computer Fiction*. The New York Times. Retrieved from http://www.nytimes.com/2001/08/02/technology/a-scientist-s-art-computer-fiction.html.

Hallinan, T. (2010). *The Queen of Patpong*. New York, NY: William Morrow.

Hamilton, S. (2010). *The Lock Artist*. New York, NY: Minotaur Books.

Harrington, H., & Knox, R. (ed.). (1929). *The Best English Detective Stories of 1928*. New York, NY: Horace Liveright.

Hart, J. (2009). *The Last Child*. New York, NY: Minotaur Books.

Hartman, G. H. "Literature High and Low: The Case of the Detective Story". In Most and Stowe, *The Poetics and Murder: Detective Fiction and Literary Theory* (pp.210-230). New York, NY: Harcourt Brace Jovanovich.

Heissenbueffl, H. (1983). "Rule of the Game of the Crime Novel". In Most and Stowe (Eds.), *The Poetics and Murder: Detective Fiction and Literary Theory* (pp.79-93). New York, NY: Harcourt Brace Jovanovich.

Herbert, R. (ed.). (1999). *The Oxford Companion to Crime and Mystery Writing*. Oxford, UK: Oxford University Press.

Huston, C. Pulpnoir http://www.pulpnoir.com/.

Huston, C. (2005). *Already Dead*. New York, NY: Ballantine Books.

Huston, C. (2009). *Mystic Arts of Erasing All Signs of Death*. New York, NY: Ballantine Books.

IProfess, [Review of the book *Fantasy in Death*]. Interface. Retrieved (2011, June 22). from http://bcis.pacificu.edu/journal/article.php?id=752#1

James, P. D. (2009). *Talking about Detective Fiction*. New York, NY: Knopf (Kindle Edition).

Jameson, F. R. "On Raymond Chandler". In Most and Stowe (Eds.), *The Poetics and Murder: Detective Fiction and Literary Theory* (pp. 122-148). New York, NY: Harcourt Brace Jovanovich.

Kellerman, J. (2003). *When the Bough Breaks*. New York, NY: Ballantine Books.

Kermode, F. (1974). "Novel and Narrative." In Most and Stowe (Eds.), The Poetics and Murder: Detective Fiction and Literary Theory (pp. 175-197). New York, NY: Harcourt Brace Jovanovich.

Kipling, R. (2011, April 2). My Boy Jack (poem). Retrieved from http://en.wikipedia.org/wiki/My_Boy_Jack_%28poem%29.

Knox, R. (2001, July 4). The Ten Commandments of Detective Fiction. Retrieved from http://www.mysterylist.com/declog.html.

Larsson, S. (2010). *The Millenium Trilogy*. New York, NY: Knopf.

Lehman, D. *The Perfect Murder: A Study in Detection*. Ann Arbor: The University of Michigan Press.

Lippman, L. (2010). *I'd Know You Anywhere: A Novel*. New York, NY: William Morrow (Kindle Edition).

Locke, A. (2009). *Black Water Rising*. New York, NY: Harper.

McCormack, D. (2011, June 28). Online Etymology Dictionary.

Retrieved from
http://www.etymonline.com/index.php?search=cyberspac
e.

Mitnick, K. D., & William, S.L. (2002). *The Art of Deception,
Controlling the Human Element of Security*. Indianapolis, IN:
Wiley Publishing.

Most, G.W., & Stowe, W.W. (1983). *The Poetics of Murder:
Detective Fiction and Literary Theory*. New York, NY:
Harcourt Brace Jovanovich.

O'Brien, E.O. (2008). *The Poetics of Murder in the Victorian Era*.
Columbus, OH: The Ohio State University Press.

Palmer, D. and Palmer M. (2006) "Disfigured." In Patterson, J. (ed.)
Thriller. N.P. Mira (Kindle Edition).

Panek, L. L. (2003). *The American Police Novel: A History*.
Jefferson, NC: McFarland and Company.

Patterson, J. (ed.) 2006, *The Thriller*. n.p. Mira.

Pizzolatto, N. (2010). *Galveston: A Novel*. New York, NY: Simon &
Schuster.

Reddy, M. T. (1988). *Sisters in Crime: Feminism and the Crime
Novel*. New York, NY: Continuum.

Reilly, J.M. (1999). "Thrillers: Action Thriller". Herbert, R. (ed.).
The Oxford Companion, 461.

Rice, C., 2006 "Man Catch." In Patterson, J. (ed.) 2006 *Thriller*. n.p.
Mira.

The Ronald Knox Society of North America, (n.d.). at:
http://ronaldknoxsociety.com/detective.html.

Rose, M. J. (2006). *The Venus Fix*. Ontario, Canada: Mira.

Sandford, J. (1989). *The Fool's Run*. New York, NY: Berkley
Publishing.

Sandford, J. (1991). *The Empress File*. New York, NY: Berkley
Publishing.

Sandford, J. (2000). *The Devil's Code*. New York, NY: Berkley
Publishing.

Sandford, J. (2003). *The Hanged Man's Song*. New York, NY:
Berkley Publishing.

Sandford, J. *The Fool's Run* synopsis. JohnSandford.org.

http://www.johnsandford.org/kidd01c.html. Retrieved July 9, 2011.

Schechner, R., & Willa, A (1990). *By Means of Performance: Intercultural Studies of Theater and Ritual*. New York, NY: Cambridge University Press.

Stevens, T. (2011). *The Informationist: A Thriller*. New York, NY: Crown Publishers

Stowe, W.W (1983). "From Semiotics to Hermeneutics: Modes of Detection in Doyle and Chandler." In Most, G.W., & Stowe, W.W. (Eds.). *The Poetics of Murder: Detective Fiction and Literary Theory*. 366-383, San Diego, CA: Harcourt.

The New York Times. (n.d.). The New York Times: Search for computer hacker from January 1990- December 1995. Retrieved from http://query.nytimes.com/search/query?frow=0&n=10&srcht=a&query=computer+hacker&srchst=nyt&submit.x=30&submit.y=8&hdlquery=&bylquery=&daterange=period&mon1=01&day1=01&year1=1990&mon2=12&day2=31&year2=1990.

The New York Times. (n.d.). The New York Times: Search for computer hacker from January 1995- December 1995. Retrieved from http://query.nytimes.com/search/query?frow=0&n=10&srcht=a&query=computer+hacker&srchst=nyt&submit.x=37&submit.y=15&hdlquery=&bylquery=&daterange=period&mon1=01&day1=01&year1=1995&mon2=12&day2=31&year2=1995.

Thompson, J. (2010). *Snow Angels*. New York, NY: G.P. Putnam's Sons.

Turner, V. (1982). *From Ritual to Theater: The Human seriousness of Play*. New York, NY: PAJ.

Turner, V. "Are there universals of performance in myth, ritual, and drama?" Richard Schechner and Willa Appel, (eds.) *By Means of Performance. Intercultural Studies of Theater and Ritual*. Cambridge University Press, 1990. Chapter 1.

Vachss, A. (2007). *Terminal: A Burke Novel*. New York, NY: Pantheon.

101

Van Dine, S.S. (1928). "Twenty Rules for Writing Detective
    Stories". American Magazine. (1928-Sept.) Retrieved from
    http://gaslight.mtroyal.ca/vandine.htm See etext at:
    http://gaslight.mtroyal.ca/vandine.htm.
Wagner, E.J. (2007). *The Science of Sherlock Holmes: From
    Baskerville Hall to the Valley of Fear, The Real Forensics
    Behind The Greatest Detective's Greatest Cases.* New York,
    NY: John Wiley and Sons.
Anonymous, Wikipedia. (2011, July 3). "MacGuffin". Retrieved
    from http://en.wikipedia.org/wiki/MacGuffin.

References II: References to reviews by the author of books mentioned in the text.

These are references to the author's book reviews in *Interface*, the
e-journal of the Berglund Center for Internet Studies, Pacific
University. They are in Alpha order by book title. (Dates are dates
last accessed)

Barlow, J. (2011, June 29). [Review of the book *Anyone You Want
    Me to Be. A True Story of Sex and Death on the Internet*].
    Interface. Retrieved from
    http://bcis.pacificu.edu/journal/article.php?id=402.
Barlow, J. (2011, June 27). [Review of the book *The Art of
    Deception, Controlling the Human Element of Security*].
    Interface. Retrieved from
    http://bcis.pacificu.edu/journal/article.php?id=419.
Barlow, J. (2011, June 27). [Review of the book *The Art of
    Intrusion*]. Interface. Retrieved
    fromhttp://bcis.pacificu.edu/journal/2005/07/mitnick.ph
    p.
Barlow, J. (2011, June 17). [Review of the book *Bangkok Haunts*].
    Interface. Retrieved from
    http://bcis.pacificu.edu/journal/2008/04/burdett.php.
Barlow, J. (2011, June 26). [Review of the book *Blue Heaven*].
    Interface. Retrieved from
    http://bcis.pacificu.edu/journal/article.php?id=698.
Barlow, J. (2011, June 15). [Review of the book *The Broken*

Window: A Lincoln Rhyme Novel]. Interface. Retrieved from http://bcis.pacificu.edu/journal/article.php?id=96.

Barlow, J. (2011, June 24). [Review of the book *Caught*]. Interface. Retrieved fromhttp://bcis.pacificu.edu/journal/article.php?id=779.

Barlow, J. (2011, June 30). [Review of the book *Cyber Terror*]. Interface. Retrieved from http://bcis.pacificu.edu/journal/article.php?id=367.

Barlow, J. (2011, June 30). [Review of the book *The Daemon*]. Interface. Retrieved from http://bcis.pacificu.edu/journal/article.php?id=659.

Barlow, J. (2011, June 19). [Review of the book *Digital Fortress*]. Interface. Retrieved from http://bcis.pacificu.edu/journal/article.php?id=379#1.

Barlow, J. (2011, June 14). [Review of the book *The Girl She Used to Be*]. Interface. Retrieved from http://bcis.pacificu.edu/journal/article.php?id=718#contents3.

Barlow, J. (2011, June 16). [Review of the book *Hacker Cracker*]. Interface. Retrieved from http://bcis.pacificu.edu/journal/article.php?id=373.

Barlow, J. (2011, June 21). [Review of the book *The Hanged Man's Song*]. Interface. Retrieved from http://bcis.pacificu.edu/journal/article.php?id=351.

Barlow, J. (2011, June 23). [Review of the book *The Last Child*]. Interface. Retrieved from http://bcis.pacificu.edu/journal/article.php?id=728.

Barlow, J. (2011, June 13). [Review of the book *The Mystic Arts of Erasing All Signs of Death*]. Interface. Retrieved from http://bcis.pacificu.edu/journal/article.php?id=718.

Barlow, J. (2011, June 17). [Review of the book *The Scarecrow*]. Interface. Retrieved from http://bcis.pacificu.edu/journal/article.php?id=96.

Barlow, J. (2011, June 26). [Review of the book *Terminal: A Burke Novel*]. Interface. Retrieved from http://bcis.pacificu.edu/journal/article.php?id=52.

Barlow, J. (2011, June 23). [Review of the book *The Venus Fix*]. Interface. Retrieved from http://bcis.pacificu.edu/journal/article.php?id=142.

Test taking or project building? Internet 2.0 in K-12 education after the bubble burst

Mike Charles
Pacific University

At the beginning of the 21st Century, a high school teacher in New Jersey named Will Richardson started reading the book *Secret Life of Bees*[1] with his junior and senior students.[2] It was a relatively new book, and so he suggested to his students that they use an emerging media tool, a weblog (or blog) to create an online reader's guide to the book. As part of the experience he contacted Sue Monk Kidd, the author of the book, to ask if she would join the students in their study of the book. So as his students read the book and began commenting on it, Sue read along with them and began responding to a series of questions they asked. One of her responses ran 2300 words. In Will's classroom a blog was not something you heard about in the news, but something you used both to engage your own learning and to reach beyond the proverbial walls of the classroom. Writing to that larger audience could help you develop much better writing skills. Internet 2.0, the read/write web (often referred to as Web 2.0), was beginning to make the kind of impact in K-12 education that some had imagined.

What happened in K-12 education with the advent of Web 2.0, after the dotcom bubble burst? After rapid expansion at the end of the 20th Century, the story of the decade from 2000-2010 involved maturing ways of using the Internet. This article attempts to describe what that maturing use looked like in K-12 education,

---

[1] Secret Life of Bees (2002) Retrieved from: http://weblogs.hcrhs.k12.nj.us/bees/
[2] Richardson, W. and Mancabelli, R. (in press 2011). *Personal Learning Networks: Using the Power of Connections to Transform Education.* Solution Tree.

both in what was hoped for, and what took place. It does so by taking a look back at previous work the author has written in *Interface* and following up on its progress through the lens of Web 2.0 tools.

On the whole, it appears that despite the availability of increasingly easier to use Web 2.0 tools such as wikis, blogs, and podcasts, the past ten years has seen a marked decline in the kind of project-based learning with technology in K-12 schools that is exemplified by Will Richardson's students' work as described above. Instead, the Internet is being used increasingly to more efficiently measure student achievement on a school-wide basis, which is part of a production mindset that is pervasive in the culture as a whole and enjoys increasing influence in education in particular. This movement has been counterpointed by the limited use of Web 2.0 tools to reach the worldwide audience promised by the Web. That worldwide audience of K-12 students is growing, in part due to effort like One Laptop Per Child. In addition there has been an increase in the sophistication of the models used to describe exemplary technology use in schools as combining new technology, progressive pedagogy, and knowledge of content for curriculum-based planning by educators. In the end, one hopes that the next ten years will see the re-emergence of more project-based work, although the outlook for change in that direction is not particularly promising at present.

Technology for testing

In the past ten years the Internet has moved into mainstream use in K-12 education across the United States.[3] The widespread use of Web 2.0 applications mean that authoring on the web requires a very accessible set of skills for the general population: if a user can write an email and attach a file, that user can author and collaborate on the Web. The combination of easier to use tools

---

[3] DeBell, M., and Chapman, C. (2006). *Computer and Internet Use by Students in 2003* (NCES 2006-065). U.S. Department of Education. Washington, DC: National Center for Education Statistics.

and widespread access in the schools has led to maturing uses of the web in K-12 schools. But has maturing use in K-12 schools in the past ten years meant better use?

Earlier in the decade the argument was made in *Interface* about how technological thinking holds the threat of reducing education from a cultural task to a production task.[4] The cell phone that has become the ubiquitous technological object of the 21st Century is a perfect example of the triumph of technical thinking. For example, imagine comparing a cell phone from 2000 and a cell phone from 2010. Both phones transfer digital information wirelessly from an expanding number of locations around the globe. What is the difference between the two, and why is the newer phone perceived to be better? The newer phone does the same task faster, more efficiently, and more cheaply; that is the essential set of values of the technical mindset. Because of that one can interact with the newer phone differently (a touch screen instead of a microphone and a speaker for voice). Today's cell phones are described in the parlance of the day as simply amazing. But at the most fundamental level, they are quite predictable. They do the same thing cheaper, more efficiently, and faster than their predecessors and thus they are able to provide new capabilities (e.g. streaming video over the Internet). Technical thinking, whose basic ethic is greater efficiency of systems, is invaluable in perfecting production tasks such as the making of a cell phone. But technical thinking has serious flaws when it comes to cultural tasks, whose means and ends are considerably more complex than simple production tasks.[5]

---

[4] Charles, M. (2007). Where are we going as we leave no child behind? La Technique and Postman, Papert, and Palmer-Part Three. *Interface: the Journal of Education, Community, and Values;* v 7 no. 3 retrieved from http://bcis.pacificu.edu/journal/article.php?id=194

[5] Charles, M. (2004). Where are we going as we leave no child behind? La Technique and Postman, Papert, and Palmer-Part Two. *Interface: the Journal of Education, Community, and Values.* April/May 2004; v 3 no. 4 retrieved from http://bcis.pacificu.edu/journal/2004/03/charles.php

The first piece of legislation passed by the George W. Bush administration with a bipartisan consensus before the events of September 11, 2001 was the reauthorization of the Elementary and Secondary Education Act (ESEA), frequently referred to as No Child Left Behind (NCLB) 2001. NCLB represented a watershed mark in a century-long movement to think of education as a production task. Standards are established for all students—analogous to a set of product specifications for a production assembly line. Curricula are written for teachers to use to build those products. Standardized examinations function as quality control checks of those products on that production line. NCLB mandates that all products from the line be raised to a certain quality standard—i.e. all students must pass the exam (no child should be left behind). It is difficult to argue against this notion of higher quality, especially when one views education as a production task.[6]

The first major piece of legislation offered by the Obama administration related to K-12 education was funding for the Race to the Top.[7] It carries production level thinking to the next step, awarding funds to states so that they may pilot different ways of rewarding teachers based on measures of their productivity. Thus as described above, standards have been set, measurements (student achievement scores) have been put in place to check for productivity of the system, and now compensation to workers will be based on increases in agreed upon measures of productivity. Typically those measures are improved student achievement

---

[6] Charles, M. (2004). Where are we going as we leave no child behind? La Technique and Postman, Papert, and Palmer-Part One. *Interface: the Journal of Education, Community, and Values*. February 2004; v 4 no. 1 retrieved from http://bcis.pacificu.edu/journal/2004/01/charles.php
[7] Race to the Top: Oregon school leaders lacking needed energy, drive. http://www.oregonlive.com/opinion/index.ssf/2010/04/race_to_the_top_oreg on_school.html

scores, though they may perhaps include some form of classroom observation in the assessment of the teacher.[8]

Thus the first ten years of the 21st Century have seen the continued extension of technical thinking on a bipartisan basis into the field of education. The major shift in the use of technology in K-12 schools through the decade has been in the use of technology as part of a comprehensive assessment tool in a production system instead of the anticipated incorporation of Web 2.0 tools for student projects. Internet connected computer labs and classroom sets of laptop computers on carts are consistently used for administering state tests at schools around the country, with results being reported to central data systems served via the Web. This means that those same computer resources are not available for students to use to employ Web 2.0 tools for projects.

Web 2.0 projects—what could be

As noted at the beginning of this article, one of the big stories of the past ten years was the emergence of Web 2.0 tools like weblogs or blogs. Will Richardson, sometimes described as "the blog evangelist," has written in great detail about how Web 2.0 tools can change education, providing the kinds of tools that allow a teacher to shift their role from the proverbial "sage on stage" to a "guide alongside" of students as they learn.

In the soon to be released *Personal Learning Networks,* Will Richardson and Rob Mancabelli take a visit to another teacher's classroom to see how the web could be used to allow students to reach beyond the classroom and become learners connected to the 21st Century world:

---

[8] Associated Press, 2011. Beyond pass-fail: Washington considers more specific teacher evaluations. Retrieved from:
http://www.oregonlive.com/pacific-northwest
news/index.ssf/2011/03/beyond_pass-
fail_washington_considers_more_specific_teacher_evaluations.html

Seventh and eighth grade teacher Clarence Fisher has an interesting way of describing his classroom up in Snow Lake, Manitoba. As he tells it, it has "thin walls," meaning that despite being eight hours north of the nearest metropolitan airport, his students are getting out into the world on a regular basis, using the Web to connect and collaborate with students in far flung places from around the globe. The name of Clarence's blog, "Remote Access," sums up nicely the opportunities that his students have in their networked classroom.

"Learning is only as powerful as the network it occurs in," Clarence says. "No doubt, there is still value in the learning that occurs between teachers and students in classrooms. But the power of that learning is more solid and more relevant at the end of the day if the networks and the connections are larger."

Without question, Clarence imbues the notion of the "connected learner." Aside from reflecting on his life and his practice on his blog, he uses Twitter to grow his network, uses Delicious to capture and share bookmarks, and makes other tools like Skype and YouTube a regular part of his learning life. In other words, he's deeply rooted in the learning networks he advocates for his students.

'It's changed everything for me as a learner," he says. "I teach in a small school of 145 kids, so I don't know what it's like to have a lot of colleagues. I can't imagine closing my door and having to generate all of these ideas on my own."[9]

This is the Web 2.0 that so many imagined. It is a tool for going public with student work, and a way for a teacher to connect with other like-minded educators to develop further as a professional.

---

[9] Richardson, W. and Mancabelli, R. (in press 2011). *Personal Learning Networks: Using the Power of Connections to Transform Education*. Solution Tree.

As we continue into the 21st Century, the number of tools and their availability seems to only be proliferating. For example, Wordle (see resources) is a tool for creating "word clouds" that many teachers are beginning to use to help students analyze their writing in a visual way. In a recent article about "growing creativity" for K-12 students, the author lists Wordle as a possible tool to help students consciously learn to focus on fluency, flexibility, originality, and elaboration in their thinking.[10] Later in the article she lists 29 different web-based tools that can be used to help "grow creativity," demonstrating the rapid proliferation of tools, with three other word cloud tools[11] included in the list. The phrase "there's an app for that," from a popular Apple commercial has become a commonplace way to refer to this proliferation. Note also that these tools are profoundly decentralized, in that Clarence is constructing his own personal program of professional development (Author, 2004) and using the Internet to do it. Personal Learning Networks[12] is a current way of describing this phenomenon of self-constructed professional development that happens through people to people connections.

This same Web 2.0 has great promise for students. For example, Silas is a 4th grade student in a relatively lower SES school in New Zealand who uses his blog and related multimedia tools to publish his work to the world (Author 2010/2011). Silas' entry "My waka animation adventure" was one of the first things that he wrote after only two weeks in 4th grade learning about how the Polynesians had migrated from one island to the next in the Pacific aboard giant double sailing canoes called waka. He created a

---

[10] Shively, Candace Hackett, (2011). Grow Creativity. *Learning and Leading with Technology,* pp. 10-15 (38, 7).
[11] Word cloud tools:
      Tagul http://tagul.com/
      Tagxedo http://www.tagxedo.com/
      Worditou http://worditout.com/
Wordle http://www.wordle.net/
[12] Personal Learning Networks (2011) retrieved from http://en.wikipedia.org/wiki/Personal_Learning_Networks

110

computer-animated drawing that showed what he learned, and that animated drawing was published as an entry on his blog that he narrated:

> While the waka was battling the odds, the numerous stormy and rough waves were crashing over them. The people were frightened and sad as waves crashed over the waka. And the fierce wind howled like a wolf's cry.

The energy in Silas' writing is palpable, and his work suggests that he might comprehend at a rather personal level at least some of the dangers of this most hazardous journey of the Maori.

Silas kept his blog throughout the school year essentially as a learning journal, similar to what many educators have envisioned blogs would be used effectively in classrooms.[13] He made over 20 blog entries (about two or three posts per month). The topics he posted on ranged from things he was learning in school (like the waka adventure, volcanoes, and using descriptive words) to things he loves to do (like his Michael Jackson moonwalk). One of his posts includes an "about me" word cloud created in Wordle, the tool described earlier. Silas' classroom only has a few computers in it that students successfully share. At the time when he wrote, there was no cart of laptops for every student to use. Internet access in his school is at a slower rate than at many schools in the United States. The educators that lead his school have plans underway to provide greater high-speed access to the Internet on more computers in his school. However, it is not for the purpose of administering standard assessments of student achievement, but instead as a tool for more students to go public with their work within in the school community and without to the larger world.

Draw and talk about what you are learning is a simple and fundamentally sound educational strategy, especially for students

---

[13] Bull, G., Bull, G., & Kajder, S. (2003). Mining the Internet - Writing with Weblogs. *Learning and Leading with Technology*. 31 (2): 32-35.

111

at the elementary school level. Having students post on their own blogs for a larger world to read and comment on is an idea that many advocate,[14] but a relatively small percentage of students in the USA actually do, often because of safety concerns. And yet at Pt England School in New Zealand, the public school where Silas attends, those safety concerns are balanced by the conviction that student voices need to be heard, and that publishing to the web is a critical part of developing students as confident, connected, and actively involved lifelong learners. Silas' blog and those of his classmates are open to the world so that any one can read and comment on them. Many of the readers are students from the school or family members of the writers, but a quick look at the map on the blog shows that readers come from several continents.[15]

In 2000 the kind of use for these emerging Web 2.0 tools that many in the USA envisioned was similar to what has been described above for Clarence as a teacher and for Silas as a student. But particularly in the USA, Internet use has instead been focused on using this technology as part of a comprehensive assessment system whose intent is to measure the productivity of students and teachers in K-12 schools. This move from project-based learning with technology to the more efficient use of these tools for measuring student achievement is part of a system-wide focus on raising test scores. What is being lost in this effort? Alfie Kohn suggests that "we should worry because of what schools are

---

[14] Richardson, W. and Mancabelli, R. (in press 2011). *Personal Learning Networks: Using the Power of Connections to Transform Education.* Solution Tree. Excerpt retrieved from http://weblogg-ed.com/2011/personal-learning-networks-an-excerpt/
[15] *Pt England School*
      Pt England School site: http://www.ptengland.school.nz/
      Pt England School blogs:
      http://www.ptengland.school.nz/index.php?family=1,451
      Pt England School—Silas' blog: http://pessilasd.blogspot.com/
      Pt England School—Silas' blog—his "about me" word cloud created in Wordle: http://pessilasd.blogspot.com/2011/03/about-me.html

sacrificing in order to focus on raising test scores: recess, music and the arts, inquiry-based science, the time to read good books, interdisciplinary projects, class meetings, field trips, discussion of current events – the list goes on and on."[16] One can add project-based computer learning to this list of things being lost in schools in the USA.

One laptop per child on a global scale

As described earlier in *Interface,* the One Laptop Per Child (OLPC)[17] initiative is an effort to improve education worldwide by creating an affordable and portable computing device (Author, 2006). OLPC is a non-profit association launched by Nicholas Negroponte of the Massachusetts Institute for Technology (MIT). To date, it has designed and produced an affordable and durable "XO laptop" and distributed it to over 2 million children in 40 different countries around the world, a distribution best viewed in a unique map display at the OLPC site that shows both locations and numbers of computers distributed in each country— http://one.laptop.org/map). According to its website:

> OLPC's mission is to empower the world's poorest children through education. We aim to provide each child with a rugged, low-cost, low-power, connected laptop. To this end, we have designed hardware, content and software for collaborative, joyful, and self-empowered learning. With access to this type of tool, children are engaged in their own education, and learn, share, and create together. They become connected to each other, to the world and to a brighter future.[18]

---

[16] Kohn, A. (2002-03). The worst kind of cheating. *Streamlined Seminar--a publication of the National Association of Elementary School Principals.*
[17] *One Laptop Per Child*
One Laptop Per Child (2011). Retrieved from http://one.laptop.org/.
One Laptop Per Child map display retrieved from
http://one.laptop.org/map
[18] One Laptop Per Child XO-3 (2011). Retrieved from
http://one.laptop.org/about/xo-3

113

Within the mission statement one sees a focus both on unique hardware and a specific educational philosophy. Regarding the hardware, note the focus on the ruggedness of the design that will stand up to the rigors of life for many children in developing countries, places where inexpensive electrical power may not be readily available. There is also a clear focus on a connected laptop that children can use for collaboration as opposed to one that runs typical "office" productivity applications. Joyful and self-empowered are prominent phrases found in this mission statement in contrast to the mission statements of education organizations in many developed nations.

In the earlier article it was noted that just as interesting as the hardware for the project is the philosophical foundations of OLPC and the ideas of informal education:

> The bold assertion of the OLPC initiative is that learning is a natural act, and that formal schooling reduces learning to a series of merely technical acts (and the teacher to the role of a technician). The computer can be part of an educational revolution that bypasses formal schooling, whose thinking is rooted in the 19th century assembly line. Seymour Papert calls this educational revolution "Kid Power," and the OLPC initiative holds the promise of taking this kid power to a global audience. (Author, 2006)

In short, the XO laptop was a tool to provide for informal learning in the developing world. Distinct from many educational technology projects, OLPC has a concisely stated philosophy of education, the key idea of which is that through using a simple, durable, and affordable connected laptop, students can "fully participate as producers of knowledge and not just as consumers of materials produced by others." [19]

Earlier three major criticisms of the OLPC plan were noted: concerns about the appropriateness of the design of the device, concerns that the distribution model for the project was not sufficiently market-based, and concerns about laptops as an agent of western cultural imperialism (Author, 2006). There was also noted a disconnect between a philosophy which relies on the potential of informal education but does so by providing laptops to schools in developing countries, the site of formal education. The worldwide economic crisis of the past three years has certainly been a difficult climate for the OLPC business model with its generous helping of philanthropy. So how has the XO laptop fared as a tool to bring better educational opportunities to the developing world in the past five years?

Perusing through the stories and news section of the OLPC site one finds hopeful signs of a maturing project of significant scale. There is hope expressed on the OLPC site for greater expansion beyond the first 2 million XO laptops in the next few years with the possible launch of an updated device (XO-3) that is more tablet-like. The OLPC website includes multimedia slideshow stories of how the XO has been recently deployed in various countries such Nicaragua, Madagascar, Paraguay, India, and Gaza. The OLPC website[20] also includes a news sections with links to external stories as well as updates from the OLPC wiki. A recent Yahoo News story about new policies of the government of Thailand included the promise of 800 000 new XO laptops for school children over six years. The story mentioned that some educators argue that the laptops do more harm than good. XO laptop distribution in Thailand dates from before a 2006 coup which

---

[19] One Laptop Per Child XO-3 (2011). Retrieved from
http://one.laptop.org/about/xo-3
[20] One Laptop Per Child (2011) Mission statement retrieved from
http://laptop.org/en/vision/mission/index.shtml

ousted the government that had completed the first laptop distributions.[21]

In the upcoming first deployment of XO laptops in the Marshall Islands[22], there appears to be a healthy emphasis on elements that make for what OLPC describes as a "solid deployment," including a clear technology plan for the Islands and plans for professional development workshops for teachers on the Islands. The acting minister of education notes that "By bridging the digital divide to an inclusive global community, our students here in the islands can share ideas with other students in the Pacific and from around world," a quote consistent with the values of the OLPC mission statement. This certainly is not informal education, but it is an education that anticipates using the XO laptop as a means for students to be active in sharing their ideas and not simply consuming the materials and ideas of others.

What is generally missing from the OLPC blog is tangible evidence of this kind of sharing beyond the multimedia slideshow "stories" section of the site. More examples of the inclusive global education community that the Minister of Education in Marshall Islands alludes to are needed. The content generated on the wiki is certainly global, constructed from a variety of voices, but the kind of collaboration that is demonstrated at sites like Pt England School in New Zealand as described above (things such as Silas' blog) are harder to find. There are pictures and descriptions of students playing with Turtle Art (a Logo-like application) and making videos, but for now that work is not being captured very

---

[21] Yahoo (2011). *Factbox - Policy pledges of Thailand's incoming government.* Reuters. Retrieved from http://au.news.yahoo.com/thewest/a/- /world/9823791/factbox-policy-pledges-of-thailands-incoming-government/

[22] One Laptop Per Child Oceania (2011). Marshall Islands prepare for OLPC deployment with national workshop. Retrieved from http://blog.laptop.org/2011/06/23/marshall-islands-1000/

often for a larger audience. The recent posting[23] about a global art contest sponsored by Nickolodeon Latin America and OLPC is a step in that direction. In the end, of course, perhaps the important thing is what happens for the students in the school with their XO laptops and not that they "publish" it to a larger world, but it would be encouraging to be able to "overhear" in some way more of what is at the heart of the educational mission of the project.

The XO laptop was remarkable not only for its design but also that it was, in the words of Seymour Papert, a "children's machine."[24] It was not a "scaled down" computer from business offices but something designed for students to use from the outset. Papert first described the possibility of such a machine that would be education specific, but now to see it produced and in use is intriguing. As an electronic device that entered mass production in 2009 but was in development in 2005, it is interesting to see the extent to which it foreshadowed the iPad and other recently popular tablets that have emerged on the global market. Small size, flash memory instead of a hard drive, an operating system that boots up very quickly and does not run all the existing office applications—in all of these ways the XO laptop designed for children in developing countries foreshadows the latest electronics gadget in the developed countries. The XO-3, still under development for possible release in 2012[25] is a further evolution of the device in the direction of current tablets.

At this writing, OLPC remains a viable project of relatively small size (on a global scale) that has weathered recent economic storms and still appears to be on track with its mission and philosophical underpinnings worked out in a pragmatic way. The 2006 article in

---

[23] One Laptop Per Child Nickolodeon (2011). Nickelodeon partners with OLPC on multimedia contest. Retrieved from
http://blog.laptop.org/2011/07/15/nickelodeon-olpc-contest/
[24] Papert, Seymour. (1993) p. 143. The children's machine: rethinking school in the age of the computer. New York: Basic Books.
[25] One Laptop Per Child XO-3 (2011). Retrieved from
http://one.laptop.org/about/xo-3

Interface concluded by saying that it would "be interesting to see if both the device and its operating educational philosophy can make a significant change in something as fundamental as world literacy. If it can, then it will have proven to be a very powerful idea dressed in a rather small package." In 2011 it seems that it has not yet made change at that scale, but that it remains on track in an encouraging way and is worthy of further attention in the coming years.

Putting together the total package

One of the encouraging trends in Internet use in education in the past ten years is the increasingly sophisticated way in which technology and content have been connected. For many years those who use technology in the schools have made the point that the question is not really about technology, but about learning.[26] To ask how one might use a particular set of technologies such as Web 2.0 tools in the schools is to frame the question incorrectly. It is an example of what has been described as technocentric thinking[27] when what really needs to be considered are educentric applications of Internet 2.0 tools in education. Richardson's discussion of the use of wikis, blogs, and podcasts earlier in this article is a good example of this notion. The idea is that the technology is essentially invisible, and the focus is on the learning. The power of Silas' blog is not that he is writing a blog, but that he is writing for a larger audience, using the Internet.

This idea of how to effectively put together technology, content, and pedagogy has been more succinctly described in the past ten

---

[26] Russell, Anne L. (1995). Stages in learning new technology: Naive adult email users, *Computers & Education*, (Volume 25, Issue 4), pp. 173-178, retrieved from http://www.sciencedirect.com/science/article/B6VCJ-3YF49Y7-1/2/f79d42d17eacfab85ec4bf8fc732d5d6)

[27] Papert, S. (1987). Computer Criticism vs. Technocentric Thinking. *Educational Researcher* (vol. 16, no. I) retrieved from http://www.papert.org/articles/ComputerCriticismVsTechnocentric.html

years with the TPACK (Technology, Pedagogy, and Content Knowledge)[28] model. TPACK has been defined as:

> Technological Pedagogical Content Knowledge (TPACK) attempts to capture some of the essential qualities of knowledge required by teachers for technology integration in their teaching, while addressing the complex, multifaceted and situated nature of teacher knowledge. At the heart of the TPACK framework, is the complex interplay of three primary forms of knowledge: Content (CK), Pedagogy (PK), and Technology (TK) (TPACK website in resources).

The key idea is that in order to use technology to create better learning opportunities for students, teachers must know their content, know how to teach (pedagogy), and know the affordances that emerging technologies provide. At the intersection of these three forms of knowledge is the "sweet spot" of effective technology use in schools, or TPACK. In an article written earlier this decade[29] this idea was referred to as putting together the total package. To really use these Web 2.0 tools effectively, a teacher needs to first draw on strong content knowledge and pedagogical knowledge in combination with technological knowledge. In the first 10 years of the 21st Century, what distinguishes the technological tools is that they are generally getting easier to use. But that does not insure better educational outcomes because the difficulty is not how to use the technology. The challenge is to put together the total package.

This TPACK model has been well defined in the educational research community as a construct for taking a more thoughtful

---

[28] TPACK website retrieved from http://www.tpack.org/tpck/index.php?title=Main_Page
[29] Borthwick, A., Pierson, M., Thompson, A., Park, J., Searson, M., Bull, G. (2008). Realizing Technology Potential through TPACK. *Learning and Leading with Technology*. 36(2): 23-26.

look at what has previously been called technology integration. As one source stated:

> Advances in technology combined with widespread user participation clearly create opportunities in education that did not exist previously. We can assist teachers in reflecting, planning, and enacting instructional strategies based on the TPACK intersection.[30]

The TPACK model may be an important part of allowing technology to realize greater potential in the schools for the paradoxical reason that it broadens the conversation beyond technology, and into content and pedagogy.

Other serious efforts at charting the intersection of technology, pedagogy, and content knowledge are underway in conversations about the importance of quality professional development for teachers.[31] The failure of previous efforts is described that can often be focused on learning the new technology. The real problem is putting technology, pedagogy, and content together. Curriculum-based educational technology professional development for teachers is an idea that has been advanced to help guide future efforts in the schools so that as millions are spent on technology infrastructure, teachers are better able to use these resources as part of a total package to improve learning.[32]

Thus if the Internet technology in use in the schools today can be freed up from the fiction that it can be used to increase educational productivity and is instead used to unleash student learning, then the TPACK model can help us move beyond the hype that the Internet will revolutionize education and on to more

---

[30] Ibid.
[31] Harris, J. (2008). One Size Doesn't Fit All: Customizing Educational Technology Professional Development. Part One: Choosing ETPD Goals. *Learning & Leading with Technology*, 35, 5, 18.
[32] Hofer, M. & Harris, J. (2009). LEARNING CONNECTIONS - Social Studies - Tech Integration in Social Studies. *Learning and Leading with Technology*, 37, 2, 26.

serious discussions of learning. TPACK and better professional development for teachers are important ideas that have developed in the past 10-year discussion that might lead the way.

What might the future be?

Over the past 30 years, critiques of secondary education have called for greater rigor in high school courses.[33] The proliferation of Advanced Placement (AP) courses in high schools across the nation has been one response to these calls. AP courses enrolled 3.2 million students in the 2010.[34] These courses offer greater rigor as assessed by a standardized examination, which students may opt to take for college credit for a fee. Yet there is no personal higher education involvement in these courses. Recent research suggests that merely taking AP courses is not a valid indicator of eventual college success.[35] The idea behind the AP system is one based on notions of productivity—students enroll in the same courses in high school that they would take in college—has been described as "learning the same stuff sooner" (Author 2011). Defining better high school courses as learning the same stuff sooner is an extension of the kind of productivity thinking described earlier in this article.

There is a different definition of more rigorous high school courses that accompanies much of the "school reform" discussion.[36] There have been many calls for the need to teach 21st Century Thinking

---

[33] National Commission on Excellence in Education. (1983). *A nation at risk: The imperative for educational reform.* Washington, DC: U.S. Department of Education.

[34] Kramer, B. (2011). Lake County part of national upswing in high-test academics. *Chicago Sun Times.* Retrieved at http://newssun.suntimes.com/news/4116941-418/lake-county-part-of-national-upswing-in-high-test-academics.html

[35] Geiser, Saul, & Santelices, Veronica. (2004). The Role of Advanced Placement and Honors Courses in College Admissions. UC Berkeley: Center for Studies in Higher Education. Retrieved from: http://escholarship.org/uc/item/3ft1g8rz.

[36] Tyack, D. B., & Cuban, L. (1995). *Tinkering toward utopia: A century of public school reform.* Cambridge, Mass: Harvard University Press.

Skills for high school students.[37] This might be called "learning different stuff deeper." To that end there is a course being offered at a significant number of high schools in Virginia called the Geospatial Semester.[38] In this semester or year-long course, high school students learn about geospatial technologies such as Geographic Information Systems (GIS), Global Positioning Systems (GPS), and Remote Sensing. They then apply this new technical knowledge to a local community based problem as the capstone project for the course. They may earn dual credit from a Virginia university in a course that is taught by a local high school teacher who is capable in the use of these tools. Higher education teachers who visit classrooms regularly as well as offering email support provide project mentoring and technical support for the course.

GSS has been underway for the past 5 years and nearly 1000 students have completed the course. In the 2009-2010 academic year the course was offered in 15 different high schools and in a total of 20 different classes in 10 different school districts. Thus while this is not a nationwide innovation, it is at least being carried out on a scale of multiple school districts that holds promise for broader implementation. Typical projects include an

---

[37] *21st Century Skills*

Assessment and Teaching of 21st Century Skills. (2009). Retrieved from http://www.atc21s.org/white-papers/
The enGauge 21st Century Skills Continua of Progress. (2003). Retrieved from http://www.metiri.com/features.html
Lemke, C. (2003). enGauge 21st Century Skills: Digital literacies for a digital age. Retrieved from http://www.metiri.com/features.html (ERIC Document Reproduction Service No. ED463753).
The Partnership for 21st Century Skills. (2004). Retrieved from http://www.p21.org/
21st Century Workforce Commission-National Alliance of Business (June 2000). Building America's 21st Century Workforce. Executive Summary, page 5.
Cited in Twenty-First Century Skills. Retrieved from http://www.metiri.com/features.html

[38] *Geospatial Semester*

Geospatial semester site: http://www.isat.jmu.edu/geospatialsemester/

assessment of the risk of fire for properties adjacent to the Shenandoah National Park. The student devised a rubric that integrated a number of factors, including proximity to forest, type of forest and amount of open terrain to develop a rating system and then displayed the differential risk on a series of maps of the properties. Another project done by a pair of students was an assessment of the traffic pattern of a Northern Virginia high school. The students took data for traffic, pedestrian and parking patterns at a variety of times before and after school, analyzed the data and developed a set of solutions and supporting maps to try to alleviate congestion.

These are the kind of projects that the Internet can help make possible in our schools, both as a source for data for projects and for project publication. The curriculum-based professional development necessary to allow a teacher to teach the GSS course relies on high quality professional development experiences for teachers.[39] To support their work with their students, teachers need online resources and communication tools—all part of a 21st Century workplace envisioned by many authors in *Interface* and other publications. The possibility of building and sustaining meaningful communities of professional practice using the Internet to support the teaching of courses like Geospatial Semester is most promising. Project-based work might emerge triumphant in the next ten years as the Internet continues to develop. But as long as productivity thinking continues to emerge and dominate the educational landscape, the Internet will be used as a more efficient tool for measuring a very confined definition of student learning called student achievement scores. The question remains: should the Web be used for test taking or project building?

---

[39] Kolvoord, R.A. & Purcell, S. (manuscript accepted for publication in 2010). What Happens After the Professional Development: Case Studies on Implementing GIS in the Classroom. In MaKinster, J., Trautman, N., Barnett, M. (Eds.), *Teaching Science and Investigating Environmental Issues with Geospatial Technology*. New York: Springer Publishing.

Open Access & Open Lives: The Changing Role of Academic Libraries

Isaac Gilman and Lynda Irons
Pacific University

Introduction

The ongoing impact of the Internet on library and information services cannot be overstated. As with print journalism, the capacity and culture of networked life has transformed every aspect of the library profession, from technical to public services. The first comprehensive examinations of the Internet's impact on libraries and library services appeared in the 1990s,[1] and by the turn of the century there was a considerable body of literature devoted to various dimensions of the topic. Not surprisingly, these examinations largely addressed the effect of the Internet on traditional library services and roles: cataloging/technical services, collection management, interlibrary loan, bibliographic instruction, and reference services.[2,3]

These changes in traditional services are perhaps best exemplified by the changing nature of the library catalog: the transition from physical index cards to machine-readable records to networked catalogs (i.e. WorldCat) alone has improved the process of bibliographic research phenomenally. With the Internet, libraries are able to provide remote access for their users not only to their local collections and catalog, but also to library collections around the nation and the world. With this capacity, metadata and

---

[1] Liu, Lewis-Guodo. 2001. *The Role and Impact of the Internet on Library and Information Services*. Westport, Conn: Greenwood Press.

[2] See Note 1

[3] Su, Di. 2001. *Evolution in Reference and Information Services: The Impact of the Internet*. Binghamton, NY: Haworth Information Press.

resource description standards have become more important as numerous libraries contribute records to shared catalogs and local cataloging practices affect access for patrons across the world. However, while such Internet-induced changes in the library catalog are worthy of examination, these changes do not fundamentally alter the role of the catalog in library services.

Indeed, library literature in 2001[4,5] reflects the fact that, as much as the Internet had changed the process and the possibilities of traditional library functions, the essential nature of library services remained the same: the acquisition, organization, and dissemination of and education about, information resources. In the past decade, though, the open culture and evolving technology of the Internet has created a set of user expectations that have presented libraries—particularly academic libraries—with opportunities to not only change their approach to traditional services, but to embrace new roles.

Openness and Online User Expectations
From its inception, the concept of openness has been integral to the success of the Internet; as some of its developers note, "A key to the rapid growth of the Internet has been the free and open access to the basic documents...."[6] Collaboration and open sharing of documentation and code enabled swift development of the early Internet, and open source programming continues to be the backbone of some of the most robust applications available to Internet users today. The openness of the Internet extends beyond sharing source code, however, at its core; the open ethos of the Internet is today expressed in two ways: openness of access and openness of identity.

---

[4] See note 1
[5] See note 3
[6] Leiner, Barry M., Cerf, Vinton G., Clark, David D., Kahn, Robert E., Kleinrock, Leonard, Lynch, Daniel C., Postel, Jon, Roberts, Larry G. and Stephen Wolff. 2001. "A Brief History of the Internet" in Liu, Lewis-Guodo, ed. *The Role and Impact of the Internet on Library and Information Services*. Westport, Conn: Greenwood Press.

In a 2010 global British Broadcasting Corporation (BBC) survey (n=27,000), 80 percent of respondents indicated that Internet access is a human right.[7] The expectation that equitable access to online resources is on par with access to clean water seems entirely reasonable—after all, like water, the Internet is freely available to anyone. It may require resources to procure the computer and hardware necessary to connect to the Internet, but the Internet itself is a free resource. Users pay for a computer and for access to cable lines or to wireless networks, but no one pays for a Web browser, access to a search engine, or to send E-mail or to visit millions of websites.

The view of Internet access as a human right is a reflection of how today's users experience the Internet, and what they expect when they go online: easy and free access to resources. The most popular Internet sites and applications like Google and Facebook are openly (freely) available to all. Many daily tasks can be accomplished on the Internet without spending a cent: Google Docs or Zoho or Open Office provide tools for work and school assignments; Hulu provides entertainment; CNN (or Fox) provide news; Skype provides a connection to relatives in Detroit; Mint provides budgeting assistance; and Pandora provides the soundtrack for it all. As a recent Wall Street Journal (online!) column notes, "we have built a country-size economy online where the default price is zero – nothing, nada, zip. ... For the Google Generation, the Internet is the land of the free."[8] As much of an economic driver as the Internet is, the expectation of free access to online tools, resources and information is hard-wired into many Internet users: the 2010 Annenberg Digital Future Study found

---

[7] Ayish, Muhammad. "Universal Internet Access is the New Human Rights Issue." *The National,* March 18, 2010. Accessed October 29, 2010. http://www.thenational.ae/news/universal-internet-access-is-the-new-human-rights-issue?pageCount=0

[8] Anderson, Chris. "The Ecomonics of Giving it Away." *Wall Street Journal,* January 31, 2009. Accessed October 29, 2010. http://online.wsj.com/article/SB123335678420235003.html

that, of 49 percent of Internet users who reported using services like Twitter, exactly zero percent would be willing to pay for such a service.[9] This does not mean that users will never pay for an online service (e.g., for a "premium" version of an online service[10]) but it supports the supposition that users' default expectation is to experience free access online.

At the same time that users have been conditioned to expect open access to online resources, the Internet (particularly in the last decade) has also encouraged users to be open about themselves online. Though it can be argued that the Internet encourages not openness about identity but rather faceless (or deceptive) anonymity, it would be difficult to argue against the predominance of online technologies and forums that enable (and expect) unprecedented individual openness. Users' full utilization of social networking sites like MySpace and Facebook is directly related to the amount of personal information users are prepared to share online and the culture of blogging and micro-blogging (i.e. Twitter) encourages people to expose their deepest (and shallowest) thoughts with ongoing immediacy. It has been noted that some online users do attempt to retain a certain level of privacy within their online activities,[11,12] and consistent flaps over Facebook privacy snafus demonstrate that many users do care about having control over their personal information. However, a recent study by the Pew Center found that only 33 percent of Internet users are

---

[9] Annenberg School of Communications. *2010 USC Annenberg Digital Future Study Finds Strong Negative Reaction to Paying for Online Services*, July 23, 2010. Accessed October 29, 2010.
http://www.digitalcenter.org/pdf/2010_digital_future_final_release.pdf
[10] Bulik, Beth Snyder. "On-Demand Generation Will Pay to Play." *Advertising Age*, April 12, 2010. Accessed November 1, 2010.
http://adage.com/digital/article?article_id=143220
[11] Lange, P.G. "Publicly Private and Privately Public: Social Networking on YouTube." *Journal of Computer-Mediated Communication* 13(2007): Article 18. Accessed November 1, 2010. http://jcmc.indiana.edu/vol13/issue1/lange.html
[12] Holson, Laura M. "Tell-All Generation Learns to Keep Things Offline." *The New York Times,* May 8, 2010. Accessed November 1, 2010.
http://www.nytimes.com/2010/05/09/fashion/09privacy.html?_r=1

concerned about what information is available about them online, and only 33 percent of users have taken any action to limit/reduce the amount of information available about them on the Internet.[13] In fact, some users are beginning to acknowledge that limiting the amount of available information may be less important than *adding* desired information to influence the nature of their online identities.[14]

Openness and Opportunities

Over the past decade, the confluence of users' willingness to share personal information (in a variety of formats) online, and their desire/expectation of receiving open access to online tools and resources (sometimes in exchange for sharing personal information) has contributed to an unprecedented culture of openness on the Internet. As users with these expectations and experiences arrive on college and university campuses (both as students and as faculty), it has presented academic libraries with the opportunity to provide services that are informed by both dimensions of this online openness—and that reach beyond the library's traditional roles.

Open Access and Academic Libraries

Traditionally, academic libraries have purchased resources from publishers and other vendors to create collections of materials for student and faculty use. In turn, libraries have been defined by their role as collector.[15] However, as the cost of library resources, particularly scholarly journals, has risen dramatically over the

---

[13] Madden, Mary and Aaron Smith. 2010. *Reputation Management and Social Media.* Pew Research Center. Accessed November 1, 2010.
http://pewinternet.org/Reports/2010/Reputation-Management.aspx
[14] Thompson, Clive. "The See-Through CEO." *Wired,* March 2007. Accessed October 29, 2010.
http://www.wired.com/wired/archive/15.04/wired40_ceo.html
[15] Gilman, Isaac and Marita Kunkel. 2010. "From Passive to Pervasive: Changing Perceptions of the Library's Role through Intra-Campus Partnerships." *Collaborative Librarianship* 2(1): 20-30.
http://collaborativelibrarianship.org/index.html

past decade, academic libraries have been confronted with stark budget realities[16] -and the openness of the Internet has emerged as a partial solution: instead of merely subscribing to journals, academic libraries are now publishing them, and are on the vanguard of the open access movement.

Open Access
Open access, in relation to scholarly publishing, has been described in various ways. The Budapest Open Access Initiative (2002) provides one of the most comprehensive definitions:

> By 'open access' to this literature, we mean its free availability on the public internet, permitting any users to read, download, copy, distribute, print, search, or link to the full texts of these articles, crawl them for indexing, pass them as data to software, or use them for any other lawful purpose, without financial, legal, or technical barriers other than those inseparable from gaining access to the internet itself.[17]

Peter Suber, a well-known open access advocate, offers a more succinct definition: "Open-access (OA) literature is digital, online, free of charge, and free of most copyright and licensing restrictions."[18] Regardless of how it is defined, the call for free and unrestricted access to online journal content is born from a very simple principle, well-articulated by John Willinsky:

> "A commitment to the value and quality of research carries with it a responsibility to extend the circulation of such

---

[16] Van Orsdel, Lee C. and Kathleen Born. "Reality Bites: Periodicals Price Survey 2009." *Library Journal*, April 15, 2009. Accessed November 1, 2010. http://www.libraryjournal.com/article/CA6651248.html
[17] *Budapest Open Access Initiative*. February 12, 2002. Accessed January 6, 2011. http://www.soros.org/openaccess/read.shtml
[18] Suber, Peter. *A Very Brief Introduction to Open Access*. December 29, 2004. Accessed January 6, 2011. http://www.earlham.edu/~peters/fos/brief.htm

work as far as possible and ideally to all who are interested in it and all who might profit by it."[19]

Willinsky also notes that a commitment to this principle and, by extension, to open access is something that is very familiar to librarians. Libraries' dedication to intellectual inquiry demands equitable access to information. Academic libraries, in particular, are sensitive to the needs of their students, faculty and researchers to have the broadest and deepest access possible to relevant scholarly literature.

Libraries' desires to provide these comprehensive collections for their users have been challenged by the rising cost of scholarly journals.[20] These price increases are exacerbated by a pricing structure colloquially referred to as "the big deal." Large commercial publishers like Elsevier, Springer and Wiley (who, as of 2002, were estimated to account for 42% of scholarly journal articles published[21]) often bundle individual journal subscriptions together, tying desirable journals with lower quality titles and forcing a larger expenditure of library funds.[22] As a result, rather than continuing to expand their collections, many academic libraries have been forced to make difficult choices about which resources to cut in order to maintain expensive subscriptions, as in this 2008 example from Washington State University-Pullman:

---

[19] Willinsky, John. 2006. *The access principle: the case for open access to research and scholarship*. Cambridge, Mass: MIT Press., xii

[20] Henderson, Kittie S. and Stephen Bosch. "Seeking the New Normal: Periodicals Price Survey 2010." *Library Journal*, April 15, 2010. Accessed January 8, 2011. http://www.libraryjournal.com/article/CA6725256.html

[21] McGuigan, Glenn S. and Robert D. Russell. "The Business of Academic Publishing: A Strategic Analysis of the Academic Journal Publishing Industry and its Impact on the Future of Scholarly Publishing." *Electronic Journal of Academic and Special Librarianship* 9(3) (Winter 2008). http://southernlibrarianship.icaap.org/content/v09n03/mcguigan_g01.html

[22] Nabe, Jonathan. "E-Journal Bundling and Its Impact on Academic Libraries: Some Early Results." *Issues in Science and Technology Librarianship* (Spring 2001). http://www.library.ucsb.edu/istl/01-spring/article3.html

The WSU Libraries have had to cancel a substantial number of journal titles in recent years. Some titles were cancelled outright. Others are now only available electronically. During this time, the library materials budget has been flat; we have not received increases to cover inflation in books or journals. Journal inflation, including access to abstracting and indexing services, is running between 5% and 10% annually. We now have this year's budget figures, and again there is no money to keep offering the access we currently have. We are going to have to cancel somewhere around $600,000 of journals, approximately 15% of our remaining subscriptions.[23]

Faced with the choice, however, some large research libraries have taken a stand, either electing to cancel subscriptions in protest,[24] or taking their pricing issues public. In 2010, the University of California Libraries recommended that its faculty stop submitting to Nature Publishing Group journals in response to a proposed 400% increase in the subscription rate for the UC system.[25]

Such unsustainable journal prices, coupled with their ethical affinity to open access, have made academic libraries into fierce advocates for more affordable models of scholarly publishing, particularly open access – a model that benefits both their bottom lines and their users. SPARC, the Scholarly Publishing and Academic Resources Coalition (founded in 1997), is "an international alliance of hundreds of academic libraries and

[23] Kaag, Cindy S. WSU Pullman Libraries Collection Development Decisions Calendar 2008. Accessed January 7, 2011. http://www.wsulibs.wsu.edu/collections/cancelcover.html
[24] See Note 19
[25] Oder, Norman. "UC Libraries, Nature Publishing Group in Heated Dispute Over Pricing; Boycott Possible." *Library Journal*, June 10, 2010. Accessed January 6, 2011. http://www.libraryjournal.com/lj/home/885271-264/uc_libraries_nature_publishing_group.html.csp

research institutions"[26] and is a driving force in the push for greater access to published scholarship, particularly that derived from publicly funded research. However, advocacy is not the most significant role that libraries have embraced; as leaders in the open access movement, academic libraries are also becoming publishers as well by providing a wide range of technological and organizational support for new (and existing) publications.

Library as Publisher
Though the costs of online publishing (in increasingly sophisticated form) have been relatively minimal since the inception of the Internet, it has only been in the past decade that many libraries have begun to take full advantage of the opportunity to become actively involved in online publishing activities. Two developments have been instrumental in this shift: the availability of publishing platforms (both open source and commercial) and, to a lesser extent, challenges to the viability of traditional university presses.

A 2008 survey of ARL (Association of Research Libraries) member libraries found that 43% of respondents were engaged in publishing activities and, of those libraries, over half were using the open source Open Journal Systems as their publishing platform.[27] Open Journal Systems (http://pkp.sfu.ca/?q=ojs) is a platform created by the Public Knowledge Project, a partnership between the Faculty of Education at the University of British Columbia, the Simon Fraser University Library, the School of Education at Stanford University, and the Canadian Centre for Studies in Publishing at Simon Fraser University:

> OJS assists with every stage of the refereed publishing
> process, from submissions through to online publication

[26] SPARC. *About SPARC.* Accessed January 7, 2011.
http://www.arl.org/sparc/about/index.shtml
[27] Hahn, Karla L. *Research Library Publishing Services: New Options for University Publishing.* Association of Research Libraries, March 2008.
http://www.arl.org/bm~doc/research-library-publishing-services.pdf

and indexing. Through its management systems, it's finely grained indexing of research, and the context it provides for research, OJS seeks to improve both the scholarly and public quality of refereed research.

OJS is open source software made freely available to journals worldwide for the purpose of making open access publishing a viable option for more journals, as open access can increase a journal's readership as well as its contribution to the public good on a global scale.[28]

As open source software, Open Journals Systems is freely available for libraries to download, install and configure to desired specifications. However, there are also affordable commercial software options that provide libraries with the same ability to easily manage and published open access peer-reviewed scholarly journals. For example, EdiKit®,[29] an editorial management and publication platform from Berkeley Electronic Press (bepress), is available as stand-alone hosted software, or in conjunction with bepress' hosted repository platform, Digital CommonsTM. As the ARL survey observed, using software like EdiKit® "frees a library from both hardware and software support, allowing staff resources to be directed to other publishing service functions such as consulting and workflow design."[30]

Whether they choose to use open source publishing software or hosted commercial software, libraries are being presented with new opportunities to offer publishing services as university presses face challenges to their sustainability[31,] creating openings

---

[28] Public Knowledge Project. *Open Journal Systems*. Accessed January 9, 2011. http://pkp.sfu.ca/?q=ojs
[29] http://www.bepress.com/edikit.html
[30] See Note 27
[31] Brown, Laura, Griffiths, Rebecca and Matthew Rascoff. "University Publishing in a Digital Age." *Ithaka Report*. July 26, 2007. http://www.ithaka.org/ithaka-s-r/research/university-publishing-in-a-digital-age/Ithaka%20University%20Publishing%20Report.pdf

for library-press partnerships. A 2007 Ithaka report, "University Publishing in a Digital Age," offered the following recommendation for university presses:

> *Recommendation 6: Collaborate with libraries to co-develop tools and programs.*
>
> Work together to identify content of institutional value. Co-develop products, tools and professional educational and training programs for faculty, researchers, and students around traditional and electronic publishing issues, procedures, etc. Co-develop joint programs for preservation and archiving or collaborate in support of third party platforms that ensure preservation. Co-develop tools for content creation and online collaboration.[32]

As they enter into these collaborations, libraries are not only offering support for open access journals, but are translating the open access model to monographic materials as well. For example, the Utah State University press recently became part of the university library and many publications will now be available open access in digital form.[33] In doing so, Utah State joins the University of Michigan and Purdue University as institutions with presses that are units of the university library. In addition to monographs, Purdue University Press publishes both subscription and open access journals. The Press utilizes bepress' Digital CommonsTM/EdiKit® platform in its open access publishing activities – both serial and monographic.[34]

Even for libraries at institutions with strong university presses (or no university press at all), support for open access publishing, both locally and globally, have been a growing trend. At Columbia

---

[32] See Note 31
[33] Jaschik, Scott. "Survival – Through Open Access." *Inside Higher Ed.* November 4, 2009.
http://www.insidehighered.com/news/2009/11/04/utahstate
[34] http://docs.lib.purdue.edu/thepress/

University, the University Libraries/Information Services unit created a Center for Digital Research and Scholarship (http://cdrs.columbia.edu/) in 2007. In addition to managing Columbia's institutional repository (another venue through which libraries provide open access to scholarly work), CDSR "offers journal hosting support services to Columbia faculty and students who want to start or continue publishing a journal."[35] CDSR supports both subscription and open access journals, and utilizes a combination of open source and commercial publishing software (e.g., CDSR uses OJS as a publishing platform, but its forthcoming Columbia Journal of Race and Law also utilizes bepress' law review submission software, ExpressO™).

The relatively low cost and scalable nature of online publishing, made possible by the Internet (and platforms like OJS and EdiKit™), means that institutions much smaller than Utah State, Purdue and Columbia have also been able to move in the direction of making publishing (both open access and subscription-based) one of their core service areas. Over the past two years, the University Library at Pacific University (Oregon) has made an intentional effort to develop the capacity and structure to support scholarly publishing activities. The Library uses Digital Commons® as its institutional repository platform, and selected it because of its dual capacity to function both as a hosted repository and hosted publishing platform.

Pacific University Library's first publication as a publishing body was an existing open access peer-reviewed scholarly journal, *Essays in Philosophy*. The journal had previously been hosted at Humboldt State University, but due to a change in editorship, the journal was seeking a new online home. This initial partnership with a faculty member from the Department of Philosophy led to the creation of a new open access journal, *Res Cogitans*, devoted to

---

[35] A brief overview of the publishing services provided is available here: http://cdrs.columbia.edu/cdrsmain/wp-content/uploads/2009/04/journalservicesv6.pdf

undergraduate philosophy papers presented at an annual conference. For both journals, editorial management related to journal content is managed by the journals' editor, but support for the final design and publication of articles is provided by the University Library.

In recognition of its developing role in a wide range of publishing-related activities, in 2010 the Pacific University Library created a new unit, Local Collections and Publication Services (LCPS).[36] While coordinating some more traditional library services – archival services and online collections (image collections and institutional repository content) – LCPS also became the home for library publishing services. The collaborative effort and strategic direction provided by the new unit (comprised of existing members of the Library's faculty) will be integral to providing support for new publishing requests. A new interprofessional healthcare journal based out of Pacific University's College of Health Professions and College of Optometry is planned for 2011, and there have also been discussions about the possibility of hosting/supporting two professional society journals.

Beyond the examples of Columbia and Pacific University, yet another indicator of the rise in library publishing activities is their visibility in conference sessions, library publications and professional development opportunities for librarians. In the last academic year, as part of a scholarly communications webinar series, ARL offered sessions on open access publishing and open access publishing support, intended to "help libraries that are increasingly involved in providing journal hosting and support services, [and to explore] transitional models for economic support from subscriptions to open access."[37]

---

[36] http://www.pacificu.edu/library/services/lcps/
[37] ARL. *Reshaping Scholarly Communications: Program 3A & 3B: Open Access Publishing & Open Access Publishing Support.* Accessed January 9, 2011. http://www.arl.org/sc/institute/iscwebseries/2010iscweb3.shtml

While there are predominant open access publishers, such as BioMed Central, it is clear that libraries are doing their part to continue the growth of open access publishing. And for open-minded librarians, the figures are encouraging: the number of open access journals is growing continuously (the Directory of Open Access Journals added more than 3 new titles per day in the last quarter[38]) and even journals which are not strictly open access are making some content openly available, either voluntarily or due to mandates from both the government and educational institutions.[39,40]

Beyond Publishing: Other Open Access Activities
As the number of open access journals grow, and mainstream publishers adapt their policies to accommodate the demand for open access literature (e.g. Springer's Open Choice option), academic librarians are also taking an active role in educating their patrons (i.e. faculty members) about new opportunities for retaining the ability to make their work openly accessible. This role is seen most clearly in both librarians' advocacy for authors' rights and in the establishment of funds to support publication in open access journals.

Publishers have long argued the necessity of possessing the copyright for articles published in their journals. Common arguments have included the need for centralization of permission requests and the need to protect publishers' ability to provide articles for indexing/inclusion in databases.[41,42] As some have

---

[38] Morrison, Heather. "Dramatic Growth of Open Access: September 30, 2010." *The Imaginary Journal of Poetic Economics.* Accessed October 4, 2010. http://poeticeconomics.blogspot.com/2010/09/dramatic-growth-of-open-access.html
[39] National Institutes of Health Public Access. Accessed November 1, 2010. http://publicaccess.nih.gov/
[40] Suber, Peter. "The Open Access Mandate at Harvard." *SPARC Open Access Newsletter,* March 2, 2008. Accessed November 1, 2010. http://www.earlham.edu/~peters/fos/newsletter/03-02-08.htm#harvard
[41] Winchester, Ian. 2009. Publishing Academic Journals in the Internet Era. *Journal of Educational Thought* 43(1):1-2.

observed, authors relinquishing their copyrights to publishers had few serious implications in a print environment – but as the Internet made sharing work openly easier and more desirable, those rights have become more precious.[43] Academic and research libraries, particularly through the leadership of the SPARC alliance have been at the forefront of arguing that authors should be able to retain the ability to share their articles openly – even if they haven't published in an open access journal. Librarians, like those at Oregon State University,[44] put on workshops to educate faculty about how to determine which journals will allow them to retain the right to share, and how to advocate for that right with journals that don't.

While many open access journals (like those published at Pacific University) do not pass the costs of operation on to their published authors, many larger open access publishers do. For example, authors published in Public Library of Science journals can expect to pay between $1,350 and $2,900 (depending on the journal). For authors with grant funding or other financial support, these fees may not be a barrier. However, for authors without such support, publication in some high-profile open access journals may be out of reach. In response to this need, some academic institutions have begun to establish open access funds to cover the cost of publishing and to ensure that their faculty/researchers are able to make their work openly accessible.[45] At some of these institutions, the library has been the leader in creating and

---

[42] Polansky, Barbara F. 1984. Responsible publishers require copyright transfer . . . and everyone benefits. *Journal of the American Dietetic Association* 84: 891.

[43] Copyright Battle Expands To New Fronts. 1999. *Chemical & Engineering News* 77 (24): 40-42.

[44] Wirth, Andrea A., and Faye A. Chadwell. 2010. "Rights Well: An Authors' Rights Workshop for Librarians". *Portal: Libraries and the Academy*. 10 (3): 337-354. http://hdl.handle.net/1957/17099

[45] SPARC. *Campus-based Open-access Publishing Funds.* Accessed January 12, 2011. http://www.arl.org/sparc/openaccess/funds/

administering the fund – a model seen both at the University of Oregon and the University of North Carolina.[46,47]

When faculty authors take advantage of open access funds or retain distribution rights through the negotiation of a copyright transfer agreement, academic libraries also offer one final opportunity for additional openness: archiving and dissemination of published work through an institutional repository. Though not formal "publication" (and many works in repositories have already been formally published), inclusion in a repository offers faculty authors the assurance that their work will remain both discoverable and accessible. For authors who have already published in an open access journal, addition of their articles to a library's open repository adds another access point and opportunity for use of their work. For authors who have published in subscription-based journals – but have retained the right to post their work in a repository – the contribution of their work provides open access to their knowledge, and an act of "publication" with the potential to increase the impact of work that would otherwise be locked behind a monetary barrier.

For libraries, the shift from passive purchasers of external resources to vital partners in the creation of new publications is truly transformational. Whether they are publishing open access journals or providing authors with the knowledge and tools that allow open dissemination of their work, academic libraries have embraced the opportunity of openness provided by the Internet and are meeting (and sometimes exceeding) users' expectations.

Readers' Advisory to Identity Advisory
While capitalizing on their own opportunity to contribute to openly accessible knowledge through online publishing activities,

---

[46] University of Oregon Libraries. *Open Access Publishing Support Fund.* Accessed January 12, 2011. http://libweb.uoregon.edu/scis/sc/oaps.html
[47] UNC Health Sciences Library. *Open Access and Scholarly Communications.* Accessed January 12, 2011.
http://guides.hsl.unc.edu/content.php?pid=121319&sid=1262572

academic libraries are also faced with the challenge of responding to their students' personal openness.

Libraries have long been privacy advocates, championing intellectual freedom and the confidentiality of their patrons' information. The American Library Association's (ALA) Code of Ethics states, "We protect each library user's right to privacy and confidentiality with respect to information sought or received and resources consulted, borrowed, acquired or transmitted."[48] However, as technology has evolved, it has become more challenging for libraries to honor that commitment, as they are faced with decisions about how best to protect patron privacy in an increasingly distributed and unsecured digital environment. While part of protecting patron privacy is certainly dependent on libraries' own policies and practices keeping pace with technological change, their users' practices must also be addressed. It is this realm that holds the greatest opportunity for a new service area for academic libraries: identity advisory.

Personal Privacy Online
Sitting at the nexus of popularity (1 billion worldwide projected users by August 2012[49]) and controversy, Facebook has been the recent face of Internet privacy concerns, with news stories detailing issues ranging from the relatively innocuous (embarrassing photographs) to the deathly serious (the potential and inadvertent risk of impacting the security and safety of the troops located in war zones by posting to Facebook[50]). A recent simple search of the LexisNexis Academic database yielded approximately 1,000 recent stories discussing Facebook and privacy settings. Yet Facebook is not alone in its sometimes light

---

[48] ALA. *Code of Ethics of the American Library Association.* June 28, 1997. Accessed January 14, 2011.
http://www.ala.org/ala/issuesadvocacy/proethics/codeofethics/codeethics.cfm
[49] Grossman, Lev. "2010 Person of the Year: Mark Zuckerberg." *Time.* 176.26 (Dec. 27, 2010): 58.
[50] Baldeor, Lolita. Troops warned of Facebook security risk. *The Oregonian.* November 21, 2010, A9.

regard for users' personal privacy—the Internet is rife with opportunities for personal information to be solicited, stolen, or bartered in exchange for services:

> The word "web" was originally an image used to describe a decentralized system of interconnected information networks. Nobody imaged that a spider would actually take up residence at its center and start spying on the activities of all Internet users.[51]

Indeed, it is difficult to visit a website without information about your activity being stored and tracked for future use. For example, marketers place cookies (small text files) on users' computers when they visit a site. Those cookies help "deliver content that is customized according to user preferences,"[52] but also represent a potential invasion of user privacy. Louis Vuitton, Starbucks, and countless others use cookies as a mechanism by which to reach more audiences with directed and relevant advertising and services.[53] But those targeted services are coupled with the reality that marketers know a user's Internet traffic patterns.

This environment, where corporations are able to track personal movements online, and Facebook "knows exactly who you are and what you're interested in, because you told it,"[54] creates a personal experience for users online and encourages users to share ever more personal information in the pursuit of further tailoring that experience – whether that is a Facebook page shared with friends, recommendations from retail sites based on purchases and ratings, or personal details shared on a blog (or in a Tweet). As more of life is shared online, users would do well to heed Google CEO Eric Schmidt, who cautioned that "If you have something that

---

[51] Riviere, Philippe. "The Magic Mirror and the Web." *Oregonian* January 9, 2011: D2.
[52] Marshall, Patrick. "Online Privacy." *CQ Researcher* November 6, 2009: 933-56. Web. 10 Jan 2011. http://library.cqpress.com/cqresearcher
[53] See Note 51.
[54] See Note 49.

you don't want anyone to know, maybe you shouldn't be doing it in the first place."[55] Openness, whether voluntary or not, appears to be the rule in the Web 2.0 world.

Such openness is not without potential consequences (beyond the simple over-sharing of information). Students, employees and potential employees have all been impacted by unfortunate photos, videos or other material surfacing online at inopportune times. Particularly for students engaged in professional programs, (such as teaching or medicine), the ramifications for a future career and employment can be disastrous.[56] Recognizing this, many colleges and universities have taken steps to prepare their students to live more private lives online. Some, like Syracuse University have even taken the proactive approach of helping their job-seeking graduates create a better image for themselves:

> Brand-Yourself.com ... created and run by four SU alumni, is an online reputation management company that builds positive web content and relevant Google search results for their clients. ...
>
> Recent SU graduates can use their Brand-Yourself account to build a personal Web site, monitor Google search results for their name, and build positive content on the web while burying the negative or irrelevant search results. Brand-Yourself also educates clients about the Google algorithm, which ranks relevant content in search results. By learning how to use social networks and outside linkage, clients can boost positive content higher on the search engine list.[57]

---

[55] See Note 49.

[56] Gilman, Isaac. 2009. "Online Lives, Offline Consequences: Professionalism, Information Ethics and Professional Students." *Interface on the Internet* 9. http://bcis.pacificu.edu/journal/article.php?id=22

[57] Waugh, Danielle. "University Helps Students Clean Up Digital Dirt." *Campus Chatter (ABC News)*. Accessed January 13, 2011. http://blogs.abcnews.com/campuschatter/2010/07/university-helps-students-clean-up-digital-dirt.html

Academic Libraries and Identity Advisory
As long-standing privacy advocates, it makes sense that academic
libraries should play a role in educating their student (and
occasionally, faculty) users about the creation and maintenance of
their online identities. Within the library profession at large, the
American Library Association (ALA) has undertaken several
initiatives to create awareness of privacy issues for library users,
including the first *Choose Privacy Week* in 2010. These activities
encourage users to utilize the Internet responsibly and to be
aware of how social networking and various other sites are
collecting/using their personal information. Although tied to a
traditional library practice (protecting privacy), this focus is
fundamentally different—it is a shift from assuring users of how
the library protects their information to advocating for how users
should manage their own information (outside of the context of a
library record).

In an academic setting, while college or university IT staff may also
have a role in educating students about the importance of
managing their online identities, this is an opportunity that college
and university libraries can, and should, welcome. Libraries
should be guided in their efforts by these questions:

> 1. How do we help students balance free speech with
> responsibility?
> 2. What kind of image does our students' use of Facebook
> present to employers, alumni, parents, and other students?
> Should this be our concern?
> 3. Can we afford to not alert our students to the
> consequences of ill-informed use of Facebook?[58]

While these questions refer specifically to the use of Facebook
(and similar social networking applications), the principles raised

---

[58] Oblinger, Diana G. and Brian L. Hawkins. 2006. "The Myth about Putting
Information Online." *EDUCAUSE Review* 41(5) (September/October): 14-15.

are applicable when considering any online activities that may involve personal information, images or other data – particularly the final question.

At Pacific University (Oregon), the University Library has taken a lead role in helping to address these questions and to provide identity advisory to incoming freshmen. Librarians have created online privacy-related instructional sessions to help emphasize that online identities cultivated during school may have an impact long after graduation. The sessions begin with ethical issues related to the use/re-use of online content (i.e. plagiarism and copyright infringement) and also touch on issues of free speech in an online environment. The idea of free speech carries over into discussions of the creation of online identities; as intellectual freedom advocates, librarians may be loath to support censorship of any form, but the relative permanence of words/thoughts shared online necessitates conversations of occasional self-censorship in the service of maintaining a "clean" online identity. Finally, the importance of careful social-networking habits is covered, with examples pulled from recent news stories of photos or other online content creating academic or employment issues for young adults. Discussion of the potential impact of online identities has carried special relevance at Pacific University in recent years due to a 2008 incident in which a student resident assistant (RA) was fired after appearing in online pictures that implied his presence during underage drinking.[59]

In these library sessions, it has become clear that students are not unaware of the risk of being too public online about their private lives. This confirms the results of a 2008 survey conducted by the College Board, which found that 74% of college-bound students had some level of concern about potential employers looking for

---

[59] Guros, Frankie. "You were drinking – Facebook told us so." *The Pacific Index.* April 25, 2008. p. 7.

online information about them.[60] As some researchers have
observed,

> Facebook is increasingly recognized as a space within
> which some precaution must be exercised, and users
> respond by retreating behind a virtual line of privacy—in
> proportion to the extent to which their awareness of has
> been raised by a concern that applies to them personally.[61]

As the level of student awareness regarding social-networking
privacy concerns continues to rise, it could be assumed that the
need for academic libraries to educate students about their online
identities and privacy would be reduced. However, precisely the
opposite is true.

Though students may be aware that their online identities are
representations of themselves that should be managed with an eye
towards posterity, skills for online identity management should
remain a core component of preparation for post-collegiate lives,
much in the same way that resume-writing and interviewing are
standard skill sets. In addition, reminders of the breadth of
possibilities for their online identities to impact their offline lives
must continue to be part of library educational efforts. A study of
first-year college students recently found that while 74.5% of
respondents had a private social networking profile, 61.5% had
not read their social networking site's privacy policy and 30.0%
did not know what personal information their social networking

[60] College Board. 2009. "Social Networking Sites and College-Bound Students."
StudentPoll 7(2). Accessed January 13, 2011.
http://professionals.collegeboard.com/data-reports-
research/trends/studentpoll/social-networking
[61] Lewis, Kevin, Kaufman, Jason & Nicholas Christakis. 2008. "The Taste for
Privacy: An Analysis of College Student Privacy Settings in an Online Social
Network." *Journal of Computer-Mediated Communication* 14: 79-100.

site was gathering about them.[62] An understanding of how others use their personal information online—whether it be friends uploading and tagging photos[63] or corporations tracking browsing/purchasing information or mining e-mail for targeted advertising—is a vital component of students maintaining privacy and control of their identity and information.

Setting the Example: Identity Protection in Academic Libraries
Leading initiatives to educate users about responsible management of their online identities and private information should serve as an additional (if hopefully unneeded) reminder for academic libraries of their responsibilities to protect those same users' information when they are using our resources. Libraries are no less susceptible than their users to the promise of new technology and applications, and to the possibility of added functionality for their users. In these moments, libraries are faced with decisions about which, and how much, user information is appropriate to surrender (or put at risk) for the sake of improved services. Whatever decisions are made, it is clear that if academic librarians are to be credible educators in this area, they must always be confident of the protections afforded to their users' private intellectual inquiries.

For example, there have been ongoing discussions in the library community regarding the use of RFID (radio-frequency identification) tags as a method inventory control. A position paper on the issue notes:

> RFID technology introduces an ethical dilemma for librarians. The technology allows for greatly improved services for patrons especially in the area of self-checkout,

---

[62] Lawler, James P. and John C. Molluzzo. 2011. "A Survey of First-Year College Student Perceptions of Privacy in Social Networking." *Journal of Computing Sciences in Colleges* 26(3): 36-41.

[63] Goodman, Tammy B. *Online Reputation Guide for College Students*. December 3, 2010. Accessed January 13, 2011. http://www.safetyweb.com/online-reputation-guide-for-college-students

it allows for more efficient use of professional staff, and may reduce repetitive stress injuries for library workers. And yet, the technology introduces the threat of hot listing and tracking library patrons. Librarians have taken extra steps to ensure that laws such as the USA PATRIOT Act cannot be used by government entities to invade the privacy of their patrons, and yet many of those same libraries are placing trackable chips on their patron's books.[64]

Proponents argue that the RFID technology is a necessary cost-saving measure while others are more conservative in their approach, arguing for the delayed implantation of the RFID chips until after standards are firmly established that can insure patrons' privacy. But whether it is RFID tags, bibliographic database vendors tracking individual users, or cloud computing services that store users' research libraries, citation and notes, the issue remains the same: how can libraries provide the best services while offering the best protection for their users' personal information?

Equally important to considerations of the impact of new services is the assurance that libraries are taking the basic steps necessary to secure private information. Libraries must responsibly adhere to privacy practices and policies and not simply point to the ALA's Code of Ethics as a blanket assurance that they are doing what they should. Simple issues to address include:[65]

- Reviewing the library's privacy policy. Does a policy even exist?

[64] Ayre, Lri Bowen. "Position Paper: RFID and Libraries." *The Galencia Group.* The Galencia Group, n.d. Accessed January 10, 2011. http://galecia.com/included/docs/position_rfid_permission.pdf
[65] Fredrick, Kathy. 2009. "Privacy Please!" *School Library Media Activities Monthly.* 15(6) (February): 44.

- Have library staff used e-mail to discuss specific patron issues?
- How secure are library computer passwords?
- Do library staff remember to logoff all systems?
- Are library sensitive to their surroundings and the need for privacy when assisting patrons?
- Are library computer search histories and caches regularly cleaned?

Libraries should also conduct regular privacy audits, determine what information is being collected in the course providing services (whether locally or by third parties/vendors), and determine an appropriate course of action for developing policies, procedures, and training related to the protection of their users' privacy.

It is vital for academic libraries to continue to play a role in educating their users (primarily students, but faculty as well) about strategies for protecting their online identities. For libraries to take advantage of this opportunity, however, they must demonstrate through their actions that they believe in the importance of what they are teaching.

Conclusion

Libraries have changed – and benefitted – in myriad ways due to the creation and continuing evolution of the Internet. And though the anachronistic stereotype of the academic library as the home of musty stacks may persist, the reality of library services (both traditional and non-traditional) continue to evolve along with it. Rather than Google and the open availability of information online sounding the death knell for libraries (students will get all their necessary information online, won't they?), the openness of online life has created transformational opportunities that are both revitalizing academic libraries and positioning them as partners – and leaders – in the production of open information and in the education of students whose lives, for better or for worse, will be shaped by their skill in navigating a Web-based environment. In the library's emphasis on free information (renewed through its role as open access publisher) and its continual attention to privacy issues (made increasingly relevant by digital dirt), the open culture of the Internet could have no more appropriate partner.

The Dawn of a New iAge in Education...or Not

Steve Rhine
Willamette University

"I am entirely certain that twenty years from now
we will look back at education as it is practiced in most schools
today and wonder that we could have tolerated anything so
primitive."

> -John W. Gardner, Secretary of Health, Education, and
> Welfare, 1968

Clarions marking the demise of traditional K-12 education have
repeatedly surfaced over the years. Technological advances are
usually the motivating culprit. In 1922 Edison profoundly wrote
that "the motion picture is destined to revolutionize our
educational system and that in a few years it will supplant largely,
if not entirely, the use of textbooks."[1] Needless to say, history said
otherwise. From televisions to VCR's to computers to handheld
devices, the promise of a new age in education always seems to
disappoint in the end. Cuban describes a cycle that is often
repeated in the quest for change in education through technology:
"exhilaration/scientific credibility/disappointment/teacher-
bashing."[2] The status quo is a powerful force. We develop comfort
with our practices and institutionalize policies and attitudes that
ensure a stable and predictable future. At the beginning of the
decade there were great hopes that the Internet would be a place
in which learners could interact and share knowledge as a way to

---

[1] From Cuban, L. (1986). *Teachers and Machines: The Classroom Use of
Technology.* New York: Teachers College Press, p. 9.
[2] Cuban, L. (1986). *Teachers and Machines: The Classroom Use of Technology.*
New York: Teachers College Press.

transform the educational process.[3] Has the rise of the Internet changed K-12 education?

As a people, we generally define "change" as something that happens with big fanfare and dramatic differences between "then" and "now"—a transformative revolution. We seem to need to see change in stark contrast with the past in order to feel like something has happened. Cuban suggests we are "a culture in love with swift change and big profit margins."[4] Accordingly, we often measure change by a number of something now as opposed to before. We can appreciate differences--we can "see" change between numbers.

When we look at the number of computers in classrooms over the past twenty years, we can see a dramatic change in the quantity of technology available to teachers and students. Ever since the first inkling that computers might have a role in classrooms, businesses have been keen on getting schools to devote an ever-larger portion of their budgets to technology. Apple began the charge change with donating thousands of computers to schools in the 1980's in the hope that students would get comfortable using Macintosh computers and their parents would buy them at home. Over time, Apple became less philanthropic and schools purchased the cheaper Windows machines instead. Seventy billion dollars were spent on school technology in the 1990's.[5] In the end, there is now an average of 1 computer for class use for every 3.1 students,[6] while there was 1 computer per 20 students at the start of the

---

[3] Kozma, R., & Schank, P. (1998). Connecting with the twenty-fist century: Technology in support of educational reform. In C. Dede (Ed.), *Technology and Learning*. Washington, DC; American Society for Curriculum Development.
[4] See note 1.
[5] Oppenheimer, T. (2004). *The Flickering Mind: Saving Education from the False Promise of Technology*. Random House.
[6] Nagel, D. (2010). Report: Mobile and Classroom Technologies Surge in Schools. theJournal. Retrieved from:
http://thejournal.com/articles/2010/05/05/report-mobile-and-classroom-technologies-surge-in-schools.aspx.

1990's.[7] We have gone from 84% of teachers having at least one computer in their classrooms at the beginning of this decade[8] to 97% of teachers by the end.[9] We have poured massive amounts of money into schools to make technology/the Internet accessible to students and teachers.

Of course, the biggest question is whether we have accomplished anything with that investment. Access is certainly not the same as productive and effective use that ultimately increases learning. Accordingly, answering that question is a multilayered process.

- How has access to the Internet changed in the past decade?
- How has the Internet changed teaching?
- How has the Internet changed learning?
- What are the implications for education for the future?

Another layer is how technology's reach extends into school learning at home as well as in the classroom. Both realms have simultaneously been influenced by the dawn of the Internet, but in different ways. As one peals through that layer, the issue of the digital divide is raised as well. In the following, I examine these layers and how or whether change has come to school via the Internet.

---

[7] Kim, S. H., & Bagaka, J. (2005). The digital divide in students' usage of technology tools: a multilevel analysis of the role of teacher practices and classroom characteristics. *Contemporary Issues in Technology and Teacher Education* [Online serial], *5*(3/4). Available: http://www.citejournal.org/vol5/iss3/currentpractice/article1.cfm.
[8] National Center for Education Statistics (2000). Teachers' Tools for the 21st Century: A Report on Teachers' Use of Technology. *Institute of Educational Sciences.* Retrieved from: http://nces.ed.gov/surveys/frss/publications/2000102/.
[9] Gray, L., Thomas, N., Lewis, L., Tice, P. (2010). *Teachers' Use of Educational Technology in U.S. Public Schools: 2009.* National Center for Education Statistics, Institute of Education Sciences, U.S. Department of Education. Washington, DC. Retrieved from http://nces.ed.gov/pubs2010/2010040.pdf.

Access

As discussed earlier with the advent of computers in classrooms, there has been a similar growth in school access to the Internet over the past 15 years (see Figure 1). Beginning with only three percent of schools with Internet access in 1994, essentially every school in the country has access to the Internet in 2011, a phenomenal achievement. This can be partially attributed to the Telecommunications Act of 1996, which aimed to decrease the digital divide by establishing the E-Rate[10] or discounts to schools and libraries to make Internet access affordable to schools. The level of discount to schools was between twenty and ninety percent depending on the level of poverty in the school. The fund subsidizes schools to the tune of $2.25 billion annually, although yearly requests for E-Rate discounts amount to three times that amount.[11, 12] To put this amount in perspective, the E-Rate fund is slightly less than what all schools spent on computers in 1999 ($3.3 billion, including hardware, software, training, and networking).[13] Needless to say, the government thought it was pretty important to get all schools wired to the Internet.

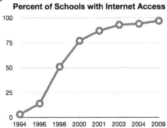

Percent of Schools with Internet Access

Figure 1. Schools with Internet Access (NCES, 2005 & 2009[14])

---

9 Formally known as the Schools and Libraries program in the Universal Service Fund of the Telecommunications Act of 1996.

[11] Gilroy, A. (2003). Telecommunications Discounts for Schools and Libraries: The "E-Rate" Program and Controversies. *Congressional Research Service.* (IB98040).

[12] Goolsbee, A. & Guryan, J. (2006). The Impact of Internet Subsidies in Public Schools. *Review of Economics and Statistics,* 88(2), 336-347.

[13] Lake, David (2000). Surfing at School. *The Industry Standard*, 117.

[14] National Center for Education Statistics (2005). Internet Access in U.S. Public Schools and Classrooms: 1994-2003. Retrieved from: http://nces.ed.gov/pubs2005/2005015.pdf.

At the beginning of the Internet decade, a digital divide in schools existed in regard to a number of computers as well as Internet access. Classrooms in schools with less than six percent minority enrollments were more likely to have 2-5 computers than schools with high minority enrollment (over nineteen percent).[15] In schools with less than twenty percent minority enrollments, teachers were more likely to have the Internet available in the classroom than teachers in schools with fifty percent or more minority enrollments.[16] By 2010, the digital divide in school shrank, as much as eighty percent of students from families with incomes of $20,000-$24,999 used computers in school compared with 86% of students from families with income of $75,000 or more. In regard to the digital divide in schools now, there is not a significant difference (less than three percent) in the number of computers available between elementary and secondary teachers, city versus rural schools, size of school, or percent of students in school eligible for free or reduced-price lunch programs.[17]

In a similar vein, Internet access at home has increased over the past decade so that it has become more a part of how students do their homework. In 2000, 41.5% of all homes had Internet access[18] while 69% did in 2009.[19] However, the digital divide at home has been significant as only 12.5% of families with household income below $20,000 used computers at home for schoolwork, while 43.8% of families with income over $50,000 did in 1997.[20] This divide remains with 51% of students with family incomes of $25,000-$34,999 having access to the Internet versus ninety percent of students in families with incomes of $75,000 or

---

[15] See note 7.
[16] See note 7.
[17] See note 8.
[18] U.S. Census Bureau (2000). Student use of computers: Table 278. Retrieved from:
http://www.allcountries.org/uscensus/278_student_use_of_computers.html.
[19] Exner, R. (2010). Sunday's Numbers: Internet now used in 69 percent of homes, mostly via broadband connections. *Cleveland.com*. Retrieved from:
http://www.cleveland.com/datacentral/index.ssf/2010/02/sundays_numbers_internet_now_u.html.
[20] See note 17.

more in 2007.[21] The divide is also reflected in educational backgrounds (only 24% of people who lack a high school diploma have Internet access versus 84% of those with a bachelor's degree[22]) and by race, as indicated in Figure 2.

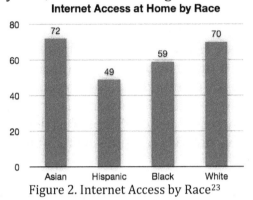

Figure 2. Internet Access by Race[23]

However, what do we mean by access? There is a raging debate in education regarding what access students should have to the Internet. Students with a constant access to the Internet scare schools. Districts have become increasingly worried about those hacking into their system and "inappropriate uses" of the Internet such as pornography and cyber bullying. In response, the Virginia Public Schools,[24] for instance, have a six page (single spaced) "Technology Resource Acceptable Use Policy" that is typical for schools. In the past decade, schools are increasingly having students sign codes of conduct upon entrance. Part of that agreement often includes something like the following:

---

[21] U.S. Census Bureau (2010). The 2010 Statistical Abstract: Table 1118. Retrieved from: http://www.census.gov/compendia/statab/cats/information_communications/internet_publishing_and_broadcasting_and_internet_usage.html.

[22] Burns, E. (2009). U.S. Census: Three in Five U.S. Households Have Home Internet Access. *Clickz: Marketing News and Expert Advice.* Retrieved from: http://www.clickz.com/clickz/stats/1694827/us-census-three-five-us-households-have-home-internet-access.

[23] See note 18.

[24] Virginia Public Schools (2011). Internet Use Policy. Retrieved from: http://vmps.org/technology-services/internet-use-policy/.

> We understand that modern information technologies offer a wealth of resources for learning, but like any tool, may be misused. We agree that the benefits of access outweigh the potential risks and responsibility for appropriate use falls on the individual user. We agree to hold the School District harmless for any misuse of its computer systems or any information that may be accessed through the School District's information technology resources. We understand that in order to administer its information technology resources, the School District can and will monitor use of those resources without notice prior to users.[25]

As a result of districts fearing inappropriate uses of the Internet, they are generally employing filters of content and not allowing wireless access. Parents are generally supportive of schools' protecting their children from pornography, hate speech, and other content they consider harmful. However, "harmful" and "inappropriate" are in the eye of the beholder. Furthermore, Internet filters are far from perfect. In a study on "Internet blocking in public schools," [26] the authors found that for every web page blocked, one or more pages were blocked unintentionally. Blocking software miscategorized about eighty percent of the pages in a sample of one million pages. For example, while one version of the software filtered sites on the Klan (36% of sites blocked), firearms (fifty percent), and slavery and genocide (33%), it also unintentionally filtered sites on pogo-sticks (46%), comedy (42%), and short poems (32%). Concerns over censorship have been heightened while fears of students being engaged or confronted with inappropriate content have not been sufficiently allayed. The report concludes:

---

[25] See note 23.

[26] Electronic Frontier Foundation (2003). Internet blocking in public schools. Retrieved from: http://w2.eff.org/Censorship/Censorware/net_block_report/net_block_report.pdf.

The use of Internet blocking software in schools cannot help schools comply with the law because schools do not and cannot set the software to block only the categories required by the law, and because the software is incapable of blocking only the visual depictions required by CIPA. Blocking software overblocks and underblocks, that is, the software blocks access to many web pages protected by the First Amendment and does not block many of the web pages that CIPA would likely prohibit.

Blocking software does not protect children from exposure to a large volume of material that is harmful to minors within the legal definitions. Blocking software cannot adapt adequately to local community standards. Most schools already have in place alternatives to Internet blocking software, such as adoption and enforcement of Internet use policies, media literacy education, directed use, and supervised use.

Blocking software in schools damages educational opportunities for students, both by blocking access to web pages that are directly related to state-mandated curriculums and by restricting broader inquiries of both students and teachers.[27]

As an alternative to filtering software, some suggest that schools take charge of teaching students critical thinking skills to help them use the Internet wisely (Doherty, Hansen, & Kaya, 1999; Weiler, 2005).[28]

---

[27] See note 25.
[28] Doherty, J., Hansen, M., & Kaya, K. (1999). Teaching information skills in the information age: The need for critical thinking. *Library Philosophy and Practice,* 1(2). Retrieved March 31, 2011 from http:// http://www.webpages.uidaho.edu/~mbolin/doherty.htm.

In summary, the Internet decade has seen schools' physical access to the Internet become essentially universal, regardless of socio-economics, with an increasing number of students able to access it in their classrooms. However, the ability of students to use Internet access for homework remains a digital divide issue if you are in a family of low socio-economic means. It remains to be seen how the tension between protection of students and First Amendment rights will be resolved in schools across the country.

Teaching

Certainly, the above data indicates that teachers have access to the Internet. However, for teachers, access is relative.

> The physical location and organization of computer technologies, whether the lab, classroom, library, or even school hallway, delimits and shapes the ways which teachers talk about and make use of their schools. As with the distribution of and access to any kind of resource, the distribution and organization of technology has an impact on the frequency and quality of teachers' integration/implementation efforts.[29]

It matters where the access to the Internet resides. If it is in a library, that leads to one kind of use for teachers. A computer lab implies a distinctive kind of use. A few computers in the classroom create still different ways of potentially using the Internet.

Has that access changed teaching? While we might naturally jump to the instruction aspect of teaching in order to address that question, in reality there are multiple dimensions of what a

---

Weiler, A. (2005). Information-Seeking Behavior in Generation Y Students: Motivation, Critical Thinking, and Learning Theory. *The Journal of Academic Librarianship*, 31(1), 46-53.

[29] Jenson, J., & Rose, C. (2008). Finding space for technology: Pedagogical observations on the organization of computers in school environments. *Canadian Journal Of Learning And Technology, 32*(1). Retrieved December 22, 2010, from http://www.cjlt.ca/index.php/cjlt/article/view/59/56.

teacher does. In considering how the Internet has influenced teaching, I propose eight aspects of the job:

1. understand the subject matter
2. understand the curriculum
3. understand the requirements of the state/district/etc.
4. understand the students
5. teach students the curriculum
6. assess students' understanding of the curriculum
7. record students' progress/achievement
8. communicate with parents, students, and administration

Understanding the subject matter

First, teachers need to understand the content of what they teach. Teachers' content knowledge is one of the few things that are actually correlated with students' achievement.[30, 31] This includes "knowledge and understanding of facts, concepts, and principles and the ways in which they are organized, as well as knowledge about the discipline; that is ways to establish truth."[32] It is impossible for teachers to know every aspect of every topic they need to teach. Accordingly, part of their preparation time is research on the topic. In this regard, the Internet has fundamentally changed how teachers prepare for their lessons. The number of teachers who 'sometimes' or 'often' use the Internet to prepare for instruction is 94%.[33] Formerly, teachers relied on books in the teachers' lounge or visited their local

---

[30] Hill, H., Rowan, B., & Ball, D. (2005). Effects of Teachers' Mathematical Knowledge for Teaching on Student Achievement. *American Educational Research Journal, 42*(2), 371-406.

[31] Moats, L. & Foorman, B. (2003). Measuring teachers' content knowledge of language and reading. *Annals of Dyslexia, 53*(1), 23-45.

[32] Even, R. (1993). Subject-Matter Knowledge and Pedagogical Content Knowledge: Prospective Secondary Teachers and the Function Concept. Journal for Research in Mathematics Education, 24(2), 94-116.

[33] See note 8.

library. Some teachers used their colleagues to understand content, but often, this is a socially complex interaction. Some are fortunate enough to have peers they can trust with those kinds of questions. With the Internet, there are video tutorials, the infamous Wikipedia, the Library of Congress, anonymous chat rooms, and more at teachers' fingertips to refresh or develop their understanding of the subject matter. Particularly at the secondary level, teachers have a wealth of opportunity to develop deeper insights into their content from a range of perspectives. Of course, there are justifiable concerns about the validity of information on the Internet, but most teachers, at this point, understand that they need to question the source of information.

Teaching is also taking place in the home, as 1.5 million students, or three percent of the population was homeschooled in 2007, up to 74% since 1999.[34] Parents of those homeschoolers feel more qualified to teach certain subjects more than others, so the Internet is vital to these families for developing understanding and networking with others. In 2007, "Fewer homeschoolers were enrolled part time in traditional schools to study subjects their parents lack knowledge to teach" (18% in 1999 to 16% in 2007).[35] Potential reasons for this may include the availability of online courses for students and parents' increasing use of the Internet to counterbalance the limits of their knowledge. In regard to developing content knowledge needed to teach, homeschooling parents are increasingly relying on the Internet as a resource for developing subject matter expertise they need to teach their children.

One other element that is growing is the use of the Internet for teacher professional development. In a recent Boston College study of 330 elementary and middle school math and language

---

[34] Lloyd, J. (January 5, 2009). Home schooling grows. *USA Today*. Retrieved from: http://www.usatoday.com/news/education/2009-01-04-homeschooling_N.htm.
[35] See note 32.

arts teachers, courses online improved teachers' instructional practices and subject matter knowledge, ultimately facilitating learning gains for students.[36] Lynn Meeks is a director of a project with Alabama Public Television: "Online courses allow busy teachers to access learning, resources, and colleagues not available locally and at a time that fits with their busy schedules. This is particularly important for rural teachers, who make up a large percentage of teachers." As teachers are distributed far and wide and have differing needs to increase their skills and knowledge, the Internet is a potentially effective tool to provide professional development.

Understanding the curriculum and demands of the state or district

The curriculum is distinct from the subject matter. Subject matter is what teachers know about the content. Curriculum is what topics are to be taught at what age level and in what order. It is the pathway to understanding the subject matter. The state or district often dictates a general guide for curricula, with the Internet becoming the primary source for distribution of state standards. There is typically different flexibility in different content areas. For instance, Mathematics is often very prescriptive in regard to a curriculum while Social Studies are typically provided with a broad curriculum in which teachers fill in the details. Figuring out the best path is often a matter of seeing what other paths have been chosen. Over the past decade, the Internet has developed into a great networking tool for examining others' syllabi or course plans as well as tapping into state and district resources. In Oregon there is an excellent website created by the Department of Education in which there are searchable state standards as well as examples of assessments and activities tied to those standards. Other states have similar curricular

---

[36] Cohen, A. & Orne, P. (2010). Report: Online Professional Development Improves Teaching and Student Achievement. *Education Development Center.* Retrieved from: http://www.edc.org/newsroom/press_releases/study_finds_online_professional_development_improves_teaching.

resources. The past decade has seen teachers and states increasingly rely on the Internet to design and access curriculum.

On a side note related to curriculum, there are many small schools and rural districts that struggle to offer the range and flexibility of courses students need. The past ten years of Internet time has also seen a great rise in virtual schools. State run virtual schools are now in 39 states. In the 2009-10 school year, there were 450,000 course enrollments (one student taking one semester long course). This is an increase of forty percent over the previous year. With North Carolina and Florida leading the way, there are currently 200,000 students attending online schools full-time.[37] In addition, many school districts are providing students with courses online to help them make up credits, Talented and Gifted programs, or to meet the needs of small and rural schools who cannot offer the same spectrum of courses that larger schools can. 1.5 million students took one or more online courses in 2009-10.[38]

Understanding the students
Teachers will likely tell you that the most rewarding and the most challenging aspect of their job is meeting each individual student's needs. There is also a sense that students' physical and emotional well-being has changed over the past decade or two, leaving teachers to cope with a range of students' behaviors that were not as present in classrooms previously.

> Over the past three decades in the United States, behavioral and learning disorders have emerged as major chronic conditions affecting the development of school-aged children and adolescents. Educators have reported a rise in

---

[37] Watson, J., Murin, A., Vashawy, L., Gemin, B., & Rapp, C. (2010). Keeping pace with K-12 online learning: An annual review of policy and practice. *Evergreen Education Group.* Retrieved from: http://www.kpk12.com/wp-content/uploads/KeepingPaceK12_2010.pdf.
[38] Wicks, M. (2010). *A National Primer on K-12 Online Learning: Version 2.* International Association for K-12 Online Learning. Retrieved from: http://www.inacol.org/research/docs/iNCL_NationalPrimerv22010-web.pdf.

the number of children with these disorders. Pediatricians have reported an increased number of children with outpatient visits related to behavioral and emotional disorders...Additionally, a marked increase has also been observed in the number of children with emotional and behavioral disorders who are treated with psychotropic medications.[39]

Some argue that the increasing numbers of students with problems, are real and others argue that they are simply due to increased awareness and diagnosis. Regardless, we do know that 5 million students were diagnosed with Attention Deficit Hyperactivity Disorder (ADHD) in 2009,[40] which amounts to approximately ten percent of the school population. Parent reported diagnoses of ADHD increased by 22% during 2003-2007, with a higher rate of diagnosis for older teens.[41] Five million students have Learning Disabilities (LD), although there is some overlap with students who have both ADHD and LD.[42] The 7.1 million students who have asthma, 9.5 million students took prescription drugs regularly for at least 3 months of 2009, and five percent of students missed over 11 days of school due to illness or injury.[43]

---

[39] Center for Disease Control and Prevention (CDC) (2008). Diagnosed Attention Deficit Hyperactivity Disorder and Learning Disability: United States, 2004–2006. *Vital and Health Statistics: Series 10, number 237.* U.S. Department of Health and Human Services. Retrieved from: http://www.cdc.gov/nchs/data/series/sr_10/Sr10_237.pdf.
[40] Center for Disease Control and Prevention (CDC) (2009). Summary Health Statistics for U.S. Children: National Health Interview Survey, 2009. *Vital and Health Statistics: Series 10, number 247.* U.S. Department of Health and Human Services. Retrieved from: http://www.cdc.gov/nchs/data/series/sr_10/sr10_247.pdf.
[41] Centers for Disease Control and Prevention (CDC) (n.d.). Retrieved from: http://www.cdc.gov/ncbddd/adhd/data.html.
[42] See note 38.
[43] See note 38.

The bottom line is that the classroom is an increasingly complex place for teachers. Each student who has unique needs requires teachers to meet with parents, psychologists, counselors, administrators, etc. to create an Individual Education Plan (IEP) which describes the challenges the student has and how teachers must meet his or her needs. In 71% of schools Individual Education Plans (IEPs) are now available through the Internet and 47% of teachers use those IEPs sometimes or often.[44] The complexity of issues that students bring with them to school requires teachers to have an understanding of medical/behavioral conditions they previously did not need to consider. Through websites such as WebMD.com, Wikipedia, and social networks, the Internet has become the 'go to' place for teachers to understand the diversity of students' needs in their classroom.

Assessing and recording students' progress
Summative assessments have been significantly influenced by the advancement of the Internet decade. States increasingly rely on the Internet for distribution of state standards and assessment of those standards. Online testing has revolutionized the evaluation of students' understanding of the standards. For instance, some states are adopting computer-adaptive testing in which students' next question is determined by whether they got the previous question correct or incorrect.[45] When testing is managed through the Internet, states and teachers get immediate feedback regarding how well students do on the state tests. In the past, teachers often didn't find out how well their students were doing until six months after the test was given, which often meant they were teaching whole new groups of students in a new school year. Immediate feedback is most effective.[46] It allows teachers to

---

[44] See note 8.
[45] Stewart, A. (2009). Computer-adaptive testing is gaining favor. *Deseret News,* July 27. Retrieved March 31, 2011 from http://www.deseretnews.com/article/705319400/Computer-adaptive-testing-is-gaining-favor.html.
[46] Hattie, J. & Timperley, H. (2007). The power of feedback. *Review of Educational Research, 77*(1), 81-112.

identify strengths and areas for needed improvement regarding achievement of the state standards with the students they are currently teaching, and focus on students with low test scores. It allows students to make adjustments while the tasks are fresh in their minds.

Since Internet based assessment is physically easier, we feel like we can do more of it. An undesired consequence, from many teachers' and parents' perspective, is that we are over-assessing our students.[47] Diane Ravitch, former Assistant Secretary of Education for the Bush Administration, agrees with that sentiment in her book *The Death and Life of the Great American School System: How Testing and Choice are Undermining Education,* stating *"Efforts to reform public education are, ironically, diminishing its quality and endangering its very survival."*[48] A huge amount of time is spent preparing for the tests, taking the tests, and then making use of the data. Is that time better spent in instruction? Another unintended consequence of Internet based testing is a coup d'état of the school computer labs. School computer lab use has been in the process of completely changing over the past few years. Instructional use of computer labs has decreased significantly as testing demands monopolize the labs for major parts of the year, decreasing teachers' ability to access computers for whole class instruction.[49]

---

[47] French, S. (2011). Are we over-testing our students? *SantaCruzPatch*, March 30, 2011. Retrieved March 31, 2011 from http://santacruz.patch.com/articles/are-we-over-testing-our-students. Benner, J. (2001). The over-testing of America? *Wired,* August 27. Retrieved March 31, 2011 from http://www.wired.com/culture/education/news/2001/08/45902. Goff, H. (2008). Teachers criticize 'over-testing'. BBC News, Monday, March 24. Retrieved March 31, 2011 from http://news.bbc.co.uk/2/hi/uk_news/education/7311863.stm.
[48] Ravitch, D. (2010). *The Death and Life of the Great American School System: How Testing and Choice are Undermining Education.* NY: Basic Books.
[49] Owen, W. (2010). Oregon school computer labs overwhelmed by demands on students. *The Oregonian*, July 23. Retrieved March 31, 2011 from http://www.oregonlive.com/education/index.ssf/2010/07/oregon_school_computer_labs_ov.html.

Perhaps one of the biggest reasons computers originally made it into teachers' classrooms is to facilitate administrative tasks. Gone are the student helpers walking around the halls of middle and secondary schools collecting attendance sheets from teachers. No more bubble sheets for grades. Approximately 94% of teachers use their computers for entering grades and attendance now in an Internet based network. Part of the appeal is that teachers can access the same records from home. There are 81 % of teachers who have remote access to student data, while 61% use this access sometimes or often.[50] Parents, students, counselors, and administrators typically can have access to that data at any time, facilitating, and monitoring the students' progress.

Communicate with parents, students, and administration
The Internet is certainly changing how teachers, parents, students, and administration communicate. About 97% of teachers reported having remote access to school email, and of these teachers, 85% used this remote access sometimes or often.[51] As more students gain Internet access at home, teachers and administrators are relying more on the Internet as the information distribution vehicle. Email and school websites promote school and classroom activities. Teachers now look first to email as a way to contact parents about students. However, the digital divide is still wide and causes schools to rely on multiple avenues of communication. Differences in teachers' use of the Internet for communication are significantly different between low and high poverty schools: email to send information to parents (69% to 39%) or to students (30% to 17%), email to address individual concerns with parents (92% to 48%) or with students (38% to 19%), a course web page to communicate with parents (47% to 30%) or with students (36% to 18%).[52]

---

[50] See note 8.
[51] See note 8.
[52] See note 8.

Instruction

Perhaps the greatest focus of efforts to increase use of technology, and more specifically the Internet, is the classroom. We know that teachers make a difference in students' learning. Accordingly, reform efforts in education usually start with the teacher. Has instruction in the classroom changed as a result of increased access to the Internet?

Teachers report that the majority of them are using computers in their classrooms for instruction: forty percent often and 29% sometimes.[53] However, there was a significant difference between elementary and secondary teachers who reported that they or their students used computers in the classroom during instructional time (74% of elementary teachers, 59% of secondary teachers). The 16% of secondary teachers reported never using computers in their classrooms for instruction versus eight percent of elementary teachers.

The National Educational Technology Plan (2010) suggests that instead of a traditional model of instruction in which the teacher transmits the same information to all students in the same way, technology makes it possible to put students at the center and encourages them to take control of their learning with the flexibility that technology can provide. Because most people will likely change jobs throughout their life, they need critical thinking, complex problem solving, collaboration, and multimedia communication skills that are developed across all content areas. Internet based tools such as wikis, blogs, and other user-generated content can help students tackle "real-world problems, develop search strategies, and evaluate the credibility and authority of websites and authors, and create and communicate with multimedia"[54] Original documents, previously only available to

---

[53] See note 8.
[54] Office of Educational Technology (2010). Draft: National Educational Technology Plan. Transforming American education: Learning powered by technology. *U.S. Department of Education*, (March 5, 2010).

historians, are now available as digital resources through such places as the Smithsonian and Library of Congress. Accordingly, students can engage with primary source documents as they develop a rich and complex understanding of historical events.

Over the past ten years, the web itself has transformed. In 1999 DiNucci wrote

> The first glimmerings of Web 2.0 are beginning to appear. … The Web will be understood not as screenfulls of text and graphics, but as a transport mechanism, the ether through which interactivity happens."[55] We have experienced a paradigm shift this decade away from the Internet as a resource to the Internet as interactive. The public has gone from consumers to creators to community. The Pew Internet & American Life Project reported by 2003, 53 million American adults, or almost half of adult Internet users had created content on the Internet.[56] In 2007, Pew reported that 64% of online teenagers had created content, up from 57% in 2004. With 1.73 billion users worldwide in 2009,[57] the potential for Internet content is mind blowing. Through YouTube (12.2 billion views per month), blogs (126 million), Wikipedia (10 billion views per month), Facebook (350 million people), etc., the Internet has become a place to put ideas out there and engage in conversation.[58] Web 2.0 is an Internet that is evolving away from being simply a library/storehouse of information and towards an interactive, worldwide connection place.

---

[55] DiNucci, D. (1999). Fragmented future. *Print, 53*(4).
[56] Lenhart, A., Fallows, D., & Horrigan, J. (2004). Reports: Online activities & pursuits." *The Pew Internet & American Life Project.* Retrieved from: http://www.pewinternet.org/PPF/r/113/report_display.asp.
[57] Pingdom (2010). Internet 2009 in numbers. *Royal Pingdom.* Retrieved from: http://royal.pingdom.com/2010/01/22/internet-2009-in-numbers/.
[58] See note 50.

The hope and vision of the National Educational Technology Plan has not transformed most teachers.[59] Teachers surveyed in the National Center for Education Statistics' study said that their students used technology in a variety of ways, many requiring Internet use (see Figure 3). However, few had their students contribute to class web pages, blogs, or wikis. Most K-12 teachers have their students make use of Web 1.0 by doing research on the Internet to find information as opposed to using it as a publishing and discussion space.

Important differences can be found within this data regarding the digital divide. Students in high poverty schools were more likely to use technology to learn or practice basic skills (61% to 83%) and less likely to develop and present multimedia presentations (47% and 36%) or write (66% to 56%).[60] There is potentially a digital divide in the way the Internet is being used within schools, not just between schools. Students in lower socio-economic status are writing less and creating fewer presentations while practicing basic skills more. This may be particularly true at the elementary level where 76% of teachers use computers to drill students versus 53% of secondary teachers.

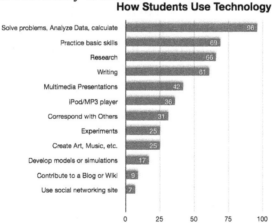

How Students Use Technology

Figure 3. How students use technology.[61]

---

[59] See note 47.
[60] See note 8.
[61] See note 8.

While the statistics imply that quite a bit of technology is being used in classrooms, my experience as a teacher educator for the past two decades leads me to believe otherwise. For instance, the data is not clear on what teachers mean by "often" or how these tools are truly being used. Terms such as "often" or "sometimes" were not defined by the researchers as meaning once a day, week, or month. Since "calculate" was included in the first question with "analysis," does that just mean calculators? That is a far cry from thoughtful analysis of data acquired from the Internet and manipulated in a spreadsheet to understand a social phenomenon. I spend quite a bit of time in schools observing student teachers and walking the halls. As I peer in classroom doors, rarely do I see students using the Internet in classes in meaningful ways. How learning may be influenced is discussed in the next section.

However, interactive whiteboards/smart-boards may be one recent technology changing teachers' use of the Internet in the classroom. These are devices that create a touch screen on the wall for a computer, making Internet access easy. Many districts are investing in interactive whiteboards for classrooms. Sales increased by 43% in 2009 for Smart Technologies, the leader in the field, to $648 million[62] in a market of $1 billion. Decision Tree Consulting estimates that by 2011, one in seven classrooms in the world will have an interactive whiteboard.[63] There are a number of studies that find teachers using interactive whiteboards can increase student achievement[64,65,66,67] so schools are jumping on

---

[62] Moritz, S. (2010). Smart Technologies: Chairing the SMARTBoard market. *TheStreet.* Retrieved from: http://finance.yahoo.com/news/Smart-Technologies-Chairing-tsmf-3933183653.html?x=0&v=2.

[63] Davis, M. (2007). Whiteboards Inc. *Education Week's Spotlight.* Retrieved from: http://www.edweek.org/dd/articles/2007/09/12/02board.h01.html.

[64] Lopez, O. (2010). The Digital Learning Classroom: Improving English Language Learners' academic success in mathematics and reading using interactive whiteboard technology. *Computers & Education, 54*(4), 901-915.

[65] Marzano, R. (2009). Teaching with Interactive Whiteboards, *Educational Leadership, 67*(3), 80–82.

the bandwagon. However, the technology encourages teacher directed instruction, so that student-to-student interaction decreases in classrooms,[68] the boards are very costly (approximately $4,000), and some believe that the studies indicating increased achievement are weak and funded by the industry.[69]

In summary, at the end of the Internet decade, teacher use of the Internet for instruction in the classroom has not changed teaching dramatically since Cuban's research (2003) found that "the integration of computers into classroom curricula and instruction techniques was minimal." The statistics on teacher use are deceptive. While preparation for instruction is certainly dominated by the Internet, teachers are not yet using the resources of the Internet for teaching students in significant ways. Interactive whiteboards are making direct instruction with the Internet more frequent in classrooms in recent years. However, multiple barriers continue to stand in the way of teachers seamlessly integrating the Internet into their instruction. In the next section I discuss some of those obstacles.

Learning
Are students learning more after the Internet decade? A number of studies show that the use of the Internet in the classroom can have positive influences on academic achievement, increased student motivation, problem solving, and information

---

[66] Schmid, E. C. (2008). Potential pedagogical benefits and drawbacks of multimedia use in the English language classroom equipped with interactive whiteboard technology. *Computers & Education*, 51, 1553-1568.
[67] Swan, K., Schenker, Kratcoski, A. (2008). The effect of the use of intereactive whiteboards on student achievement. In J. Luca & E. Weippl (Eds.), *Proceedings of the World Conference on Educational Multimedia, Hypermedia, and Telecommunications 2008*, 3290-3297.
[68] Latane, B. (2002). Focused interactive learning: A tool for active class discussion. *Teaching of Psychology*, 28(1), 10-16.
[69] McCrummen, S. (June 11, 2010). Some educators question if whiteboards, other high-tech tools raise achievement. *Washington Post*.

handling.[70,71,72] Internet use for searching for information is positively correlated with achievement while using the Internet for recreational and social purposes impacts academic achievement negatively.[73] Over the past decade, students' scores in math have been increasing and in reading they have remained generally flat on the National Assessment of Educational Progress (NAEP) (see Figure 4). No study directly correlates Internet use and NAEP scores, but this data suggests that schools are moving in a somewhat positive direction.

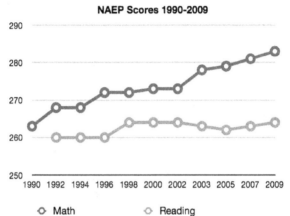

Figure 4. Scores on the National Assessment of Educational Progress, 1990-2009.[74]

[70] Cifuentes, L., Murphy, K., & Davis, T. (1998, February). *Cultural connections: Promoting self-esteem, achievement, and multicultural understanding through distance learning.* Proceedings of Selected Research and Development Presentations at the National Convention of the Association for Educational Communications and Technology, St. Louis, Missouri.

[71] Gragert, E. (2000, September). *Expanding international education through the Internet: No longer limited to the global studies and language curriculum.* Washington, DC: White Paper prepared for the Secretary of Education's Conference on Technology in Education.

[72] Pittard, V., Bannister, P., & Dunn, J. (2003). *The big pICTure: The impact of ICT on attainment, motivation and learning.* Nottinghamshire, England: Department for Education and Skills.

[73] Chen, S., & Fu, Y. (2009). Internet Use and Academic Achievement: Gender Differences in Early Adolescence. *Adolescence, 44,* 797-812.

[74] National Assessment of Educational Progress (2010). The Nation's Report Card. Retrieved from: http://nces.ed.gov/nationsreportcard/.

In spite of those reports, there have been a number of critics that posited we have achieved very little and sacrificed a lot. In Stoll's High Tech Heretic (2000) he argues "the Internet takes our time and energy away from more communal activities."[75] A Kaiser Family Foundation Study supports that concern as they find that 8-18 year olds devote an average of 7 hours and 38 minutes to using entertainment media in a typical day (i.e., music 2:31, television 4:29, computers 1:29, and video games 1:13)—which adds up to more than 53 hours a week.[76] In Oversold and Underused (2003), Cuban found that very few of the teachers they studied in high technology access schools modified their instructional practice, instead, using "a familiar repertoire of instructional approaches."[77] Healy, in Failure to Connect (1998), fears that children are being exploited through new, manipulative forms of advertising during Internet use. In Oppenheimer's, The Flickering Mind (2004) he describes the New York School District's choice in 2001 to lay off administrators and cut after-school and arts programs to make up for a $406 million deficit. That budget included $250 million for technology. These are valid concerns that must ultimately be addressed in conversations about the cost/benefit ratio of technology integration in schools.

My experience in the classroom over the past decade has paralleled Cuban's findings and has not alleviated concerns about how computers are being used in schools. At the elementary level, students are often on computers in learning centers at the back of the room. They participate in computer activities that have formerly been stand-alone applications at the beginning of the decade, but are becoming more prevalent on the Internet now. Varied sites such as Scholastic, Public Broadcasting, and

---

[75] Stoll, C. (2000). *High Tech Heretic: Why Computers Don't Belong in the Classroom and Other Reflections by a Computer Contrarian.* Doubleday.
[76] Rideout, V., Foehr, U., & Roberts, D. (2010). GENERATION M2 Media in the Lives of 8- to 18-Year-Olds. *A Kaiser Family Foundation Study.* Retrieved from: http://www.kff.org/entmedia/upload/8010.pdf.
[77] Cuban, L. (2003). *Oversold and Underused: Computers in the Classroom.* Cambridge, MA: Harvard University Press.

CoolMath4Kids provide many "educational games" and have different motivations for attracting students to their sites. These programs have been generally dubbed "edutainment" for supposedly being entertaining while simultaneously being educational. They include text, graphics, audio, video, and animation to engage students. Proponents claim that edutainment is an effective teaching method that increases motivation while encouraging students to learn, particularly for those who have low motivation or don't know much about a subject.[78] These games have the advantage of students being able to play them at their own pace, adjust to the students' level of learning, and can be effective for teaching specific knowledge.[79] However, if the games are structured more like complex simulations rather than simple games, there can be greater retention or breadth of knowledge.[80,81,82] These more sophisticated games take significant amounts of time to play in order to get the learning benefit, so are not necessarily feasible for classroom use.

Opponents claim that edutainment websites use behavioristic reward systems, relying heavily on extrinsic motivation rather than intrinsic motivation or real interest in the subject matter. Rewards typically are presented for completing levels rather than having any connection to the learning, so students play with a focus on the gaming experience rather than understanding the content. Edutainment presents information in a very simplistic, straightforward manner for students, typically in a drill and practice routine rather than encouraging deeper understanding.

---

[78] Egenfeldt-Nielsen, Simon (2007a). *Beyond Edutainment: The Educational Potential of Computer Games.* Continuum Press.

[79] Gander, S. (2002). Does learning occur through gaming? *Electronic Journal of Instructional Science and Technology, 3*(2).

[80] Buch, T. & Egenfeldt-Nielsen, S. (2006). The learning effect of "Global Conflicts:" Palestine. Conference Proceedings Media@Terra, Athens, April 2006.

[81] Egenfeldt-Nielsen, S. (2007b). Third Generation Educational Use of Computer Games. *Journal of Educational Multimedia and Hypermedia, 16*(3).

[82] Squire, K., Barnett, M., Grant, J. M., & Higginbotham, T. (2004). Electromagnetism supercharged! Paper presented at the International Conference of the Learning Sciences 2004, Los Angeles.

"Edutainment is usually more about training than learning."[83] The "design of the software is intended to ensure that the pleasures of the software are experienced in the process of playing and are not necessarily dependent upon any identifiable acquisition of skills and knowledge to be taken away from the experience afterwards."[84] Technology can lead to bad pedagogy when it is used to simply drill students, which research indicates occurs more with lower-socioeconomic students.

As students get older, into the higher levels of elementary and into middle school, researching topics on the Internet is a common activity in classrooms and school libraries. Earlier statistics citied in this chapter indicate that secondary students use the Internet less than elementary students. At the secondary level, once in a while, there will be a big project, typically in a Social Studies class, in which students go to the library to research a topic. This might happen once a month or less. As part of the research process, students often spend inordinate amounts of time making flashy PowerPoint presentations with minimal content, although not necessarily at the expense of classroom time. In my observation of students' presentations of their Internet research, bullet points are often simplistic and generally do not demonstrate thoughtful analysis. This personal finding is supported by research: "In many schools, PCs have failed to aid students' learning or improve test scores, or equip them with the analysis and communications skills that today's workplace demands, according to studies. The problems include a reliance on paper lesson plans that don't factor in technology, and inadequate teacher training and technical support. Also at fault, say educators, is American classrooms'

---

[83] See note 74.
[84] Facer, K., Furlong, J., Furlong, R., & Sutherland, R. (2003). Edutainment software: A site for cultures in conflict. In R. Sutherland, G. Claxton & A. Pollard (Eds.), Learning and Teaching Where Worldviews meet. London: Trentham Books.

occupation with teaching kids strategies for raising standardized test scores to meet provisions of the No Child Left Behind Act."[85] One learning area that is in the process of changing significantly is homework. "Help" with homework is being transformed by the Internet. Parents decry multitasking (engaging in multiple tasks simultaneously) as detrimental to learning. Students are listening to music, typing a paper, researching on the web, and chatting with friends on Facebook simultaneously. Recent research echoes those concerns as studies indicate that multitasking diminishes the quality of learning that takes place.[86] However, most of the studies on multitasking create situations in which subjects are doing disparate tasks like counting beeps while sorting cards. Students, on the other hand, are often using multiple tools to accomplish a single task. Social networking sites such as Facebook might be considered 'study groups' that are continuously meeting. As a student types up a paper they can quickly ask others questions and discuss homework topics. That is certainly not all they are doing, but social networking can serve as a learning purpose as well as a social purpose. Furthermore, there are numerous web sites that are now resources for students doing homework that include video on how to solve an algebraic word problem, Sparknotes for understanding literature, Grammar Girl, and Wikipedia. The Internet, for better or worse, is taking the place of parents helping with homework. We know that parents' educational level is correlated with students' success in school. Perhaps this might level the playing field a bit for students with less educated parents.

Research documents a number of bright spots in which teachers demonstrate the potential power of the Internet in learning. In

---

[85] Ricadela, A. (December 16, 2008). Rethinking Computers in the Classroom. Bloomberg Businessweek. Retrieved from http://www.businessweek.com/technology/content/dec2008/tc20081215_37 1267.htm.
[86] Foerde, K.; Knowlton, B.; & Poldrack, R. (2006). Modulation of competing memory systems by distraction. *Proceedings of the National Academies of Science (PNAS)*, 103 (3), 11778-83.

most of the critics' books, they acknowledge the fact that worthwhile learning is possible with technology; it is just that the vast majority of teachers are not accessing that potential and the cost is currently not necessarily worth the benefit. Why is that? Michael Fullan (2006) claims that those interested in change in schools must address "the harder questions—'Under what conditions will continuous improvement happen?' and, correspondingly, 'How do we change cultures?' (or) they are bound to fail."[87] In response to Fullan, I suggest two areas of consideration in order to move towards effective Internet integration in schools:

1. Changing cultures: Professional development
2. Conditions for improvement: Access

Professional Development
"Schools are enthusiastic about the technology's promise, but short of the money and trained faculty to extract many of its benefits."[88] Teaching is a complex culture. There are an incredible amount of areas to take into consideration in planning and implementing instruction. For instance, it is one thing to understand mathematics. It is another to understand mathematics within a curriculum in ways that meet the demands of the state and the needs and character of students so that it can be taught in a way that increases achievement. Historically, "teachers' subject knowledge and pedagogy were being treated as mutually exclusive domains."[89] However, Shulman[90] introduced the idea of

---

[87] Fullan, M. (2006). Change Theory: A force for school improvement. *Centre for Strategic Education Seminar Series Paper No. 157*, November. Retrieved from http://www.michaelfullan.ca/Articles_06/06_change_theory.pdf.
[88] See note 78.
[89] Mishra, P. & Koehler, M. (2006). Technological Pedagogical Content Knowledge: A Framework for Teacher Knowledge. *Teachers College Record, 108*(6), 1017–1054. Retrieved from:
http://www.tpck.org/tpck/index.php?title=Main_Page.
[90] Shulman, L. (1987). Knowledge and teaching: Foundations of the new reform. *Harvard Educational Review, 57*, 1-22.

Pedagogical Content Knowledge (PCK), which blends content and pedagogy and includes teachers' understanding of why some students experience difficulties when learning a concept while others understand relatively easily.[91] PCK is also knowledge of effective ways to represent[92] and explain a concept[93] based on students' understanding.

There is still another dimension of the teaching culture to consider when teaching using technology. Researchers describe it as Technological Pedagogical Content Knowledge (TPACK) (see Figure 5), which builds on Shulman's PCK. "The relationships between content (the actual subject matter that is to be learned and taught), pedagogy (the process and practice or methods of teaching and learning), and technology (both commonplace, like chalkboards, and advanced, such as digital computers) are complex and nuanced. Technologies often come with their own imperatives that constrain the content that has to be covered and the nature of possible representations."[94]

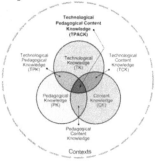

Figure 5. Technological Pedagogical Content Knowledge[95]

[91] Shulman, L. S. (1986). Paradigms and research programs in the study of teaching: A contemporary perspective. In M. C. Wittrock (Ed.) *Handbook on Research in Teaching*. New York: MacMillan.
[92] Feiman-Nemser, S. (1990). Teacher preparation: Structural and conceptual alternatives. In W. R. Houston, M. Haberman, & J. Sikula (Eds.), *Handbook of Research on Teacher Education* (pp. 212-233). New York: MacMillan.
[93] Leinhardt, G. (1987). The development of an expert explanation: An analysis of a sequence of subtraction lessons. *Cognition and Instruction, 4*(4), 225-282.
[94] See note 82.
[95] See note 82.

Technology has often been considered an impetus for reform of teaching towards more student-centered instruction.[96] However, in order to achieve that reform, teachers need to understand TPACK—the dynamic between technology, content, and pedagogy and what it takes to effectively make use of the Internet with today's students. Without investment in professional development that focuses on the complex aspects of technology integration, it is difficult for the majority of teachers to achieve effective and thoughtful integration on their own. Professional development in the form of mentorship, workshops, readings, etc. is critical if teachers are to feel comfortable with a new culture in their classrooms that maximizes learning when students make use of technology. Needless to say, these things take time and resources to achieve.

Access

Productive use of the Internet in schools will only happen when it is seamless and ubiquitous. Teachers and students can get to the Internet today, but it requires planning and determination when there are a handful of computers for multiple students in classrooms or the lab is across the school and in demand. The current school access for most classrooms is also problematic when it may take only 5 minutes to get what a student needs from the Internet. There are many virtual manipulatives in mathematics, for instance, that would be useful to help students construct understanding of a concept, but just take a few minutes in the midst of a larger lesson. As in the case of homework, described earlier, students are becoming accustomed to 'just-in-time' assistance through social networking and supportive websites that facilitate their learning. If teachers have to plan and arrange time on the Internet for students, it is less likely to happen than when it is readily available in a teachable/learnable moment.

---

[96] Jonassen, D., Peck, K., & Wilson, B. (1999). *Learning with technology: A constructivist perspective.* Upper Saddle River, NJ: Prentice Hall.

While the world outside the classroom is currently evolving so everyone will have 24/7 access through handheld devices, many schools are nervous about wireless access for students. About "78% of public schools reported having some form of wireless network on campus, but only 39% said their wireless access was available across the entire campus."[97] District information technology security personnel have less control than with desktop computers so they are hesitant to allow students on the network. Teachers have many legitimate concerns about distractions caused by students' full and continual access to the Internet.

These concerns will need to be resolved, because ubiquitous access is coming like a freight train down the tracks. Tablet computers are the game changer. They are immediately on. The form factor of a touch screen significantly changes the dynamic with the computer. They can serve multiple purposes such as book readers, graphing calculators, word processors, scientific data entry, research, hands on manipulatives, communication and networking, publication, and learning support such as language translation and word definitions. Teachers around the country are finding powerful uses for tablets and iPods that are having positive impact on test scores.[98] Major publishers are ready and waiting with eTextbooks for schools. As soon as the cost/benefit ratio becomes reasonable for districts, students will affordably have all their textbooks on tablets that will be interactive and constantly updated. India is pushing the envelope with their $35 tablet available to university students next year: "The 23 centimeter (nine-inch) wide touch-screen device, weighing 1.5

---

[97] See note 5.
[98] Eaton, K. (2011). Schools turning to iPads for learning, safety. Retrieved March 31, 2011 from http://washingtonexaminer.com/news/2011/03/schools-turning-ipads-learning-safety. Creer-Harris, L. (2011). New iPads are learning tools for Payson High School. *Daily Herald*, January 22. Retrieved March 31, 2011 from http://www.heraldextra.com/news/local/south/payson/article_2db375a6-598b-544d-b510-bc2e419796b4.html. Also see the Canby School District http://wiki.canby.k12.or.us/groups/ipodusergroup/ and

kilograms, is packed with open source software including internet browsers, a PDF reader, video conferencing platform, open office, media player, remote device management capability, multimedia input-output interface option, and multiple content viewer based on the open source Linus operating system. The device will also be able to run on solar power besides the usual battery-operated system."[99] Ubiquitous access to the Internet will become the standard in schools. When teachers have the option of having students simply click a button on their tablet to move from their textbook to web resources, teaching practices will, undoubtedly change to incorporate the educational potential of the Internet. "Teachers and students with more computers or computers connected to the Internet in their classrooms generally used these technologies more often than teachers with fewer computers or Internet connections."[100]

In 2003, four percent of the U.S. school districts had started 1:1 laptop implementations in which every student had a computer. By 2006 more than 24% of school districts were in the process of transitioning to 1:1.[101] With 1-1 laptop initiatives we have research that suggests higher achievement and increased engagement are possible.[102,103] "All of the studies that examined the impact of 1:1 computing on student achievement found that students in the 1:1 settings outperformed their traditional

[99] Mishra, A. (2010). INDIA: $35 laptop a revolution in university learning? *University World News.* Retrieved from: http://www.universityworldnews.com/article.php?story=20101210220253700.

[100] See note 7.

[101] Greaves, T., & Hayes, J. (2006). America's digital Schools 2008: A five-year forecast. Shelton, CT: Market Data Retrieval. Retrieved from: http://www.ads2006.org/ads2006/pdf/ADS2006KF.pdf.

[102] Boston College (2010, January 22). A computer per student leads to higher performance than traditional classroom settings. *ScienceDaily.* Retrieved December 20, 2010, from http://www.sciencedaily.com-/releases/2010/01/100121171415.htm.

[103] Livingston, P. (2009). *1-to-1 learning: Laptop programs that work.* Eugene, Or: International Society for Technology in Education.

classroom peers on English/Language Arts standardized tests by a statistically significant margin. Study authors also reported on evidence of increased student motivation and engagement, as well as changes in teachers' instructional practices."[104] If these studies are any indication, the tablet era may make a difference in education.

The Future

Has the Internet changed education? Absolutely. In a myriad of ways described in this article, the Internet has altered how teachers communicate, research ideas, manage records, and prepare to teach. The Internet has altered schools' reach into the home as well. Homework and homeschooling have been significantly transformed while virtual schools have risen significantly. Has the Internet changed learning in schools? Not so much…

Ever since Marshall McLuhan suggested "the medium is the message" our society has a heightened awareness of how the characteristics of the medium for content influence the perception of the content. The vehicle shapes the process of thought. It determines how we think and act with the content. That is certainly the case with the Internet and education.

My school generation took an hour to get to the library, talk to the librarian, look up a book in the card catalogue, go get the book, read the book to find information we wanted to use, take notes, and then type them up on the typewriter. The current generation Google's the idea and finds it in seconds along with numerous links to things that relate to the idea in multiple sources and cuts and pastes it into their current work, hopefully citing the work and not plagiarizing. As a result, Nicholas Carr, in his book *The Shallows: What the Internet is Doing to Our Brains*[105] asks whether Google is

---

[104] See note 94.
[105] Carr, N. (2010). *The Shallows: What the Internet is Doing to Our Brains.* W. W. Norton & Company.

182

making us stupid. The Internet is "chipping away my capacity for concentration and contemplation.... Once I was a scuba diver in the sea of words. Now I zip along the surface like a guy on a Jet Ski." He suggests that his persistence in reading long documents is diminishing. Instead of deeply engaging in text, the Google generation skims a text and then clicks another link for more information, bouncing from a few paragraphs here, a few paragraphs there. Teachers suggest this is the new mentality of students. Patience for reading long texts/books is becoming a lost virtue.

Our instinct is to place a value of judgment on this phenomenon. It is tradition in our country to malign younger generations as less this and less that than "our generation." However, over time we come to see that things are different, not necessarily worse. Consuming information is clearly a different process for students in the Internet age. History will ultimately tell us whether that was a good thing or not as they enter into their adult lives.

Gary Small, in a study at UCLA, finds that experienced web users actually are using their brains extensively, but in different ways when they search the web.[106] The process of searching requires continual decision-making and complex reasoning, brain activities that occur much more than when reading a book. Cascio adds that new technologies are changing our brains towards a more "'fluid intelligence'—the ability to find meaning in confusion and to solve new problems, independent of acquired knowledge."[107] The facts and knowledge that we could store in our memories is no longer as useful to us as the ability to organize and make meaning of new information. Is it important to memorize the 50 states when you can pull that information up in a few clicks? In classrooms around

---

[106] The New York Times (2008). Is Google making us smarter? *New York Times Opinion Pages: Freakonomics.* Retrieved from: http://freakonomics.blogs.nytimes.com/2008/10/16/is-google-making-us-smarter.
[107] Cascio, J. (2009). Get Smarter. *The Atlantic.* Retrieved from: http://www.theatlantic.com/magazine/archive/2009/07/get-smarter/7548/.

the country they spend a week drilling states and capitols. It seems to me that isn't necessarily the best use of our teachers' or students' time in school. The ability to pull facts out of your head in a moment's notice has lost its cachet. Our brains are changing. Information is changing. As Internet access becomes part of the flow of life for everyone, facts and knowledge bytes become much less important than what you can do with that information. How should schools adapt? We aren't having that national conversation...

I visited schools in Japan a number of years ago to try to understand a little bit better the differences in success in mathematics between our two countries on international assessments. Japan is typically near the top. The USA is typically near the upper-middle. After our observations our group met with the mayor of a town near Tokyo and I discussed with him the reasons for that difference. He said, "Our students take our national test and do extremely well. However, when given an open-ended math problem, all students in the country solve it the same way. They do it accurately, but they don't do it creatively. How do you prepare entrepreneurs and divergent thinkers like Bill Gates?"

Teachers are caught in the middle of a national battle/conversation over what education ought to be. Should we be preparing our students to do well on multiple-choice tests, demonstrating their proficiency in math and reading or do we prepare creative and critical thinkers? The pendulum is currently swinging towards the former with a move for a national curriculum (The Common Core State Standards) and national testing. Thirty-one states have agreed to use the SMARTER Balanced Assessment Consortium's national test, designed courtesy of $160 million of our tax dollars. As Will Richardson notes, "the choices that people are making in terms of school policy and programs are totally regressive when it comes to technology and these global, on-demand learning environments. And the choices that they're making about curriculum are totally counter to self-directed, self-organized, independent learning."[108,109] The direction the country has been going with education in the past ten years is in direct contrast to the way the Internet is going—narrowing the world of information rather than expanding the possibilities.

Yet change can be subtle. In education, it can be like altering the course of a large ship. It takes miles before you sense that you are heading in a new direction. With each new advance, change does occur in small, but increasingly significant ways. Change is also in the eye of the beholder. For some, things seem pretty much the same as they always have been. For others, things are radically different. Change can sneak up on you. Like a plant that you didn't perceive before on the way to work, the Internet's role in education is suddenly in full bloom, as if it came out of nowhere, but you know it must have grown there for months without you seeing it. We are not in full bloom yet.

As I look into my crystal ball I see tablets in the hands of every student in America in the next ten years. Finally, with technological tools ubiquitous and textbooks integrated into those tools it will be hard to not make use of the wealth of educational potentialities the Internet promises.

Then again, Edison was wrong...

---

[108] Richardson, W. (2010). *Blogs, Wikis, Podcasts, and Other Powerful Web Tools for Classrooms.* Corwin Press.
[109] Rebora, A. (2010). Change Agent. *Education Week.* Retrieved from: http://www.edweek.org/tsb/articles/2010/10/12/01richardson.h04.html.

The Internet and the "just-in-time" Mind

David J. Staley
Ohio State University

However you may feel about its politics, Garry Trudeau's *Doonesbury* is particularly good at identifying broad social trends in our culture. One of my favorite strips takes place in a college lecture hall. A student sits in his chair furiously typing away at his laptop, obviously distracted from the lecture. His device pings him: a fellow student warns him "Head's up dude—professor just asked you a question." None of his friends seems to know what the question is, since no one in the room apparently is paying attention to the professor. One of the student's electronic classmates overhears the question and chats back "name four major greenhouse gasses." The student pings his friend "stall her while I Google the answer." From the back of the auditorium, we hear "Professor, we couldn't hear the question back here, could you repeat it?" "I asked Mr. Harris to name four major greenhouse gasses," replies the teacher, after which comes the immediate reply from Mr. Harris "Water vapor, CO2, ozone and methane." The professor concedes "uh...right." Triumphantly indifferent, our student chats back to his friend "If this keeps up, I'll never get through my email."

I have shown this cartoon to a number of teachers over the last few years. They immediately light upon the behavior of the students, and decry the use of laptops in their classes. The students are distracted from the class, are having their attention drawn away from the lecture, indeed are not even engaged in the class, but are rather chatting with friends or emailing or web surfing. When pressed, teachers express concerns over classroom management and control in such an electronic setting. Not only are the students distracted from the lecture, this appears to be a

186

coordinated distraction, as the students are engaged in a subterranean conversation extraneous to the formal class. The students come across as wily and duplicitous, conning the professor with their clever use of technology.

But upon deeper examination, many teachers also see an issue with the professor's behavior, or at least with the entire pedagogical architecture of the class. The professor has asked a relatively simple question, one that can be easily looked up. The underlying pedagogical assumption as expressed in the behavior of the professor is that the student, having diligently read the material the night before or having been attentive to the lecture, should have such information ready to recall at the professor's insistence. This is, of course, a standard way to think about education: information and knowledge is deposited in student minds, ready to be recalled upon demand. (It is the underlying logic of standardized testing.) This student, Mr. Harris, clearly does not have this information at ready recall, in his memory, at any rate. A quick check of Google, of course, yields the answer as quickly as if it were embossed upon his memory. Teachers understand the implications: if such answers, if such information is so readily available on the Internet and if students have easy access to that Internet through a laptop or some other portable device, perhaps the "deposit" model of teaching and educational assessment needs to be reexamined.

Given that I am an historian and a futurist, I cannot help but to place events in a wider and deeper context, which is what I would like to do with Doonesbury's visual anecdote. As an educator, I am particularly interested in the effects of the Internet on knowledge. These effects should be placed in a wider historical context, certainly that of the emergence of electronic communications generally (starting with the telegraph), and perhaps even longer. I would like to argue here that the Internet represents the next great extension of the "external symbolic storage system" humans have developed since the beginnings of civilization. For all of the dramatic and disruptive change that the

187

Internet surely represents, placing it in this long-term historical context renders this change more familiar, perhaps even less jarring.

When considering the status of knowledge, the present moment might be described as the era of "just-in-time knowledge." The situation described in the Doonesbury cartoon is an example of what I mean, that it seemingly becomes unnecessary to retain information in our physical, biological memory. Since information and knowledge can be stored on the Internet, and since I can easily access that knowledge wherever I might be, then I need only access this "external memory" when called upon. Obviously, this has all sorts of implications for education as we currently conceive it. Is the Internet "making us stupid," as Nick Carr would have it, by messing around with the brain's wiring system, making us all as attention-deprived as the Doonesbury character? Observers remark that we live in the era of cloud computing, but one could easily make the case that we have been surrounded by an informational "cloud" for much of recorded history; since the first Venus figures and cave paintings, humans have been devising ways to create and store "tokens of memory" in visible, external form. The human mind conceives and constructs tools of cognition, like art and writing and books and libraries. These cognitive tools, in turn, reshape the very mind that conceived them, a process that has spanned millennia. Far from "making us stupid," the Internet represents (merely) the next step in a much longer cultural and historical process.

As an educator, I am interested in what this all means for the status of knowledge and education. I'd like to place the Internet as an external symbolic storage system in the context of other such systems, especially the Library. For academics, the Library remains our dominant metaphor for the University: indeed, the Library is assumed to physically and conceptually sit at the center of the University. The Internet as cloud, the Internet as a system that facilitates just-in-time knowledge challenges that central metaphor: we no longer need travel to a central physical location to access knowledge, since that knowledge now swirls around us, accessible from whatever location. There are, of course, disquieting implications for the University, especially if we adhere to the idea that the University is grounded in place. A placeless Cloud of information and knowledge might force us to reimagine the University as similarly placeless and just-in-time.

All of this raises important questions: Is the knowledge on the Internet any good? The shelf life of electronically preserved information seems volatile and short; can we live with "evanescent information?" Is this move into a just-in-time cloud healthy for humanity?

And what of the Gutenberg Galaxy? What is the fate of "typographic man," whose knowledge was tethered to physical books and its larger systems of storage (like libraries) and the pedagogical assumptions that followed? Rather than seeing such a cognitive system disappear, as many fear, I suspect that typographic culture but will probably become a vestigial part of our cognitive system, vestigial to an electronic system that features sound and movement and other (actually ancient) forms of knowledge.

To understand what the future holds for the Internet, beyond the present moment, we must place it in a much wider and deeper historical and temporal context. To do so will, I believe, make us less alarmed by the impact the Internet is having on our minds and on our culture, and more balanced in our assessments.

The "deep history" of the Internet

In this essay, I would like to take the provocative (?) step of placing the emergence and maturation of the Internet in a much wider historical context: beyond the beginnings of human civilization to around 40,000 BC. One could, of course, interpret the Internet in the context of the medium-term scale of the "electronics communication revolution." This would situate the Internet within an historic context defined by television, radio, film and, before all these, the telegraph. Had Marshall McLuhan lived to see its explosive growth, I am certain he would have placed the Internet centrally within the electronic Global Village he identified in the 1960s. But I have been more influenced by Daniel Lord Smail, who asks historians to extend their notions of historical time deep into the Paleolithic. Smail makes this temporal move in particular so he may use the history of the brain as a way to organize the narrative of such a "deep history."[1] One of my goals in this essay to understand how the Internet is affecting the human brain, and the best way for me to understand these changes is to situate our present moment at the appropriate scale of understanding.

Following the approach of Fernand Braudel, I would like to situate "Internet time" within the scale of the *longue duree*. Braudel divided historical time into three scales: the scale of events, where change occurs rapidly; the scale of broad cyclical changes, and a long-term scale of time he called the *longue duree*. "Traditional history," wrote Braudel, "with its concern for the short time span, for the individual and the event, has long accustomed us to the headlong, dramatic, breathless rush of its narrative."[2] Braudel considered history from the scale of historical processes that were so slow or that extended over centuries that they were, in effect, stable structures that appeared to undergird the rapid movements of events. My particular interest in placing the Internet within a long-term historical scale is to draw our attention away from the dramatic, breathless narratives that Internet time enforces on many commentators.

Considering the Internet within the context of "deep history" provides a corrective to the distorting effects of "Internet time." Andrew Odlyzko identified Internet time as "the perception that

---

[1] See especially the chapter "The New Neurohistory," in Daniel Lord Smail, *On Deep History and the Brain* (University of California Press, 2008).
[2] Fernand Braudel, "History and the Social Sciences: The Longue Duree," in Fernand Braudel, trans. by Sarah Matthews, *On History* (The University of Chicago Press, 1980), 27.

product development and consumer acceptance were now occurring in a fraction of the traditional time. Closely related to the concept of Internet time was the idea of 'first-mover advantage...' If indeed seven years of traditional product cycles were now compressed to one year, then anything might change in the blink of an eye."[3] Even before Internet time, the culture of computing had enforced a sped up notion of time; Gordon Moore's Law conditions us to think of change as quick and instantaneous, enforcing a time horizon of only a few months. I would like to interpret the meaning of the Internet by situating it not within the nanosecond scale of electronic culture, but the "slow time" of the historical long term. If gastrophiles can champion a "slow food" movement, perhaps an historian can champion a "slow time" interpretation of the Internet?

If the Internet is the epoch-defining technology I believe it is, then I would like to place it within the context, not of the next cool app, but of other such epoch-defining technologies: the printing press, the alphabet, even all the way back to the earliest Venus figurines and cave paintings. If we place them within the temporal scale of other such technologies, the changes wrought by the Internet appear as disruptive—and, yet, as familiar—as those caused by other technologies.

Civilization and External Memory

I have found the observations of Merlin Donald, in his book *Origins of the Modern Mind*, particularly helpful to me in situating the Internet in a broader historical context, in helping me to think through the larger history of the evolution of the mind, and especially in understanding the symbiosis between the mind and culture. Donald argues that "The modern human mind evolved from the primate mind through a series of adaptations, each of

---

[3] Andrew Odlyzko, "The myth of Internet time," (preprint version) http://www.dtc.umn.edu/~odlyzko/doc/internet.time.myth.txt

which led to the emergence of a new representational system."[4] Representational here means that humans, unlike other species, have devised ways to represent reality in tangible form exterior to what could be stored within their biological brains. "Each successive new representational system," he continues, "has remained intact within our current mental architecture, so that the modern mind is a mosaic structure of cognitive vestiges from earlier stages of human emergence."[5] These representational systems, for Donald, are the key to understanding the evolution of the modern mind. "Humans did not simply evolve a larger brain, an expanded memory, a lexicon, or a special speech apparatus; we evolved new systems for representing reality."[6] These systems have surrounded human beings to such an extent that "the structure of the primate mind was radically altered; or rather, it was gradually surrounded by new representational systems and absorbed into a larger cognitive apparatus."[7] We typically identify those larger representational systems—art, writing, music etc.— as products of human culture. Psychology—among other disciplines—has taught us to make a separation between the individual mind and the larger "culture" in which that mind resides. Donald, however, wants us to see the two as linked together in a single "cognitive apparatus." Where psychology would define the mind as existing within the physical apparatus of an individual human brain, Donald extends that definition to include the external representational systems that humans have invented. One important implication of this theory is that it joins together the realm of individual human psychology with human culture in a complex interplay that defines our species' cognitive architecture. It is within this context that I would like to understand the long-term historical significance of the Internet and its relationship to our human mind.

---

[4] Merlin Donald, *Origins of the Modern Mind: Three Stages in the Evolution of Culture and Cognition (Harvard University Press*, 1991), 2.
[5] Ibid., 2-3
[6] Ibid., 3
[7] Ibid., 4

The early hominid brain, like all primate brains, was episodic, the kind of mind characterized by our closest evolutionary kin, the great apes. "Their lives," notes Donald, "are lived entirely in the present, as a series of concrete episodes, and the highest element of their system of memory representation seems to be at the level of event representation."[8] By event, Donald means an occurrence tied to a specific time and a specific location. Most mammals have developed "procedural" memories as well, meaning memories of a concrete set of actions that might be generalized over time and space. If episodic memories refer to specific events, then procedural memories are generalizations of events. Neither form, however, involves a system of signs that can be used to reflect on these events, or to pass the memories of these events on to others.[9] Only humans, it seems, have developed "semantic" memory, which are memories captured with signs or in some other representational form. "Animals excel at situational analysis and recall," contends Donald, "but cannot re-present a situation to reflect on it, either individually or collectively.... The cognitive evolution of human culture is, on one level, largely the story of the development of various semantic representational systems."[10]

Homo erectus developed the capacity to exchange information through gestures, hand signs, facial expressions and other extra-linguistic forms of communication that Donald describes as mimetic. *Erectus*, of course, was a tool making species, and Donald reminds us that to manufacture such tools required a system of communication more elaborate than an episodic mind could develop. *Erectus* did not possess language, but did develop mimetic skills, which Donald defines as "the ability to produce conscious, self-initiated, representational acts that are intentional but not linguistic...mimesis is fundamentally different from imitation and mimicry in that it involves the invention of intentional representations. When there is an audience to

---

[8] Ibid., 149
[9] Ibid., 151
[10] Ibid., 160

interpret the action, mimesis also serves the purpose of social communication."[11] Acts of mimesis are expressions of thought without language; indeed, Donald maintains that before humans could develop language, before we had anything to say, "there had to be some sort of semantic foundation for speech adaptation to have proven useful, and mimetic culture would have provided it."[12] At this stage in human cognitive evolution, represented by mimetic culture, we are still referring to representational systems of thought that remain grounded in the human body, without material foundation. Facial expressions and ritualized dance did not yet exist as physical, tangible objects external to the human body. Nevertheless, "the brain structures supporting mimetic action...constituted the archaic human brain, the brain that would be *further modified* to incorporate linguistic skill into its armamentarium of systems and modules.[13] [emphasis added] The emphasis here is to draw attention to the long history of brain modifications that have defined the evolution of the human mind.

Modern *Homo sapiens* added linguistic ability and greater "semantic skill" to this growing cognitive architecture. With the development of spoken language, "the human mind had come full circle, starting as the concrete, environmentally bound representational apparatus of episodic culture and eventually becoming a device capable of imposing an interpretation of the world from above"[14] through language. Humans built upon the episodic and mimetic mind by weaving stories and myths that would bring order to the world through language.

Importantly, and especially for our understanding of the possible effects of the Internet both on the human mind and human culture, mimetic skill and mimetic culture did not "disappear" when humans developed more advanced cognitive systems. Aspects of

---

[11] Ibid., 168
[12] Ibid., 199
[13] Ibid., 200
[14] Ibid., 268

mimetic thought—vocal tone, mime, facial expression and gesture, eye movement, sport and other ritualized movements—remain a vital part of our cognitive architecture. Donald describes mimetic culture as "vestigial," meaning that mimetic skill was not lost when newer, more advanced forms of thought and communication were developed. Rather, such skills were enveloped by the new culture, an additive process. Indeed, Donald's schema rests on the idea that these earlier forms of representation remain embedded within the larger human cognitive architecture. "Episodic culture," for example, "would have been surrounded by, *and largely preserved*, within the larger context of mimetic culture…the transition to mimetic culture involved adding to the cognitive architecture already in place."[15] [emphasis added]   For those who wonder about the fate of the Gutenberg Galaxy and of typographic thought and culture in the Age of the Internet, it may be useful to think of written culture as potentially vestigial to that culture, embedded within but not eliminated by that culture.

The episodic and mimetic minds remained biologically based. That is, whatever systems of representation humans developed, these older systems remained tied exclusively to the human body; the representational signs and symbols were contained in the physical, biological apparatus of the human brain, and were expressed through the body. This suggests that any information and communication was time and space dependent, because eye movements or ritualized dance or hand signs were not captured in material form, any thought or communication expressed was evanescent. Thus, an important cultural shift occurred around 40,000 BC., when humans began to create "tokens of memory" that gave physical form to thoughts, ideas and information. Earlier humans were decorating their bodies with paint, and these decorations more than likely carried cultural meanings. But when humans began carving Venus figurines and painting animal figures on cave walls, we took an important evolutionary step in that our

---

[15] Ibid., 197

mimetic gestures were now preserved outside the human body, outside the biologically based brain.[16]

The preservation of thought and memory in external material form advanced in turn. After painting on walls, humans developed pictographic and hieroglyphic writing systems and, as speech and visual symbol were united, the first alphabetic writing systems. We developed token counting and other systems of account, musical notation, mathematics, all of which are based on creating visual representations of signs and symbols. Once preserved outside the body, these visual and material representations could be looked at, shared with others, reflected and commented upon and, importantly, "remembered" without the reliance on biological memory. It is often said of the first counting systems, for example, that as long as what needed to be counted was small in number, what needed to be remembered could be contained in the biologically based human memory. However, as societies grew larger and more complex—that is, as more objects needed to be

---

[16] For an interesting history of the idea of information, see Michael E. Hobart and Zachary S. Schiffman, *Information Ages: Literacy, Numeracy, and the Computer Revolution* (Johns Hopkins University Press, 1998). The authors argue that "the invention of writing gave birth to information itself, engendering the first information revolution. Writing created new entities, mental objects that exist apart from the flow of speech, along with the earliest, systematic attempts to organize this abstract mental world." (2) It was the action of preserving human thought in material form that constituted "information." The authors write "Both writing and speech constitute communication, but of the two only writing extracts the sounds of speech from their oral flow by giving them visual representation...Because information separates mental objects from the flux of experience, it follows that different information technologies can single out different aspects of experience in different ways, generating different kinds of information." (4-5) This analysis strikes me as very similar to what Donald was suggesting about the movement toward semantic representation and the creation of the ESS. Hobart and Schiffman see writing as the prime mover event in the creation of information, but, as I note above, I see this invention with the first stone figurines and cave paintings. To follow their definition, these were mental objects separated from the flow of experience. However we term it, there was an historical development from evanescent forms of communication that were not preserved in material form versus those that were so preserved.

counted and remembered—a system of visual, material numerical notation was necessary to supplement human memory. For Donald, this supplement to memory should not be distinguished from our biologically based memory. Indeed, it should be viewed as an extension of that memory, our biology extended outward through our technologies.

Donald refers to this ever-expanding corpus of material representations the "external symbolic storage system." (hereafter, ESS) This concept pertains to "all memory items stored in some relatively permanent external [to the human brain] format, whether or not they are immediately available to the user."[17] What we might identify as the products of human culture and civilization, Donald would like us to view as extensions of the human mind, inseparable from that biologically based entity. This external symbolic storage system has surrounded human beings since the beginnings of civilization, with additions over the millennia. All the objects we associate with culture—art, music, architecture, as well as books and, it must be said, the Internet— are contained in this representational storage system, a "cloud" of information that surrounds each individual human mind.

Interestingly, Donald evokes the metaphor of the computer to conceptualize this human mind defined by both its internal biologically based memory and its external memory. The computer clearly has its own hardware and software stored on the client (think of Microsoft Office and the Vista operating system), but computers also rely on external memory devices (like a USB drive or portable hard drive) which extend the functionality of the computer beyond that stored on the client. (Indeed, computer specialists speak of "external memory" in this way.) Donald was writing before the rise of the World Wide Web, but understood the implications of networked computing, especially its ability to extend the functional power of the individual computer. "If a computer is embedded in a network of computers, that is, if it

---

17 Donald, 306

interacts with a 'society' of other computers, it does not necessarily retain the same 'cognitive capacity.' That is, the powers of the network must also be taken into account when defining and explaining what a computer can do."[18] Similarly, "individuals in possession of reading, writing, and other visuographic skills thus become somewhat like computers with networking capabilities; they are equipped to interface, to plug into whatever network becomes available. And once plugged in, their skills are determined by both the network and their own biological inheritance."[19] At one time, "plugging into" our cognitive network meant interacting with a book or browsing the stacks at the library. Today, "plugging into" our collective external symbolic storage system can also mean, like Doonesbury's student, plugging into the Internet.

Donald uses this metaphor of the computer to describe the human mind as it has developed since the Neolithic. Interestingly, his metaphor is not necessarily that shared by some AI researchers, who have long sought to replicate the mind in the computer, or at least to view the mind as a kind of computer. Rather, Donald's analogy is the inseparability of internal and external memory storage as a way to understand the computational power of the entire computer. In the same way that we cannot separate the totality of the computer's processing power into hardware and software stored in the machine, on the one hand, and its connection to other machines via a network on the other, neither can we separate the biological portion of the human mind from the larger "external storage system" humans have developed to extend that mind. The products of human culture must be viewed as "hardware" every bit as much as the biologically based brain is hardware.

Donald is at pains to point out the symbiosis of internal and external memory storage as the way to conceptualize the

---

[18] Ibid., 310
[19] Ibid., 311

individual human mind. "In the traditional view of psychologists," he writes:

> The mind has clear biological boundaries. "External storage" might be seen as just another term for the culture or civilization within which an individual exists [and, thus, of interest to historians and anthologists and sociologists]. The individual picks and chooses, acquires skills and knowledge from society, but nevertheless exists as an easily identifiable unit within that society. In this view, while society influences memory and thought, memory and thought occur only in the individual mind or brain and therefore are to be regarded as attributes of the individual, and studied in the individual....But external memory is not simply coextensive with culture in general, or with civilization...External memory is best defined in functional terms: it is the exact external analog of internal, or biological memory, namely a storage and retrieval system that allows humans to accumulate experience and knowledge.[20]

Furthermore, "The major locus of stored knowledge is out there, not within the bounds of biological memory."[21] This suggests that the external symbolic storage system is vastly more important to memory than whatever is contained internally in our brains. And it also suggests, importantly, that for millennia, the human mind has been both "in here" (contained in our brains) and "out there" (in the ESS), long before the Internet was developed.

I would like to place the development of the Internet within this much longer history, and contend that the Internet must be considered an important part of the human mind that is "out there," the next step in the longer historical process of storing symbols, information, culture and memory in material form

---

[20] Ibid., 309
[21] Ibid., 314

outside of our bodies. What I describe as "just-in-time" knowledge should be understood within this long-term historical process. More and more information and knowledge is migrating to the Internet and even more is being created in situ. I am reminded of the doctor I saw once in an emergency room, consulting a pocket version of his Physicians' Desk Reference in order to check on potential risks of prescribing two drugs. Doctors are not expected to keep all of this information in their heads, and thus the need for a pocket "memory device." Of course, those pocket editions of the Physicians' Desk Reference are now found on smart devices, meaning that it is even easier for doctors to access that information "just-in-time."

The "cloud" is the ideal metaphor for this historic development. In computing terms, the Cloud refers to data that is stored on an external server, as opposed to on a local client device. It is what Donald had in mind, I think, when he employed the metaphor of a computer to describe the relationship between brain, mind and ESS. It is exactly what I have in mind in describing just-in-time knowledge: rather than relying on internal, biological memory, we have devised a new way of accessing information from an external storage medium. In effect, information, knowledge and culture are migrating to The Cloud. This medium promises to be the most "portable" ESS system we have yet devised: we can, in effect, carry entire libraries around in our pockets. When Doonesbury's student used his device to locate information quickly, one could argue that he was enacting a new version of a ritual several thousand years old.

Of course, placing the Internet within this historical long view raises a whole host of important—and unsettling-- questions.

Reconfiguring the Brain

If the mind comprises both the physical brain inseparable from the larger external symbolic storage system, then it would seem that changes in that external system have important implications for the mind. For purposes of this essay, I am less interested in how

200

the Internet connects individual users or how the network transmits that information, important as these might be. I am, however, interested in the relationship between the individual biological mind and the larger representational system the Internet represents. To that end, I am more interested in the line of thought begun by Nicholas Carr, who asked in a widely-read article (and now extended in a thoughtful book) whether "Google is making us stupid." His concern is that the Internet (and especially how we use the internet) is dulling our capacity for deep reading, and, thus, deep thought and reflection. Users of the Internet do not so much read as flit from hyperlink to hyperlink, voraciously consuming content, but not digesting it with the patience and thoughtfulness we associate with reading books or long-form articles. More worrying for Carr is that the Internet is, perhaps without our knowledge and consent, rewiring our brains.

Carr's is an important argument, and is not the standard way we think about the impact of new technologies or new media. Many commentators have documented how new tools change our culture: the development of the mechanical clock, for example, altered our natural biological rhythms and enforced a "clock culture" of mechanized time on humanity. The Industrial Revolution required of workers less artisanal skill and more "machine tending," a de-skilling of their labor, according to economic historians. What is new in Carr's estimation is that we now understand more about how these tools directly affect the synaptic patterns in our brains. Carr cites important new work that measures the ways in which prolonged Internet use creates new synaptic connections, literally rewiring our brains. If this new research demonstrates anything, it is that the brain is a far more plastic organ than we previously imagined. And because we can now measure the extent of the changes wrought by this new technology using brain scanning technologies like fMRI (functional Magnetic Resonance Imaging), it seems all the more dastardly and insidious. Technophobes and Luddites—and I am not convinced that Carr is one of these—have long decried the deleterious effects of technology on human culture and society; it would seem that these critics have a new—and, ironically, technologically-determined—way to legitimate their concerns. As Carr notes, "for all that's been written about the Net, there's been little consideration of how, exactly, it's reprogramming us."[22]

Carr cites in evident agreement the thoughts of Richard Foreman, who elegizes the end of the individual personality in a culture wired to the Internet. "I come from a tradition of Western culture in which the ideal (my ideal) was the complex, dense and 'cathedral-like' structure of the highly educated and articulate personality—a man or woman who carried inside themselves a personally constructed and unique version of the entire heritage of the West," begins Foreman.

> But today, I see within us all (myself included) the replacement of complex inner density with a new kind of self-evolving under the pressure of information overload and the technology of the "instantly available". A new self that needs to contain less and less of an inner repertory of dense cultural inheritance—as we all become "pancake people"—spread wide and thin as we connect with that vast network of information accessed by the mere touch of a button.[23]

I cannot read Foreman's thoughtful quote without thinking of the long history of the external symbolic storage system. We have always—at least as long as we have been *Homo sapiens*—connected to a vast network of information. It is just that the scope and nature of that network and the manner in which we connect to it has changed over time. I am a bibliophile; to what

---

[22] Nicholas Carr, "Is Google Making Us Stupid?" The Atlantic, July/August 2008, http://www.theatlantic.com/magazine/archive/2008/07/is-google-making-us-stupid/6868/ See also Nicholas Carr, *The Shallows: What the Internet is Doing to Our Brains* (W.W. Norton and Co., 2010).

[23] Richard Foreman, "The Pancake People, or, 'The Gods are Pounding my Head,'" *Edge, The Third Culture,* http://www.edge.org/3rd_culture/foreman05/foreman05_index.html

degree is the Self that is "David Staley" bound up with and indistinguishable from his books, his personal library, and his connection to a library at his disposal at his university? How has the particular configuration of books I have read defined my mind? With each book I add to my network, with each book I read or write, how has the definition of my "inner self" been altered? Am I truly able to wall off my mind from the books I have read and that continue to surround me? Am I defined in part by my books? Given the importance of the ESS in defining the mind, it seems we have never been able to so fully separate ourselves, to isolate our mind from our information storage networks.

Foreman expresses what the philosopher Mark Rowlands calls a Cartesian view of cognition. According to this view, "cognitive processes—the category of mental processes with which cognitive science is concerned—occur inside cognizing organisms, and they do so because cognitive processes are, ultimately, brain processes." This assumption—that the mind and all of its cognitive activities reside strictly within the biological body, and in a highly localized portion of that body—has been influential for centuries among both philosophers and cognitive scientists. In contrast, Rowlands identifies a "new science of the mind," a new way of thinking about cognition "inspired by, and organized around, not the brain but some combination of the ideas that mental processes are 1) *embodied*, 2) *embedded*, 3) *enacted*, and 4) *extended*."[24]

Rowlands' non-Cartesian cognitive science is not yet a fully developed scientific approach; he is only identifying the philosophical and conceptual outlines of this new approach to cognitive science, one based not on the idea of a mind that resides exclusively in the brain, but which has for a very long time extended outward toward an information environment.

---

[24] Mark Rowlands, *The New Science of the Mind: From Extended Mind to Embodied Phenomenology* (MIT Press, 2010), 3.

> The idea that mental processes are embodied is, very roughly, the idea that they are partly constituted by, partly made up of, wider (i.e., extraneural) bodily structures and processes. The idea that mental processes are embedded is, again roughly, the idea that mental processes have been designed to function only in tandem with a certain environment that lies outside the brain of the subject.... The idea that mental processes are extended is the idea that they are not located exclusively inside an organism's head but extend out, in various ways, into the organism's environment.[25]

Echoing the thoughts of Merlin Donald, Rowlands observes that human beings often "offload" portions of our cognitive activities to technologies residing in this external environment. His example is a GPS system or a Mapquest map, which Rowlands accesses rather than retaining spatial directions solely within his biological memory. He terms technologies like GPS systems "external forms of information storage," observing that they "reduce the burden on my biological memory."[26] But to reiterate: this off-loading of cognitive activity did not begin with Mapquest or even with the recent electronic communications revolution. The human mind has, in Rowlands' estimation, always been so extended and embodied, at least since the development of writing (although we can extend this cognitive off-loading even further in our history). It is a conceit of Western thought since Descartes that the mind is sheltered and isolated within the cathedral of the brain. The Internet, in this reading, is simply the next feature of our external environment onto which we are off-loading cognitive activity.

It seems that the concern expressed by Carr and Foreman and others is that we lack autonomy from our technologies. Considered in terms over the historical long-view, the human mind has never been as isolated as Foreman supposes. He

---

[25] Ibid.
[26] Ibid., 14

concludes his reflections with a question: "Can computers achieve everything the human mind can achieve?" He continues: "Human beings make mistakes. In the arts—and in the sciences, I believe?—those mistakes can often open doors to new worlds, new discoveries and developments—the mistake itself becoming the basis of a whole new world of insights and procedures."[27] But framing the question in this way again assumes that our information technologies are as autonomous as the Self supposedly is. This is a typical rhetorical move, I think: we position technology—and especially new media—as in opposition to humanity, the Other that enslaves us (if we are a Luddite) or liberates us (if we are a technophile). Our retelling of the history of civilization, however, suggests that information technology—that secretion of the human mind—is intertwined with the mind, not in separation and isolation. Computers can only achieve what we can achieve with them in partnership.

Only if one believes in an autonomous Global Brain could Foreman's scenario play out, and I have my doubts about such a scenario. Nick Carr quotes, with some alarm, the musings of Google's founders, Sergey Brin and Larry Page, who, in the words of Carr, "speak frequently of their desire to turn their search engine into an artificial intelligence, a HAL-like machine that might be connected directly to our brains." Carr quotes Page as saying "The ultimate search engine is something as smart as people—or smarter," and quotes Brin as suggesting "Certainly if you had all the world's information directly attached to your brain, or an artificial brain that was smarter than your brain, you'd be better off." "Their easy assumption that we'd all 'be better off' if our brains were supplemented, or even replaced, by artificial intelligence is unsettling," writes Carr. "[In this view] the brain is just an outdated computer that needs a faster processor and a bigger hard drive."[28] I share some of Carr's worries here, but I am less concerned than he is about some of these implications. Carr is

[27] Foreman, op. cit.
[28] Carr, op. cit.

concerned, I think, with 1) the idea of a competing brain to the human brain and 2) the seemingly unnatural connection between the two.

In the first case, even in the wake of Deep Blue's historic defeat of chess champion Garry Kasparov, many AI researchers acknowledge that the idea of replicating or surpassing the brain in silicon remains a daunting challenge.[29] One lesson we learned from the Deep Blue-Kasparov competition is that computers are powerful aids to the human mind. Kasparov himself has said that he views computers as partners with humans to explore the intricacies of chess in ways not possible before. That is, powerful computers are tools that allow us to do some things faster or better, in the same way a shovel or bulldozer allows us to move more earth than our physical bodies alone can. Such tools have, historically at least, extended—rather than supplanted—our minds. If the Internet is a global brain, then it is an extension of our biologically based brain, not an autonomous intelligence.

As for the brain and the computer being connected, I suppose there is the uncomfortable thought of computers being wired directly to our brains (and there is some early research here that suggests this is a possibility) or that we will do something like what occurred in *Neuromancer* or the Matrix. But, in one way, our brains have already been "connected" to the larger ESS. If there is a more direct physical link, this might be unsettling, but it would be an advance on the metaphorical links that have long been established.

---

[29] Computer success at chess is one thing; throwing a ball or skipping rope, however, remain relatively simple cognitive tasks beyond the ability of a computer, in part because it lacks a body. A large part of human intelligence comes from the fact that we possess bodies that move through space. An interesting meditation on this idea is George Lakoff and Mark Johnson, *Philosophy In The Flesh: The Embodied Mind And Its Challenge To Western Thought* (Basic Books, 1999).

206

I cannot help but to hear in these musings about a Global Brain doing our thinking for us the debates that mathematics teachers had (continue to have?) about the place of the calculator in mathematics education. When the first inexpensive handheld calculators began to proliferate, some educators argued that they were harming students' ability to acquire mathematical knowledge. Since school kids could simply punch in numbers, they no longer needed to memorize multiplication tables. Other educators argued that calculators freed students from such rote drudgery, meaning that teachers could move on to advanced mathematics concepts, ultimately improving the quality of mathematics education. Does a calculator do our thinking for us? Or is it a tool that supplements our thinking, a technology of external memory storage that can only be activated by our biological brain?

I suspect we will have the same sorts of discussions about the just-in-time external knowledge storage system represented by the Internet. Evoking the Doonesbury character who does not hold knowledge in his biological memory but who resorts to Google for answers to the professor's question, there will no doubt be teachers who lament how little our students are remembering and how dependent they have become on the Internet for their memories. Indeed, in such a scenario, it is easy to understand why some would wonder if the Internet were doing our thinking for us. But I suspect there will be a growing number of teachers who will fashion a new pedagogy focused not on rote memorization but on the new kinds of thinking that can be "freed up" once rote memorization is replaced by this globe-spanning technology of external memory storage.

Foreman also fears a "flattening out" of the self. It implies the individual mind is being hollowed out as it no longer needs to serve as a repository of knowledge. Memory, the storage of knowledge in the individual mind, has always been a feature of humanity, of course. We are still, at our core, episodic and mimetic creatures, with biological memories. But we have never been so

207

fully dependent upon that memory, that inner cathedral, as Foreman might have imagined it, even, I would contend, during periods where memory was highly prized—among oral cultures, among the ancient Romans, etc.. The human mind has long depended upon external systems to expand its memory, its capacity. The Internet, in one telling, is emptying us of our knowledge, but only if we were to conceive ourselves as cut off from—in opposition to—that external system.

I wonder if the concern that the Internet is rewiring our brains is implying that the brain is a pristine organ that has never been rewired before, has never been so "violated" by our technologies? We should point out that our external symbolic storage system has historically had a similar effect on our brains. The cognitive neuroscientist Stanislas Dehaene concludes that the invention of writing repurposed the human brain for the task of reading the written symbols. Our brains are evolutionarily not far removed from our primate brains, Dehaene argues, and thus humans developed a "reading brain" by re-ordering a brain that had developed for other purposes. "If books and libraries have played a predominant role in the cultural evolution of our species," he writes, "it is because brain plasticity allowed us to recycle our primate visual system into a language instrument. The invention of reading led to the *mutation* of our cerebral circuits into a reading device."[30] [emphasis mine] Dehaene advances what he calls the neuronal recycling hypothesis. "According to this view, human brain architecture obeys strong genetic constraints, but some circuits have evolved to tolerate a fringe of variability. Part of our visual system, for instance, is not hardwired, but remains open to changes in the environment. Within an otherwise well-structured brain, visual plasticity gave the ancient scribes the opportunity to invent reading....When we learn a new skill, we recycle some of our old primate brain circuits—insofar, of course,

---

[30] Stanislas Dehaene, *Reading in the Brain: The Science and Evolution of a Human Invention* (Viking, 2009), 302.

as those circuits can tolerate the change."[31] It would seem that "changes in the environment" means especially the cultural/informational environment, an environment of our making that, in turn, requires our brains to be recycled and reordered. If such a process defined the origins of writing, there is every reason to think that a similar process is ordering our brain's adaptation to the Internet.

We see evidence of this reordered and repurposed brain as we observe children learning to read. In miniature, and with brain-imaging tools, we can witness the recycling/repurposing process, the "mutation" process, at work.

> If one could zoom down to the scale of single neurons or cortical columns, one would see a major upheaval in the neuronal microcode. According to the recycling view, each reading lesson leads to a neuronal reconversion: some visual neurons, previously concerned with object or face recognition, are committed to letters; others to frequent bigrams; yet others to prefixes, suffixes, or recurring words. In parallel, the neural code for spoken language is also in flux. Somehow, as phonemic awareness emerges, the code explodes into a more refined structure where phonemes are explicit. Finally, if we could track nerve fibers during development and sort them out depending on function, we would see a regular, comb like projection appear that links each visual unit to its corresponding pronunciation.[32]

The acquisition of reading alters and rewires the brain. Children learning to read reenact an ancient process of repurposing the brain. I suspect that if we had access to fMRI devices when the first writing systems were developed, we would probably see evidence of brain rewiring at work. As part of an historical

---

[31] Ibid., 7
[32] Ibid., 205

process, the Internet, like all the creations of our external symbolic storage system, reorders the brain.

For Dehaene, the brain is not infinitely plastic, only selectively plastic. That is, we developed our ability to read by altering those portions of our brain that were prepared to be refashioned for other purposes, like portions of our visual system that could be repurposed to understand written signs. These areas of plasticity are limited, and thus put constraints on the kinds of writing systems that could emerge. Dehaene notes that, despite their seeming variety and diversity, all of the writing systems human have developed are morphologically very similar. (He notes, for example, that the signs of written systems, from the alphabet to Chinese symbols, are very similar in size, in the kinds of stroke marks used to create each symbol, etc.) He contends this is because of the structural limitations imposed by our brains; our writing systems were limited by what our brains were able to manage given its genetic makeup and its limited plasticity.[33] It strikes me that this has important implications for how we might understand the evolution of the Internet. While we might fuss over the Internet's impact on our brains and fret about how it is uncomfortably rewiring them, we might pause to consider how our own cognitive architecture is setting limits on how the Internet is and will develop. If the Internet fosters just-in-time knowledge, then this is, in part, because our brains allow it to do so.

Perhaps the issue here is a discomfort with the direction that rewiring is leading us. Carr, especially, laments the decline of sustained reading in depth, that our brains may appear unable to sustain thought, but rather flits around like a gnat from this bit of data to this to this. The judgment that the Internet is "making us stupid" is based upon the idea that the reading brain is the ideal brain. Although it is so frequently evoked in such circumstances that I hesitate to do so again, I feel I must draw attention to the oft-

---

[33] Ibid., 304

quoted dialogue between Socrates and Phaedrus that spells out the former's objection to writing, in the form of a parable:

> But when they came to letters, This, said Theuth, will make the Egyptians wiser and give them better memories; it is a specific both for the memory and for the wit. Thamus replied: O most ingenious Theuth, the parent or inventor of an art is not always the best judge of the utility or inutility of his own inventions to the users of them. And in this instance, you who are the father of letters, from a paternal love of your own children have been led to attribute to them a quality which they cannot have; for this discovery of yours will create forgetfulness in the learners' souls, because they will not use their memories; they will trust to the external written characters and not remember of themselves. The specific which you have discovered is an aid not to memory, but to reminiscence, and you give your disciples not truth, but only the semblance of truth; they will be hearers of many things and will have learned nothing; they will appear to be omniscient and will generally know nothing; they will be tiresome company, having the show of wisdom without the reality.[34]

Socrates feared that, in relying on an external system of symbolic storage, the young will lose the ability to remember with their biologically based memories. If I might baldly paraphrase him, was Socrates asking "Is writing making us stupid?"

Carr gives eloquent expression to the real fear of the loss of reading (books) as a central cognitive activity in an Internet-saturated culture. As an avid reader myself, I share this lamentation, but I should also hasten to point out that deep reading is but one way humans read. The digital humanist

---

[34] Plato, *The Phaedrus*,
http://www.units.muohio.edu/technologyandhumanities/plato.htm

Matthew Kirschenbaum asks "What is reading?" and correctly observes

We do not, after all, read a novel the same way we read a reference work. We do not even read a novel the same way we read a poem; for a piece of verse by William Carlos Williams, a scholar will linger over every word, even its physical placement on the page. This is not the way we typically read *War and Peace*. Some books are read for immersion...but not all, indeed not most, books are destined for this kind of reading.[35]

Indeed, the "flitting about" process of reading seems to predate the Internet, but is certainly made much easier by the Internet. Kirschenbaum evokes images of medieval scholars in their studies with devices that held open several books at once so that the reader might read between them simultaneously, or Thomas Jefferson's device that held multiple books open at once, with Jefferson's leaping between them. "Books are random access devices par excellence, "concludes Kirschenbaum," and the strict linear sequences of reading we associate with sitting under the tree [becoming "lost" in a book] are the exception, not the rule."[36] Even if we are losing the ability to read deeply—and I am not yet convinced this is the case—we could argue that what is being lost is but one type of reading among many different variations.

We might also wonder, pace Donald, if deep reading—and the brain structure that supports this activity—is becoming a vestigial part of our minds? That is, deep reading is not lost so much as it is subsumed under the new brain activities fostered by the Internet. I understood Donald's use of the word vestigial here not to mean "leftover and without apparent use," like the human appendix, but rather a trace of something older. He described mimetic skill, like

---

[35] Mathew Kirschenbaum, "The Remaking of Reading: Data Mining and the Digital Humanities," p. 1-2
http://www.cs.umbc.edu/~hillol/NGDM07/abstracts/talks/MKirschenbaum.pdf
[36] Ibid., 2

facial expressions and gestures, as vestigial in this way, as older skills that were long supplanted by vocal language and written signs, but that are nevertheless retained as important forms of communication. Language and writing were layered upon gesture, but this did not eliminate gesture from the architecture of the human mind. Similarly, I can envision a scenario where deep reading does not disappear; rather the kind of thought encouraged by the associative "leaping about" across the Internet is layered over the deep reading apparatus. Historically, the architecture of the mind accumulates rather than eliminates.

As I write this essay, researchers at UCLA, publishing in the Proceedings of the National Academy of Sciences, have proposed that the brain does not operate like a top-down hierarchical system, a view that neurologists have held for decades. Rather, these researchers contend that "the brain appears to be a vastly interconnected network much like the Internet."[37] This is still preliminary research, and would need to be replicated and confirmed, but there are ironic implications here: of an Internet-like brain structure that is being rewired by the Internet.

The associative mind

The Internet does indeed enforce a kind of mental leaping about between bits of data. Our minds seem to flit about like a gnat when we are surfing this new external symbolic storage system. The Internet would appear to be structured to function in a nonlinear and associative manner, in contrast to a book which is organized to be linear and logical (even if it is not always read in that fashion). One of the chief concerns about the Internet and the electronic communications system generally is that it stands in contrast to The Book, which, since the development of the printing press, has served as Western culture's symbolic representation of the human mind. As J. David Bolter writes,

---

[37] Jason Palmer, "Brain works more like internet than 'top down' company," *BBC News*, 10 August 2010, http://www.bbc.co.uk/news/science-environment-10925841

> Because writing is such a highly valued individual act and cultural practice, the writing space itself is a potent metaphor. In the act of writing, the writer externalizes his or her thoughts. The writer enters into a reflective and reflexive relationship with the written page, a relationship in which thoughts are bodied forth. Writing, even writing on a computer screen, is a material practice, and it becomes difficult for a culture to decide where thinking ends and the materiality of writing begins, *where the mind ends and the writing space begins.* With any technique of writing—on stone or clay, on papyrus or paper, and the computer screen—the writer may come to regard the mind itself as a writing space. The behavior of the writing space becomes a metaphor for the human mind....[38] [emphasis mine]

It is unsurprising to me that Bolter finds the boundary between the mind and the writing space difficult to discern; in the language we have been using here, we indeed cannot separate the biologically-based mind from its systems of external representation. Whenever we write, we preserve our thoughts in external symbolic form. That external writing space is not a neutral medium for our thoughts, however. Depending on whether we are writing on clay tablets or papyrus scrolls or upon the pages of a book, the material surface of our writing space shapes our thoughts. As we have noted above, these different reading and writing practices have real effects—not just metaphorical ones—on the physical structure of our brains.

So, what sort of writing space does the Internet represent? And if our writing spaces are metaphors of the mind, what sort of mind does the Internet represent? "Hypertext" is probably the best word to describe our reading experiences on the Internet. Hypertext is not a currently fashionable word to use (it sounds too

---

[38] J. David Bolter, *Writing Space: Computers, Hypertext, and the Remediation of Print*, second edition (Lawrence Erlbaum Associates, 2001), 13

1990s), but in the context of deep historical time we are employing here, hypertext is as good a descriptive term for both the reading/writing style of the Internet and the kind of metaphor of the mind it represents.

Hypertext refers to the linking of different texts together, with the reader able to choose a reading path by selecting different links to follow. Hypertext allows us to easily move from text to text to text. Recall that this style of reading long predates the rise of the Internet. Thomas Jefferson built a device that held open several books at once for him to swivel between; the Internet makes it easier for us to "swivel between" a potentially infinite number of texts. The connections we make when we read in this fashion are just as likely to be associational and analogical rather than linear and logical.

Associational thinking has always been a part of the writing process, usually at the stage of what writing teachers call "prewriting." As Bolter maintains,

> What students create [in such prewriting exercises] is a network of elements. The computer can maintain such a network of topics and reflect the writer's progress as he trims his network by removing connections and establishing subordination, until there is strict hierarchy. When the goal is a printed text, associative writing is considered only preliminary…. The hierarchy (in the form of paragraphs, sections, and chapters) is an attempt to impose order on verbal ideas that are always prone to subvert that order. The associative relationships define alternative organizations that lie beneath the order of pages and chapters that a printed text presents to its reader.[39]

---

[39] Ibid., 33

One could follow from Bolter's observation that the Internet has
had the effect of bringing the primordial associative organization
of texts back to the surface, of foregrounding association as
"finished writing" as opposed to "prewriting." During the age of
the Gutenberg Galaxy, Western culture prized the hierarchies of
sequence, linearity and logic as the hallmarks of an educated
person because these were among the structural features of the
printed book. Part of our discomfort with the Internet might stem
from the fact that it does not appear and behave like a
hierarchically ordered printed book.

Given its associational nature, perhaps it would be more useful to
not think of the Internet as a writing space at all? Indeed, there
are some thoughtful observers who would argue that comparing
the Internet to a book or any other kind of writing space is the
wrong analogy. For these observers, the Internet looks more like
the "cabinets of curiosity" that were fashionable in Europe from
the 16th to the 18th centuries. These cabinets contained odd
objects collected together, in a seemingly disorganized fashion, but
in fact were linked together via association rather than taxonomic
logic.[40] Cabinets of curiosity, as with many other artistic forms,
work via analogy, meaning the ability "to see coordination across
separation ... to couple data that is not effectively or invariably
coupled by causal laws." Stated another way, thinking via analogy,
means having the ability to understand similarity in the midst of
apparent difference. For the art historian Barbara Maria Stafford,
curiosity cabinets "embody with great power and clarity the
central idea of the analogical world view, namely that all physical
phenomena ... can be cross-referenced, linked in reconciling
explanation by the informed imagination."[41] When placed in the
context of deep history, perhaps it makes more sense to view the
Internet not as a writing space but as a globe-spanning analogical

[40] This is the observation of Horst Bredekamp, in *The Lure of Antiquity and the
Cult of the Machine: The Kunstkammer and the Evolution of Nature, Art and
Technology* (Markus Wiener Publishers, 1995), esp. 113.
[41] Barbara Maria Stafford, *Visual Analogy: Consciousness as the Art of Connecting*
(The MIT Press,1999), 169

curiosity cabinet, a collection of curiosities that are cross-referenced and associatively linked, which would suggest a very different metaphor of the mind.

Many of the assumptions underlying the work in cognitive science assume a linear logical, text-like brain. But Stafford wonders, correctly, "Why does [cognitive science] look primarily to text-based fields, rather than the imaging arts, for insight on how cognition actually works?" "Cabinets of curiosities, Piranesi etchings, cubist collages, dada-inspired boxes, even the Netscape browser or Macintosh's mosaic toolbar [she was writing in 1999] all provide information about some *connective aspect of cognition* that are not well captured by the scientific approaches currently adopted."[42] [emphasis added] In privileging linearity over association, Western book-centric culture has either denigrated or ignored the many ways the mind works via analogy and associative connections. If the Internet is a representational space that enforces association, then it is simply mirroring our underappreciated associative brain.

The associative "hypertextual mind" might appear to be an evolutionary step back from the logical textual mind enforced by the Book. But thinking of the mind as like a writing space may conceal from us its real configuration: perhaps the mind is not a book but rather a work of art. Conceiving of it in this fashion allows us to better understand "the connective aspects of cognition" not as a disease, not as a symptom of a "stupid brain" but as a more realistic reflection of how the brain has always worked. Yes, the brain is linear and logical and capable of deep reading. But the brain is also analogical and associative, capable of making connections between disparate objects and data points, and indeed has long been doing so. The Internet has not dulled our minds but has instead unleashed this pre-existing, if undervalued, portion of our cognitive architecture.

---

[42] Ibid., 139, 138

Formal Education

I do not believe that the Internet is making us stupid, but I do believe that it is redefining what it means to be educated. By this I mean that the Internet is altering our relationship to knowledge. Donald argues that among the earliest civilizations, those that had developed writing systems, the sheer volume of external-to-the-brain symbolic materials they created necessitated a system of formal education. "Compared with the monotony and redundancy of the hunting-gathering lifestyle," he writes, "these early centers of graphic invention exploded with symbolically encoded things to be mastered. Large state libraries were already a reality in ancient Babylon, and by the time of the Greeks ESS products had been systematically collected and stored in several world centers of learning. At this point in human history, standardized formal education of children was needed for the first time, primarily to master the increasing load on visual-symbolic memory. In fact, *formal education was invented mostly to facilitate use of the ESS.*"[43] One could claim that this has been the very definition of formal education ever since: that as humans accumulated more "symbolically encoded things," they required systems for acquiring, managing, manipulating and demonstrating facility with those things. Education, in this formulation, is defined as a relationship between our biological minds and the external storage system; education means learning to manage the dance between our biologically based minds and the larger extension of our minds.

By "relationship to knowledge," I mean a kind of logistic relationship between the individual human mind and the larger external symbolic storage system. For much of human history, the products of the ESS were concentrated in relatively few locations. In the example cited above of the earliest civilizations, despite their growing volume, symbolically encoded things remained limited in location; to access the ESS, one needed to be in proximity to those great state libraries. Indeed, "The Great

---

[43] Donald, 320

218

Library" has long served as our principle metaphor for this extension of the human mind, the external symbolic storage system par excellence, and our external "cloud" that stores our symbolically encoded things outside our bodies. The Library, to use Donald's phrasing, has been one of the outstanding examples of how human beings have been able to extend our minds.

Among all of its effects, the emergence and maturation of the Internet has reconfigured the meaning of The Library, perhaps making this physical embodiment of the ESS increasingly vestigial. This admission—which is difficult for me to state—carries with it a whole host of implications, especially about the changing relationship between our biological minds and this towering example of external symbolic memory system.

One could write the history of formal education as the spreading out of the ESS from centralized locations. If we think of formal education as a logistical problem—how to locate externally preserved symbolically encoded things, how to access it, how best to manage it, how to demonstrate facility with it—then it is clear to see the potential implications of the Internet. In the first place, information and knowledge is starting to migrate from libraries, museums and other repositories of knowledge outward into the "cloud." In doing so, our proximity to that knowledge is changing. The Internet can be viewed as part of this larger narrative of spreading out knowledge and information from central locations, so that proximity to the sites of knowledge becomes less of an issue. Universal education is an historically recent phenomenon, and has been dependent upon, in part, the logistical question "How do we make the products of the ESS easily available to more people?" The printing press was one step in this direction: rather than being tethered to a large library or scriptorium at a monastery, one now had the ability to develop a personal library, a mini version of the ESS. When Andrew Carnegie lavished millions to build public libraries across the country, he was similarly seeking to broaden the proximity to knowledge, to our system of external memory. The ESS has always represented an external "cloud" of symbolically encoded things outside our bodies, but that cloud has had a somewhat constricted shape. Throughout history, the configuration of the ESS has altered, and there is reason to suspect that the Internet reflects the next stage of this larger reshaping of our external memory systems.

To restate: the Internet reconfigures formal education by altering its logistics. That is, to be "educated" still means to access, manipulate, manage, and to demonstrate facility with the external symbolic storage system. But how we will access and manipulate and manage and demonstrate facility will change. Of course, much of the information and knowledge migrating to the Internet is still read and viewed and experienced as it always has been. Accessing Shakespeare's plays via the Internet still requires one to read them; accessing a Picasso still requires one to look at the painting.[44] However, our proximity to these objects is now different, meaning that how we access these symbolic things has changed. As more and more symbolic objects move to the Cloud, as the logistics of access to information changes, the meaning of formal education is also changed.

I am reminded of my experiences teaching history at Heidelberg College in the small town of Tiffin, Ohio. I was asked to teach the historical methods course, which required a substantial research paper from each student based on archival research. As you might imagine, there are relatively few archives in and near Tiffin, thus limiting the kinds of research my students could undertake. When I made online archives part of the assignment, like the collections of the Library of Congress, my students could now expand their potential research subjects. This new proximity to information is already having profound effects on the way we think about history education at the K-12 level. There is a growing push for students to actually "do history" in middle and high school history classes, meaning engaging in primary source research of the kind all

---

[44] I understand, of course, that there are also new ways to "read" and "look" facilitated by the affordances of digital technology.

historians engage in, and primary source research being a more authentic way to learn history. This vision of authentic history teaching depends upon proximity to primary documents, usually physically stored in archives and large libraries, a logistical problem for teachers serving in small towns and other areas at some distance from repositories. Making archival materials available on the Internet reduces the proximity issues. This one narrow example demonstrates how the logistics of knowledge are altered by the Internet, with enticing potential effects for formal education.

Academics have long situated The Library at the physical and conceptual center of the University. The current discussion about Google Books, for example, is as much about the future of the library as much as anything. As the Library migrates to Google's Cloud environment, if The Great Library can be accessed from anywhere outside of Cambridge, Ann Arbor and Oxford, what does this suggest about the logistics of the University? Do students still need to be proximate to cathedrals of learning? Proximity to knowledge will, of course, continue to matter. But it strikes me that the real revolution here is in the way formal education may no longer be required to be rooted in a specific place. This may explain in part why some academics worry about Google Books. Aside from copyright concerns—and I don't wish to overlook this very serious issue—I think some of the concern comes from the perceived conceptual hollowing out of the University. If the Library stands at its center and if that center is being dispersed into the Cloud, then will the University suffer the same fate as The Library? I understand that Universities are more than their libraries, and that much of the above are really symbolic statements, but the symbolism is important. The issues of proxemics and logistics associated with libraries can be equally applied to Universities. The current debates about online education—facilitated by the Internet—are usually fashioned as questions of access that students can learn anytime/anywhere, and this is deeply troubling for some academics. We associate education as the meeting of a student and a professor, and have associated the physical proximity of teacher and learner as the most effective form of pedagogy. Those who reject online education do so, in part—because there other many other objections to be sure—because they believe that one cannot learn at an anonymous distance. (Of course, this assumes that books are poor pedagogical tools, because writer and reader are separated by both time and space.)

Advocates for online education assume that formal education need not be tethered to a specific location. While they do not use this specific language, these advocates are making the case that the diffusion of our external symbolic storage systems should continue to spread infinitely. Anya Kamenetz has been observing this movement of formal education into the Internet cloud. She draws upon her experiences with the TED Talks that are now easily accessible on the Internet, and observes that "TED has become the new Harvard:"

> If you were starting a top university today, what would it look like? You would start by gathering the very best minds from around the world, from every discipline. Since we're living in an age of abundant, not scarce, information, you'd curate the lectures carefully, with a focus on the new and original, rather than offer a course on every possible topic. You'd create a sustainable economic model by focusing on technological rather than physical infrastructure, and by getting people of means to pay for a specialized experience. You'd also construct a robust network *so people could access resources whenever and from wherever they like*, and you'd give them the tools to collaborate beyond the lecture hall. Why not fulfill the university's millennium-old mission by sharing ideas as freely and as widely as possible? [45] [emphasis mine]

---

[45] Anya Kamenetz, "How TED Became the New Harvard," *Fast Company* 82, Sept 2010, p. 148

Just as the symbolically encoded things contained in the Library are migrating to the Cloud, some of the best features of the University would also seem to have the potential to move to the Cloud. Our proximity to these great minds and great ideas is no longer tethered to place. The logistics of the University seem destined to be altered by the Internet.

Evanescent memory

If so much information and knowledge is ascending to this electronic cloud, one potentially ominous concern—more so than the question of whether or not the Internet is making us stupid—is the seemingly volatile shelf life of this information. As an historian, I come from an academic tribe that values the book in part because, as a storage medium, books seem to have long shelf lives. If I publish a book today, there is every reason to anticipate that, if properly stored, that book will be around hundreds of years from now. For scholars who value the past, this information longevity is an important facet of knowledge and knowledge creation.

But what of information in the cloud? There are some futurists who imagine a doomsday scenario where unusually high sunspot activity wipes out our electronic networks. Other scenarios include cyberwar and cyberterrorism, where rogue elements hack into and disrupt electronic networks. Other futurists have posited an impending "energy crisis" in electricity in the developed world. Because of ever increasing demand for electricity—from electronic gadgets and, potentially, electric powered cars— Western countries could see the kinds of daily power outages and rationed electricity that we associate with post-war Baghdad. Clearly, an external memory system like the Internet dependent upon electricity has many—at this stage only remotely possible— vulnerabilities, with an electronic "burning of the Library at Alexandria" an ever present threat.

But we need not focus on doomsday scenarios to understand the volatility of electronically based information. I like to tell my students the story of my dissertation. While you can read a bound copy of my work, completed in 1993, the electronic version is harder to access. My 250-page dissertation is stored on seven (yes, seven) 5.25-inch floppy disks, and so one would need to have access to a computer with a 5.25-inch drive to read them. The dissertation was written in WordStar, which was an obsolete program even in the early 1990s, but must be even more difficult to find today. Even after less than twenty years, this electronic information is very difficult to access.

This remains one of the more significant challenges of the web for librarians, archivists and other curators of digital information. Once information has been electronically encoded and uploaded to the Internet, who is going to maintain it? How will this information be maintained? Who will pay for it? Perhaps more importantly, why should such information be maintained? The Library of Congress has recently agreed to begin archiving Twitter feeds, but as the curators are well aware archiving in an electronic environment is not the same as archiving books. As new versions and upgrades of familiar applications inevitably come along, how easy will it be to migrate electronic information to these new environments? After I publish my book or journal article, there is no Book 2.0 that an archivist needs to contend with. There is reason to be cautious about information in the electronic cloud being as difficult to access as my 1993 dissertation.

And what of all the information on the web that has been intentionally created to be short-lived? Over the last three years, I have designed two site-specific, digitally based installations mounted at humanities conferences, as opposed to art galleries or museums. (I did not design these to be art installations, that is, they were not constructed for aesthetic reasons. I intended to make a scholarly argument visually.) Both of these were intentionally disassembled when the conferences were complete; they were intended to be scholarly performances of the moment. In addition to the actual argument presented in both pieces, much of the conversation surrounding the installations focused around the idea whether these installations could be called scholarship, as we traditionally understand the term. The consensus was that, yes, the installations were making a scholarly argument and were more than simply interesting things to look at. But can something be called "scholarship" if it does not sit on a library shelf someplace, or if it only exists for a short time? Both of the installations were "preserved" in digital form (and both are on the web now, although not at all in their original forms) but the "originals" are both gone, both one-off events, more like a theatrical or musical performance than a book.

What if more and more of the information that is created for the Internet is similarly understood to be fleeting and short-lived, like a mayfly? At a session during the 2010 The Humanities And Technology Camp (THATCamp) unconference, we discussed such "end-of-life" issues with electronic information. We asked, What if we decided not to preserve our digital works? We note that museums save and preserve objects, but do not save or preserve exhibitions. Is the Internet a kind of giant electronic exhibition? Can we plan for scholarship, information and knowledge as an ephemeral performance? What are the protocols of accepted and acceptable loss of digital information? That we were even having this conversation suggests that in the realm of the Internet there is less of a concern with long-term preservation. The Internet may foster a here-today, gone-tomorrow approach to information and knowledge, information as fleeting and temporary, more temporally situated than the book and the library. Creating information on the Internet becomes the gesture of an historical moment; when we say that knowledge and information on the Internet is "just-in-time," we might also refer to its ephemeral, at-this-moment quality. The whole notion of "external symbolic storage" is based around the idea of storage. What kind of meaningful symbolic *storage* does the Internet represent? I think a more important question to ask about the Internet is not is it making us stupid, but is it making it possible for us to forget?

A culture of forgetting leaves open the possibility for a high-tech Dark Age.[46] Dark Ages—and there have been several in history—were not necessarily "dark" for those who lived through them. They were, rather, "dark" for us, because not as much physical information survives, and usually very little in the way of archived written information. Because of this lack of information, it is we who are in the dark about them. Dark Age cultures—think of Homeric Greece or the early Middle Ages in Europe—were typically oral cultures, and only when those stories were written down were we able to access them. Oral culture, in this sense, is an evanescent culture, dependent upon its survival by the transmission of stories from one generation of storytellers to the next. Our electronic culture could be just as "dark" to future generations as these oral cultures are to us.

The quality of mind

To this stage, I have been trying to affect a neutral tone in my assessment of the historical meaning of the Internet. That is, I have tried not to make judgments about the quality of the kinds of changes the Internet is fostering—in our reading habits, in the wiring of our brains, in the way we access information, in the way we think about formal education—I have only tried to understand these architectural changes historically, and point out ways in which the maturation of the Internet fits within historical patterns. History does not repeat itself, said Mark Twain, but it sometimes rhymes, and I have attempted here in this essay to identify these historical "rhymes." If the future of our systems of external memory storage is tied to the Internet, are the symbolically encoded things that are stored there any good? Is this move into a just-in-time cloud is healthy for humanity?

To attempt an answer to the above questions, allow me three historical quotes, the first from Martin Luther in 1569, in the early throes of the Gutenberg revolution:

---

[46] I am grateful to the historian Alan Beyerchen for introducing this idea to me.

The multitude of books is a great evil. There is no measure of limit to this fever for writing; everyone must be an author; some out of vanity, to acquire celebrity and raise up a name; others for the sake of mere gain.

Edgar Allen Poe wrote in 1845:

The enormous multiplication of books in every branch of knowledge is one of the greatest evils of this age; since it presents one of the most serious obstacles to the acquisition of correct information by throwing in the reader's way piles of lumber in which he must painfully grope for the scraps of useful lumber.

And finally, the thoughts of the novelist Harvey Swados, when discussing the rise of cheap paperbacks in the early 1950s:

Whether this revolution in the reading habits of the American public means that we are being inundated by a flood of trash which will debase farther the popular taste, or that we shall now have available cheap editions of an ever-increasing list of classics, is a question of basic importance to our social and cultural development.[47]

I will not even bother to quote the similar kinds of lamentations about the rise of movies and television. The point is that junk information is hardly unique to the Internet; clearly, before the Internet, there were all sorts of cheap paperback novels, libelous posters, confusing propaganda, and vitriolic rants. Our external symbolic storage system has always harbored quality information and knowledge as well as "incorrect information." But the speed of transmission and the relative lack of barriers to entry (practically anyone can upload anything to the Web) mean that in addition to high-quality information there is at the same time a proliferation of poor information. Given the exquisitely complex

---

[47] All three of these quotes are cited by Clay Shirky in *Cognitive Surplus: Creativity and Generosity in a Connected Age* (The Penguin Press, 2010), 47, 50.

interrelationship between our biologically based brains and our systems of external storage, we must also wrestle with the question of the historic role of junk information, and how its ease of creation and transmission via the Internet can pollute our minds.

There are obviously many outstanding sources available to us on the Internet. However, there are toxic sources as well. Consider the rise of Wikpedia, for example, and the millions of crowd-sourced articles it has produced.[48] We should correctly ask whether the information produced on Wikipedia is of any value? That crowd-sourced publication is very good at producing articles on celebrities and athletes, but there are relatively few articles on history and sociology. Will the information about greenhouse gasses that our cartoon student accessed be subsumed under mountains of silly YouTube videos and Wikipedia articles about Lady GaGa. Just as our bodies require nourishment and are harmed when we ingest junk food, junk information has analogous effects on the mind. Similar arguments were made about television, of course, but this should not prevent us from raising these questions again regarding the Internet, and especially consider the potential for the rapid expansion of new forms of junk information.

Another issue with Wikipedia concerns the nature of crowd-sourced information itself. Studies show that many of the articles on Wikipedia are as accurate as those found in Britannica, the gold standard among encyclopedia. The thinking here is that, when you have lots of eyeballs looking at the same information, each with the ability to edit that information, after enough iterations, the collective judgment of a crowd can be as accurate as an individual

---

[48] I should state that I have written favorably elsewhere about the value of such self-organizing sites of knowledge. See David J. Staley, "Managing the Platform: Higher Education and the Logic of Wikinomics," *EDUCAUSE Review,* vol. 44, no. 1 (January/February 2009): 36–47;
http://www.educause.edu/EDUCAUSE+Review/EDUCAUSEReviewMagazineVolume44/ManagingthePlatformHigherEduca/163579

expert.[49] This is one of the great promises of Wikipedia, but also contains the germ of potential junk information. Just because a group has democratically decided on the truth value of a topic does not necessarily make it truthful. (The comedian Stephen Colbert described this as "wikiality.") We could, as a group, collectively agree to say that the Baltimore Orioles won the 2009 World Series, but this is obviously not true. What are the effects on our minds of having just-in-time access to mountains of potentially untrue information?

We should, of course, be concerned about what "counts" as information on the Internet. It would seem that, more than ever before, we need curators, gardeners and other caretakers of our external symbolic storage systems. As Kamenetz suggests in her TED-based model, the Internet needs responsible groups to serve as a filter, or at least to provide an imprimatur certifying the quality of information (not unlike what *Interface* does). It is also necessary that each individual user of the Internet act as their own curator, exercising their own judgment as to the value and worth of data they are accessing from the Cloud. Perhaps being educated in such an environment means developing the skills necessary to thoughtfully judge the quality of the symbolically encoded things one is accessing on the Internet. Perhaps that has always been the goal of formal education?

From a deep historical perspective, I finally must ask whether the growth and maturation of the Internet is "good" for humanity? I would rather not make this judgment based on personal preference: I happen to like books very much, but would prefer to refrain from judging the worth and value of the Internet from the perspective that it is "not-Books." Since we are thinking in terms of deep historical time, what if we think of the emergence of the Internet in evolutionary terms? We might ask whether the development of the Internet reflects the natural workings of some

---

[49] See especially James Surowiecki, *The Wisdom of Crowds: Why the Many Are Smarter Than the Few and How Collective Wisdom Shapes Business, Economies, Societies and Nations* (Doubleday, 2004).

inexorable process. If the historical movement of information and cognitive objects in the ESS is Darwinian in nature, then perhaps the transition from writing on papyrus to moveable-type printed books to Internet Cloud all reflect purposeless adaptations to a particular cultural environment? If this is the case, then questions about the quality of mind or whether the Internet is making us stupid seem out of place: in this Darwinian formulation, the Internet exists because of a particular set of historical circumstances. It is neither an improvement nor denigration, and we should thus resist efforts to ascribe a larger meaning.

I cannot subscribe to this view. Because we are referring to human minds, human culture, human information technologies, I am convinced that humanity exercises control over this process. In this sense—and I choose my words carefully—perhaps the evolution of our ESS is driven by a purpose, a series of choices we have made as humans. The process does not operate outside of our choices, and we have collectively chosen the path of just-in-time access to an electronically-enabled ESS. Are we comfortable with this choice?

I do not want this section of my essay to be titled "Is Wikipedia Making Us Stupid?" I do not believe that to be the case. But make no mistake: the Internet—and both the valuable and junk information it stores--is now an inexorable part of the larger architecture of the human mind. I ask this final question as a futurist: what will be the quality of a human mind tethered to an Internet-based external symbolic storage system?

Conclusion
One of the staff in my Center is a very bright, very capable young programmer. I am in awe of his range of talents and abilities, which far exceed my own. One day, I was looking over his shoulder as he was working on a coding problem I had laid out before him. He was surfing the Internet (and not working?). When I asked what he was doing, he said he was looking to copy several lines of code from someone in a user group who might

know the answer. It seems that my programmer does not hold all of that knowledge in his head: when he does not know how to do something, he will Google a query that reads something like "How can I create something that operates like Flash without using Flash?" He then chooses from among the best-looking responses (a judgment he has honed over the years) to locate someone's post or blog who has answered the question and has provided the code he needs. "This is how most coders work," my assistant informed me. "When we don't know how to do something, we look it up on the Internet."

Since I began this essay with a cartoon, perhaps it is fitting that I conclude with one as well. Although it is not as widely syndicated as Doonesbury, XKCD also captures larger technologically influenced cultural trends. The particular cartoon I have in mind is an open letter to "non-computer people":[50]

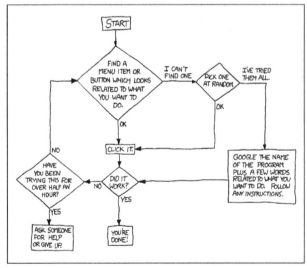

---

[50] XKCD, http://imgs.xkcd.com/comics/tech_support_cheat_sheet.png

Note in the lower right where the instruction reads "Google the name of the program plus a few words related to what you want to do. Follow any instructions." Reflect on the truth of this cartoon. "Computer people," like my student assistant, frequently rely on the Cloud for their information and knowledge, knowledge they access just-in-time to solve a problem at hand.

In my subsequent conversations with my student assistant, it is clear he takes a similar just-in-time attitude toward other academic subjects. Although he is not a history major, he has nevertheless taken some history courses, and has expressed his frustration to me that he is asked to remember details about the past. After taking an in-class exam where he was asked to recount a narrative and to write out short-answer identifications of important historical events, this student asked me with some exasperation "Why should I have to remember all of this stuff when it is just as easy for me to look it up on the Internet over my smartphone." To reiterate, I consider him to be a very good student and an exceptionally intelligent young man. I would never describe him as lazy or intellectually slothful, like the Doonesbury character I described in the introduction. Yet it is clear that he takes a very different attitude toward the acquisition and use of information and knowledge. For my young assistant, intelligence is not a matter of "know what" but of "know how." He seeks out the right information that he has adjudged to be useful and applies it to solve the problem at hand. This, to me, is the very definition of the "just-in-time" ethic that defines the Internet generation, an ethic, it turns out, is the result of a long history.

About the Authors

David F. Anderson, Ph.D.
David F. Anderson is Distinguished Service Professor of Public Administration and Informatics at the State University of New York (SUNY) Albany. His areas of research include public administration and policy, System Dynamics modeling, and digital government applications. He is a recipient (with a coauthor team from the Center for Technology in Government, University at Albany) of a three-year NSF grant on data interoperability and social systems. A 2010-2011 Carlos Rico Fulbright Scholar, he is on sabbatical in Montreal, Canada and Cholula, Mexico (Universidad des las Americas Puebla) for 2010-2011 academic year.

Deborah L. Anderson, Ph.D.
Deborah L. Anderson is Associate Professor of Information Studies and Informatics at the State University of New York (SUNY) Albany. Her areas of research include international information policy, public libraries, and education in library and information science. She is a recipient (with a coauthor team from the Center for Technology in Government, University at Albany) for a three-year NST grant on data interoperability and social systems. A 2010-2011 Carlos Rico Fulbright Scholar, she is on sabbatical in Montreal, Canada and Cholula, Mexico (Universidad de las Americas Puebla) for the 2010-2011 academic year.

Jeffrey G. Barlow
Jeffrey Barlow has been the Director of the Berglund Center from 2000 to the present. He is the founding editor of several peer-reviewed scholarly e-journals, including the Journal of History and Computing, now housed at the University of Michigan and E-AsPac, the e-journal of the Association for Asian Studies on the Pacific Coast. He has given invited lectures in the U.S., Canada, and China on topics related to the Internet.

Jeffrey's academic training at the University of California, Berkeley, was in Modern Chinese History. He is also a recognized authority on Chinese immigration into the Pacific Northwest, and on Chinese use of the Internet. He taught at the University of Oregon and at Lewis and Clark College before coming to Pacific in 1994. He has worked with the Berglund Center since its beginnings.

Mike Charles, Ph.D.
Dr. Mike Charles is an educational media and technology specialist with a background in curriculum and instruction. He taught in grades K-6 for 15 years in Phoenix, Arizona, working as a K-6 computer resource teacher for the final six years. His research interests include the way that technology enables student-initiated project learning environments, uses of visualization tools in teaching mathematics and science in K-12 education, and the complexities involved in changing teacher practice.

Isaac Gilman, MLIS
Isaac Gilman is Assistant Professor and Scholarly Communications & Research Services Librarian in the Pacific University (Oregon) Library. In addition to teaching courses in research methods and scholarly publishing, he manages Pacific University's institutional repository, *CommonKnowledge*, through which he also provides editorial support for the publication of both student and professional peer-reviewed journals. He received his Master of Library and Information Studies degree from the University of British Columbia in 2006 and his scholarly interests include information-seeking behaviors, scholarly communications, open access publishing and the legal and ethical aspects of information use.

Lynda Irons, MLIS
Lynda Irons, Assistant Professor, has been the Reference & Information Services Librarian for Pacific University since 1996.

Steve Rhine, Ed.D.
Steve Rhine, Ed. D. is a Professor of Education in the School of Education at Willamette University in Salem, Oregon. Dr. Rhine was part of the writing team for the National Educational Technology Standards for Teachers in 2000. He directed the Oregon Technology in Education Network (OTEN) from 2001-04, which was then funded by the Preparing Tomorrow's Teachers to Use Technology (PT3) program. He has been instrumental in the Teacher Quality Enhancement Partnership grant that currently funds OTEN. He has taught courses in Educational Technology, Educational Psychology, Action Research, and Mathematics Education.

His current research includes work on conducting online dialogue with student teachers based on digital video clips of their teaching, the role of Web 2.0 in classrooms, and the transition of Mexican and Ukrainian immigrant students into Oregon schools. He has recently published two

234

books. The first, *A Brilliant Teacher*, an engaging account of his year-long trip around the world with his wife and three children. The second, *Integrated Technologies, Innovative Learning: Insights from the PT3 Program,* an edited book of stories of efforts by institutions to integrate technology in the development of preservice teachers.

David Staley, Ph.D.
David Staley is Director of the Goldberg Center and an adjunct associate professor of history at The Ohio State University. He also serves as National Dean for General Education at Harrison College in Indianapolis. In addition to his work as a scholar/administrator, Dr. Staley is principal of the DStaley Group, a strategic foresight consulting practice, and serves as president of Columbus Futurists. He is a writer and essayist, whose work includes *History and Future: Using Historical Thinking to Imagine the Future,* and *Computers, Visualization and History.*

www.ingramcontent.com/pod-product-compliance
Lightning Source LLC
Chambersburg PA
CBHW071419050326
40689CB00010B/1898